Media Management

Media Management

Mittika Singal

RANDOM PUBLICATIONS
NEW DELHI (INDIA)

Media Management

ISBN 978-93-5111-241-9

Published in 2014 in India by

RANDOM PUBLICATIONS

4376-A/4B, Gali Murari Lal, Ansari Road
New Delhi-110 002
Phone : +91-11-43580356, +91-11-23289044
e-mail: randomexports@gmail.com, sales@randompublications.com, info@randompublications.com

Reprinted 2024

Type Setting by : Keystoneprintads, Delhi-110051
Digitally Printed at: Replika Press Pvt. Ltd.

Preface

Media management is a general job title that describes people who manage talent for media professionals like those who work in photo, sound, and video. It is a form of entertainment management, a field that manages talent in show business. Professionals in the media management field work with many types of media-related talent, including actors, artists, writers, and musicians. Media management in business differs from media management in computers because the computer term refers to activities that involve processing computer media files like music, video, and picture files.

Managers of this type are common in entertainment and print media because they facilitate contact between those seeking talent and those providing media talent. The media management field can include many types of management, including managing the finances of a popular band or controlling the royalties in the estate of a deceased movie star. A media manager might also work as an agent for a writer of books or magazines, contacting publishers who might want to buy clients' writing work.

Media managers usually have a number of copyright and trademark laws that guide and restrict the way they conduct business within their media field. In most places, the laws that govern music copyrights differ from laws that control copyrights of motion pictures and photographs, so some media managers specialize in only one type of media. A media professional can benefit from the use of a manager because it allows the talent to focus on media work instead of promoting the work. Because managers specialize in promoting talent to industry professionals, they often have better and more reliable industry contacts that facilitate promotion and management of the media professional's work.

A large part of the job of a media management professional is to promote and control the media image of managed talent. Job titles for media managers include broadcast media managers, Internet media managers and public relations managers. Professionals in this field may also handle negotiating contracts and collecting payments, including royalties. In many regions, governments require a talent management professional to have a license in order to negotiate or sign contracts on behalf of a media professional. Management professionals can suffer invalid or negated contracts or prosecution if they do not operate within local laws.

I thank all members of my team who have helped in the preparation of the book. My special thanks go to "Random Publications" who have published the book.

– *Mittika Singal*

Contents

1

Introduction to Media

It's 7:30 a.m. You wake up and turn on the radio, then open your local newspaper to see what has been happening in the world. During breakfast you turn on the television to catch a few minutes of the morning news shows. Before heading off to work you check your e-mail on the Internet. On the train to work you listen to the local radio station on your walkman, looking out of the window at a few outdoor billboards on the highway that you pass by. In that brief time span, you have been immersed in the world of media. Very broadly, that world includes radio, Internet, television, newspapers, magazines, and outdoor billboards.

Although you selected the radio to listen to music, or the newspaper to read the latest news, or the television to watch a programme, what you also did was receive information through a means of communication, or a medium. Given this broad definition, you can see that there are in fact hundreds of different media available, such as direct mail, skywriting, coupons, stadium signs, key rings, and food containers. All of these, and many other media, offer us ways of communicating information to an audience. As advertising media professionals, we are interested in looking at the media as a means of conveying a specific kind of information-an advertising message-about a product or service to consumers.

The media play a very important role in our lives. Media help fulfill two basic needs-they inform and they entertain. We turn to the media when we want to hear the latest world news or what happened in financialmarkets, forinstance. We also look to the media to fill our evenings and weekends with escapist fare to get us out of our everyday, humdrum routine. So television entertains us with movies, dramas, comedies, game shows, and sports. Radio offers us a wide variety of music, talk, and entertainment to listen to. We turn to magazines to find out more about our favourite hobbies and interests. Newspapers help us keep up with the world around us. And the Internet provides limitless information on any subject you are interested in. The media's informational role is perhaps best illustrated by considering what happens during a national or international crisis, such as the Balkan War in the late 1990s or the 2001 terrorist attack on the World

Trade Centre and Pentagon. On each occasion, millions of people were glued to their television sets, clicking to favourite web sites, tuned in to their radios, and reading newspapers and magazines for daily in-depth coverage and subsequent follow-up stories.

The media also affect our lives through their entertainment function. Television situation comedies such as All in the Family and Mary Tyler Moore not only reflected what was happening in U. S. society in the 1970s, but also helped to influence attitudes and behaviors concerning the issues of race and equality. Stories appearing in magazines such as People or InStyle let us know what is happening in other people's lives, both famous and ordinary. And we take our radios with us to the beach or park so that we can listen to live sports coverage while we relax.

WHAT MEDIA ARE OUT THERE?

The world of media can be very broadly divided into two types-print and electronic. Print media include magazines and newspapers, whereas electronic media cover radio, television and the Internet. Other media types are not quite as easily categorized. Thus outdoor billboards are generally defined as a print medium, whereas out-of-home options such as transit ads, or stadium signage, are variously classified as nontraditional, alternative, or ambient media.

ROLE OF MEDIA IN BUSINESS

It is important to emphasize here that the focus of this book is commercial media. That is, the communications media we talk about are not there simply to beautify the landscape or fill up the pages of a newspaper. They are designed to sell products to customers. Of course, there are also media that convey information but are not commercial in intent. Consumer Reports is a magazine that does not carry any advertising. Neither does public television. The white pages of the telephone directory, web search engines, and airline safety instructions are all informative yet are not advertisements in and of themselves.

And books certainly communicate information to their readers. Here, however, we concentrate on those media that currently accept advertising messages. It is worth emphasizing the word currently. Twenty-five years ago, you did not find commercial messages at supermarkets, schools, doctors'offices, or ski slopes. Today, advertisers can reach people in all of those places.

Even novels are not immune. A popular British author wrote Bulgari Jewelers into her fictional story, in 2000, for which the company paid her. And Hasbro paid young, hip preteens to use its Pox video game and talk about it with their friends to encourage additional sales. Although these ventures were criticized by the public, that does not mean other similar attempts will not be tried again in the future. For what is true for today may very well change by tomorrow. The generic term media (or medium in the singular) means different things to different people. To Joe Smith sitting at home on a Friday evening, the "media"mean whatever TV shows he watches or magazines he leafs through. For the local Chevy car dealer, the media provide a way to advertise this week's deals on Impalas and Blazers. And the Podunk Electric Utility Company uses the media to remind its customers that they can get free replacement lightbulbs.

Strictly speaking, a "medium"may be defined as a means by which something is accomplished, conveyed, or transferred. This deliberately broad definition means that consumer media would cover everything from handbills passed out in parking lots to "For Sale"signs taped to lampposts, to the 10-page advertising supplement that fell out of the last copy of Business Week you read, to electronic flashing signs in Times Square.

MEDIA VERSUS COMMUNICATIONS

In the business world, we think of a medium as a way to transfer and convey information about goods or services from the producer to the consumer, who is a potential buyer of that item. There are various ways to accomplish that in business besides using radio, television, or magazines. Product or company publicity, sales brochures, or exhibits can all be useful ways of conveying information to potential buyers.

It is increasingly important to think of media in the broadest terms, as communications. Advertising media used to be thought of solely as traditional, or mass. That is, planners and buyers worked with television, radio, magazines, newspapers, and outdoor. Anything beyond that was considered more specialized. Direct mail was handled by one group, event marketing by another, and promotions by a third. Today, most agencies look for integrated ways to make contact with consumers, perhaps including traditional advertising in Friends on TV, sponsoring a blimp flying over a popular beach in the summer, and putting the brand's message on coffee cup holders in Starbucks. The goal of these disparate efforts is to surround the target audience with a holistic campaign that presents them with the same message about the brand in various creative ways.

THE ROLE OF MEDIA IN CONSUMERS'LIVES

As our lives grow increasingly busy and demanding, and as technology moves ahead with ever more sophisticated ways to improve our lives, it seems that the media are playing a more and more important role in what we do, where we go, or how we behave. Many of us wake up to the sound of the clock radio; we read the newspaper while watching morning television and eating breakfast; and we connect to our offices via e-mail and the Internet. We commute to work either in the car listening to the radio, or on the bus or train surrounded by posters with advertising messages on them (or listening to a portable radio during the commute). At work, we are likely to see a broad array of Internet advertising or e-mail advertising messages, and many of us watch (or videotape) our favourite soap operas at lunchtime. When we get home in the evening, we'll probably turn on the TV to catch the local news, and after dinner we'll forget about our daily worries by watching some prime-time TV and catching up with the daily newspaper. Before we go to sleep for the night, we may check some information online, and then we'll probably glance through a couple of magazines while lying in bed.

When you sit down to watch TV and see a commercial that then appears in the magazine you are reading and on the web site you are browsing, and is mentioned again in that night's evening newscast because of the tie-in to a local charity event, you generally don't think about the effort that went into coordinating all of those elements. In fact, if the "seams"between them are too obvious, then something probably isn't working right! Although you, as a member of the reading or listening or viewing audience, are interested primarily in the particular programme or publication, the medium is interested in you as a potential buyer, offering you up to advertisers who wish to talk to you.

The role of media in conveying information through advertising messages is not something consumers generally consider. Indeed, when they do think about it they are likely to complain about being inundated by commercial messages! Yet despite the fact that no one has yet proven "how advertising works, "businesses continue to believe in its power, as evidenced by the $244 billion spent in this country on advertising in 2000.

MEDIA W0ORK WITH ADVERTISING

Advertising in the media performs the dual role of informing and entertaining. It informs us of the goods and services that are available for us to purchase and use. And, along the way, it often entertains us with some humorous, witty, or clever use of words and pictures. For example, let's say you have created a catalog for college students that features music, clothing, and household goods. You've shown it to some friends and neighbors, all of whom are convinced that it would be extremely useful to that target group. You have talked to several distributors and manufacturers of the items you want to include. Now, however, the question arises of what to do next. How do you inform people you don't know personally about this wonderful new product?

This is where the media can help. You could place an advertisement in several college newspapers or magazines, or perhaps buy some time on local college radio or TV stations. You'd want to put up a web site for your catalog that allows students to purchase online directly from the site. Your message, that "Student Stuff has everything for today's students, "would then be disseminated to an audience of hundreds, or possibly thousands, depending on your location. You might also generate additional publicity by holding student contests on key college campuses with prizes from the catalog, contests to which you could then invite local reporters.

Or perhaps you would decide to send personal letters to several influential student leaders, offering them a free sample in exchange for their opinion of the product. Whatever form of communication you use, all involve sending a message through a medium of one kind or another. Again, it is important to keep in mind that we are talking of media in the broadest sense. So in trying to promote your Student Stuff catalog, your radio ads or web site can show people what the product looks like and demonstrate how it works. Then, you might sponsor a fashion night at the mall as a public relations effort to heighten awareness of the clothes you have in the catalog. You could send out press releases in advance to notify the media of the event and thereby generate additional publicity both for the show and for your catalog.

You could offer retailers a special deal, such as contributing funds to the ads that they run (an advertising allowance), if they will promote the catalog in their weekly newspaper ads. You might also arrange for catalogs to be handed out on campus so that people can learn more about Student Stuff. By advertising the catalog in a wide variety of media, each one fulfills a slightly different role, but your overall message-that "Student Stuff has everything for today's students "-is conveyed clearly and consistently. Media advertising also performs another vital function. It helps offset the cost of the media communication itself to consumers.

If we did not have commercials on television or radio, the cost of programming would have to come through sponsorships, taxes, or government monies. Public broadcasting in the United States derives most of its income through semiannual pledge drives, during which viewers and listeners are asked to give money to pay for the services. Government funding provides additional revenues.

But even here, more and more public broadcasting television stations are accepting restricted forms of paid commercials as long as they are image oriented and not hard-sell. Indeed, there is even a network available, Public Broadcasting Marketing, to help advertisers place their spots on public TV stations across the country.

TASKS IN MEDIA

The broad field of advertising media can be broken down into three primary tasks:

- Planning how best to use media to convey the advertising message to the target consumer (the media planner).
- Buying media space and time for the message (the media buyer).
- Selling that space or time to the advertiser (the media seller).

Most large companies handle the media planning and buying functions through an advertising agency. Smaller firms will usually handle this task themselves, through their marketing director, or public relations coordinator. The role of the planner is to decide where and when the message should be placed, how often, and at what cost.

The plan is then implemented by the media buyer, who negotiates with the media providers themselves to agree on the space and time needed and to determine or confirm where the ad will appear. That buyer will, of course, be dealing with the salesperson at the media company, whose job it is to sell as much advertising space or time as possible.

2

Media in the Marketing

The media specialist through the planning and buying of media, those functions do not occur in a vacuum. Both media and advertising are part of the bigger picture of the world of marketing. The primary goal of marketing is to increase sales and profits. To return to our earlier example, where we were wondering how to market our student-oriented catalog, Student Stuff, we had considered many elements beyond which media to use. To market any product effectively involves not simply advertising it, but also figuring out how much to charge for it, where to distribute it, and how to manufacture it. In marketing jargon, these four critical elements are known as the "Four P's": Product, Price, Place (distribution), and Promotion. Although your job as a media specialist does not necessarily involve making the decisions on all of these criteria, it is critical that you have a clear understanding of how they work and, more importantly, how they can impact the media decisions and strategy.

In order to sell anything you must first have a product or service. You have to decide how much you need to charge for it (the price) so that you can make a profit. You must also figure out how and where the product will be made available to people (place, or distribution). And last, but not least, you must consider how you will let potential buyers know what you are offering (promotion). Within that last category, there are several key channels of communication: advertising, personal selling, sales promotion, direct marketing, event marketing, and publicity.

All can be thought of as media, or ways of conveying information to potential buyers. One of the most important things to remember here is that the arrows move in many directions. Almost any decision you make concerning media will have an impact on something else in the marketing mix. For example, if you decided to advertise on network television, you would have to ensure that your product was in fact available throughout the country. Or if you chose to concentrate your advertising efforts during holiday periods, you might consider lowering your price at that time to boost sales even further. The task of the media planner is to consider all of the marketing information available on the product and use that information to determine how best to reach the target audience through advertising media. In this way, the media plan can be thought of as the pivot point, or hub, of the overall marketing plan.

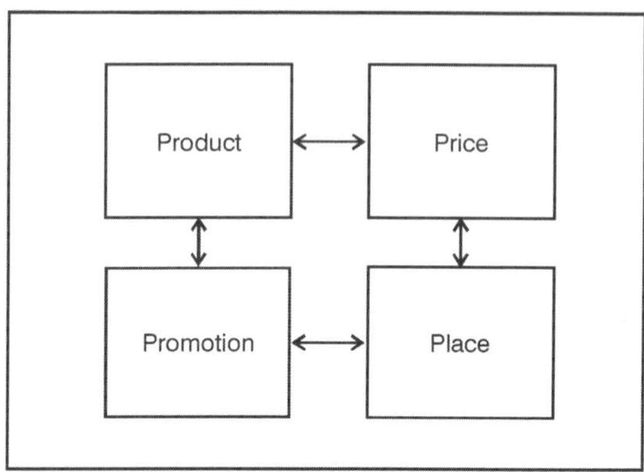

Fig. The Marketing Mix

GETTING TO KNOW THE CONSUMER

One of the most important pieces of information that marketing can provide for you as a media specialist is an understanding of how your consumers view and use your product or service. To do this you must know more about the brand and the product category. A brand is the individual product or service that you are trying to sell. It can be thought of as the name on the label. So Campbell's tomato soup is a brand, as is their chicken noodle soup, or their clam chowder variety. The product category could either be defined as all brands of tomato soup, or all kinds of soup. In the case of a service, such as insurance, the product category could be one type of insurance, such as life or home or auto, or all types. The brand would be one particular company such as Allstate Insurance, or State Farm.

One way to think about brands is to consider your own behaviour. When you go to the grocery store, you are usually not thinking in terms of product categories or brands. More likely, you are thinking about buying a container of Minute Maid orange juice, three Lean Cuisine frozen dinners, or a box of Kellogg's Frosted Flakes cereal. Similarly, when you have to decide which restaurant to go to, you will not categorize them the way marketers do, into quick-service, family-style, or steak houses, but will instead think in terms of the types of food-Chinese, Mexican, Indian, and so on. And within those groups, you will probably categorize them by geography, thinking of the specific restaurants by area.

What we need to know as marketers and media specialists, however, is how the consumer decides which brands and products to buy, as well as the process he or she goes through when purchasing an item. This will vary, depending on the type of product. Although a consumer might pick up any brand of windshield washer, the decision process she goes through to select the car she drives will take far longer because there are more elements to consider. Understanding these decision processes will help you decide which media might best be used both to reach your target and convey the desired message at the right time. For selling your student catalog, you could probably use a traditional medium such as college newspapers to increase awareness of your product. An automotive company, however, will use a wide variety of communication forms to sell its product.

Here, we take a general look at how consumers view and use brands. Then we can establish some foundations for the media plan. We do this by going back into the past and looking at what has happened in the marketplace both to the brand and the product category in which we are interested. In looking at how consumers use brands, we must answer several key questions: How much do consumers already know about the brand (brand and advertising awareness)? And when, where, and how often do they buy it (purchase dynamics)?

PEOPLE KNOW ABOUT THE BRAND

People have the opportunity to be exposed to at least 5,000 ads every week, so it isn't surprising that they don't remember many of them. In fact, a study conducted by the Newspaper Association of America in the 1990s shows that the percentage of people who can accurately remember the name of the brand they last saw advertised on television has fallen to an all-time low of 4 per cent of those surveyed. And although we talk about "great"ads that we saw on television last night, or read in a newspaper or magazine, we are probably unlikely to remember the brand which was being advertised.

Is Michael Jordan the spokesman for Gatorade or Powerade? Does Britney Spears advertise Coca-Cola or Pepsi? In today's increasingly competitive marketing climate, consumers are also likely to be exposed to more than one brand name in an ad. This comparison advertising is extremely common in categories such as analgesics, automobiles, and detergents. But while your brand, Brand A, emphasizes how much better it is than Brand B, will your target audience remember A or B?

How the Media Specialist Gets to Know Consumers

Finding out how aware your consumers are of your brand and its advertising is quite straightforward, although not without pitfalls. The easiest way to do this is through a survey (mail, telephone, or in person), in which you simply ask people what they remember about certain ads. You can do this in one of two ways-either unaided, where no prompts or assistance are provided, or aided, where you offer some kind of memory aid, such as mentioning something from the advertisement or giving an actual list of brand names and asking for further information on the advertising. The unaided method demands more on the part of consumers, asking them to tap deeper into their memories to recall the information you are seeking. With the aided method, you are basically asking people to recognize a brand and/or advertisement when it is placed before them, and then prompting them for additional information about it.

There are other issues to keep in mind with brand-awareness research. The most important is that you cannot expect complete accuracy. That is, there is always the danger with any kind of memory check that you will not get full information from the people you survey. Obviously, the longer the time between when people see or hear an ad and when they are questioned about it, the less they will remember about it. Human memory is highly fallible. People may attribute pieces of one ad to another ad, or recite a list of brand attributes from Brand A that really belong to Brand B. So if you do test consumer awareness of your ads, be sure that you keep in mind the possibility of inaccuracies in the responses.

In addition, you must remember that all of these responses are what consumers claim to recognize or recall. Even if you give people a questionnaire to fill out on their own they may not put down their real feelings or thoughts. They might not want to offend the interviewer or admit how they really feel, or for whatever reason do not want to tell the truth. For instance, they may have a vague recollection of your brand's name, but write down that they are very familiar with it. Having said that, awareness checks do play a vital role in letting you know more about how your consumer interacts with the brand and its advertising.

If no one can recall your brand name after it has been advertised on television every day for the past year, then you have a problem. It could be the message isn't convincing at all, or it could be you are advertising it in the wrong medium. Perhaps people can recall the brand name very easily but nothing about the advertising has stuck in their minds. The goal of increasing brand awareness should not be understated. It is commonly accepted that without consumer awareness of your brand, even the most spectacular media plan will be unlikely to generate many sales. People are far more likely to purchase a brand whose name they have heard before than one about which they have no information. There are many companies that conduct this kind of research.

Some of the larger ones are listed in the appendix. If you want to probe further into people's responses, you can find out more through focus groups, which are groups of 5 to 10 people who are interviewed together by a moderator. They are probed for their beliefs, attitudes, or feelings toward a given brand or product category and its advertising to help in development of the creative message as well as the marketing and media strategy. A newer, more in-depth technique for understanding consumers, at least in the marketing world, is the use of ethnography. Developed in sociology and anthropology, the technique involves close observation of what consumers are doing. This may include visiting their homes to watch them prepare a meal (for a brand like Kraft salad dressing) or spending a few hours with them in the gym (for a brand like Nike). The idea is to see up close how the brand or product category really fit into people's lives.

THE CONSUMER DECISION PROCESS

Many research studies have been conducted over the years to demonstrate the decision process that a consumer typically goes through when buying a routine product. In its simplest form, this process has three steps:

- Think.
- Feel.
- Do.

People must first think about the item (i.e., be aware of it and know it exists). They must then develop some kind of attitude or feeling toward it (i.e., like it and prefer it to others); and finally they must take some action with regard to it (decide on it, and actually buy it). This latter stage is the do part of the model.

The process is in fact far more involved than this. We can break these three stages down further, coming up with eight stages the consumer goes through in buying a product or service. These are:

- Need.
- Awareness.
- Preference.
- Search.
- Selection.
- Purchase.
- Use.
- Satisfaction.

To begin with, the consumer must first have a need to fulfill. He or she then becomes aware of the brands available to satisfy that need. After that, several brands are considered acceptable, and a preference developed for one or more of them. The consumer will then search for the brand(s) desired, and make a selection of one over the others. A specific brand is purchased and used. Finally, the level of satisfaction obtained with that purchase helps determine whether that brand is bought on a future occasion.

Of course, in reality, life isn't always as simple. There are occasions (and products) where people think about a product, buy it, and only at that point do they develop attitudes toward it. This is especially true for new product launches, where consumers have not had a chance to develop emotional bearings for the brand or category. Another point to keep in mind is that the decision process can sometimes get stalled at a stage before purchase. In our Student Stuff example, students may be made aware of the catalog, decide that they'd like to buy an item from it, but be unable to find the web site to make the purchase, and give up. Or they could get a copy of the catalog, look through its contents, and decide they actually prefer getting their books from Borders or Barnes & Noble.

THE CONSUMER BUYS PRODUCTS

One of the main drawbacks to using surveys or holding discussions with consumers about how they buy is that they are telling you what they think they do which may be very different from what they actually do in real life. Moreover, measuring their brand awareness of brand and advertising recall often ends up being a poor predictor of sales. So in addition to looking at awareness, or the top of the decision tree, you should also pay attention to what is happening at the bottom of the tree, with the purchase cycle. When are people buying your product? How much is bought? Is there some kind of seasonality to their purchases? All of this information will prove to be critical in planning and buying your media, and will have a major impact on how and when you schedule your ads.

When Do People Buy?

The answer to this question is more complex than it seems at first. You might say, "Well, they buy my product all the time. "But if you look more closely at purchase behaviour you will probably detect some kind of pattern. Although people are buying houses "all the time, "they are more likely to do so when interest rates are low and prices are depressed. People buy cars "all the time, "but sales increase when the new models come into the showrooms in the fall. And more sales occur in the second half of the month than in the first. Even everyday kinds of items have a timing component to purchases. Sales of cheese are higher at the weekends and around paydays because that is when people have more money to go shopping. Moving companies are busiest between May and October because that is when most people change their residence. Greeting card sales go up before every holiday.

If you know when consumers are most likely to buy your product, you can time your media advertising to take advantage of that purchase cycle. For major purchases in particular, you might also want to consider when people are thinking about buying. This might occur several weeks, or even months, before they make the actual purchase. So although Mr. and Mrs. Smith might buy a new Carrier air conditioner in July, they will probably start to think about which one to get several months prior to that. This provides you with a valuable opportunity to get your brand's message to the Smiths early in their decision-making process.

How Much Do They Buy?

The size of consumer purchases is another important element of the purchase cycle for the media specialist to know. That is, what proportion of your brand's sales comes from each size of the product? For Coca-Cola, it offers numerous sizes of its soda, from 12-oz cans, to 2 liter bottles, to sixpacks. The company needs to know which one is most popular? Do most people buy their soda in plastic bottles, glass bottles, or cans? Does Coke sell three times as many cans as bottles, perhaps suggesting that this is where the majority of messages should focus? It turns out that, twice as many adults buy the beverage in cans as buy it in plastic bottles (24 per cent vs. 12 per cent), and very few consumers are purchasing the glass bottles according to Mediamark Research, Inc. This kind of information is not only important for production and distribution purposes it can also play a key role in your media planning, for the users of each size are likely to be different kinds of people, with different media habits. The casual drinker who picks up the individual can is more likely to be a working professional female who is married, college educated, and living in the north central region of the country, whereas those who purchase the plastic bottles are more likely to be parents and to live in the south. Young working women prefer to watch programs such as The West Wing and Friends, and read Cosmopolitan and Glamour; older adults are more likely to choose 60 Minutes and Reader's Digest. Based on these differences in media preference, you may well end up with two media plans, one for the occasional purchaser of the single can, and another for the frequent user who consumes several plastic bottles per week.

LOOKING AT THE MARKETPLACE

Once you know about how consumers view and use your brand, the next step for the media specialist is to examine what has been happening to that brand in the marketplace in recent times. Given this information on past efforts to sell your product, you can decide whether to continue along the same path or try something different in terms of your media planning and buying. Examining the marketplace involves doing an analysis of historical data on both the brand and the product category. As the famous philosopher George Santayana said, those who do not learn from the past are condemned to repeat it.Some of the basic questions the media specialist might ask include the following:

- How long has this brand been available?
- How successful has it been throughout its history?
- How has it been positioned in the past?
- What do you know about the company that makes this brand?

You can think of this as genealogical work-trying to dig up as much "family background"on the brand as possible. You may find that the company has been in business for 150 years, suggesting possible leverage to be gained by emphasizing in the message the long heritage the brand possesses and even placing it in media vehicles that have also been around a long time. Or perhaps the company has been around forever, but is now moving in a different direction, starting to explore new opportunities, suggesting the use of new or different media. The Wrigley Company, for example, has for many years just made chewing gum. More recently, it entered into a joint venture with Crest toothpaste to produce a gum that is also beneficial to your teeth (part of the growing'neutraceutical'industry).

Yet all of its products might be considered to lie within the original and overarching purpose of the company: to provide consumers with convenient and tasty gum products. But the new product may be targeted at different groups of consumers, which, in turn, may result in a need for more diverse and/or more selective media. Perhaps its Doublemint brand would be advertised in women's service magazines such as Good Housekeeping or Woman's Day, while the new product, in contrast, may be better promoted in fitness books such as Shape or Men's Health, appealing more to young people concerned about their health.

What Are the Competitors Up To?

In doing a historical analysis of the brand you must also deal with competitive issues. That is, you should not only explore and uncover as much marketing and media information as possible about your own brand, but you also need to do the same for all the brands against which you do or plan to compete. The marketing part of these issues may be divided into three main areas:

- Product category trends.
- Brand trends and share of market.
- Brand's share of requirements.

Product Category Trends

Whether your brand has been available for half a century, 2 years, or is about to be launched, one of the most important pre-planning considerations for the media specialist is what is happening in your product category. If you are creating a media plan for the manufacturer of a Cannondale mountain bike, you would want to know whether sales of bicycles are increasing, decreasing, or flat. That will immediately influence your media budget, who you choose to target, and how you go about trying to reach them.

In some instances, in order to determine how the category has fared, you will have to decide what your "category"really is. If you are selling an oatmeal cookie, then it might seem obvious that it belongs in the cookie category. But perhaps this is a low-calorie, low-cholesterol cookie that belongs more appropriately in the "diet and health food"classification. Does a yogurt drink fit better into yogurt products or milk drinks? And what about children's software? Is that with software or children's media such as books and videos? How you define your product category will determine not only your assessment of the strengths or weaknesses of that category, but also the direction and potential marketing and media strategies you employ for your particular brand. To take the software example, if you decide it is part of the general software category, you might want to send direct mail to people who have registered their own software and indicated they have children in the household. As a children's product, however, you will probably do consumer advertising in parenting books such as Child magazine. You could also work with schools and libraries to offer special deals offering a free CD if they purchase three titles. Or you might choose to advertise the product to both target groups using a combination of those media.

There are numerous stories in advertising lore of how the redefinition of a product category gave new life to a moribund product or service. Amtrak had been witnessing declining sales for years as the country's sole passenger train in the face of stiff competition from the airlines. However, by redefining itself in the travel and recreation market instead of merely a method of transportation, the company was able to redirect its market in gand media focusso successfully that sales turned up considerably. Perhaps the most renowned case of redefinition is that of Arm and Hammer baking soda. By finding a new use for an established product (keeping refrigerators smelling fresh), the brand in effect positioned itself in two completely distinct categories-baking products and home fresheners. Today, it has a huge market share in the latter category, and has expanded into numerous other cleanser-related areas, from carpet freshener to toothpaste.

Once you have determined to which product category your brand rightfully belongs (or the category to which you wish it to belong), you are then in a position to examine trends in that category. You can do this in one of several ways. You may have access to product category sales from a trade association or manufacturers'group of some kind (such as the Juvenile Products Manufacturers Association if you are marketing children's toys, or the Electronics Industry Association if you are marketing electronics sales). You can often find such data in trade journals in your particular field (such as Supermarket News for supermarket food sales or Chemical Week for sales of liquid nitrogen). One invaluable source for this type of information is the journal Sales and Marketing Management, which comes out several times a year with overall category sales. Advertising Age also produces an advertising-to-sales ratio in all major product categories annually that shows spending on advertising relative to sales. In many larger companies, these data are routinely collected, usually within the marketing department.

In looking at category trends, be careful to look back beyond the past year. In fact, if you can find five to ten years of data, you'll be in a much stronger position to see what the real trends are. Another important point to remember is that there will be many factors to explain the rise or fall of product sales. These trends do not occur in a vacuum.

Intepreting Sales Trends.

Four factors that help explain sales trends are economic, social, political, and cultural trends. And each will, in turn, influence your media choices. For instance, if you are selling a new high-end digital Olympus camera with lots of fancy features, the overall health of the economy is going to have a large impact on whether people feel they can afford to spend the money to purchase such a piece of equipment. If you decide that despite the economic downturn you want to emphasize a sophisticated image for your product, aiming it at innovators who always want to buy the latest equipment, then you might use magazines targeted to camera aficionados, such as Darkroom and Creative Camera Techniques. If, on the other hand, you choose to emphasize the great value-for-money your camera still represents, you might look to a broader audience and use more popular, broad-based vehicles such as Popular Photography.

Politics can play an important role in the marketing of goods and services. For satellite TV services trying to promote themselves to rival cable subscribers, what happens in Washington at the Federal Communication Commission, or in state or local politics, will affect what they are allowed to sell and whether consumers are likely to buy the service. In 1999, satellite TV companies were allowed, for the first time, to beam local channels to their subscribers, a feature that had previously been banned and therefore impeded the growth of satellite services. They were quick to advertise this new benefit to prospective customers.

Cultural changes, although slower to occur, can also explain movements in product sales that have implications for media planning and buying. This is seen in the growth of ethnic foods, such as Mexican or Chinese dishes. The increasing popularity of different ethnic food products can be attributed in part to the enormous growth of the Hispanic and other immigrant populations in the United States, leading to a greater diversity of cultures that are gradually intermingling and changing tastes and preferences. Salsa now outsells ketchup in many areas of the United States, for example. People living in the West are 15 per cent more likely than the average to consume salsa, and 22 per cent less likely than the norm to eat ketchup. The marketers of these foods try different ways of reaching their target audiences, through product sampling in stores or sponsorship of community events.

Finally, social changes, which also tend to happen slowly, can ultimately have a major impact on media activities. The cigarette companies of today have a much tougher job selling their product than they did 20 or 30 years ago, primarily because smoking is no longer considered socially acceptable due to the proven health risks it carries. The marketing task is made more difficult because since 1971 they have been forbidden, by law, from advertising on television at all, and since 1999 from being on any outdoor billboards.So although you as a media specialist may not have to pinpoint all the reasons behind category trends, it is important for you to gain a broad understanding of what is really happening in the category and not simply limit yourself to whether sales are up or down. Having this additional background information will help you decide which media you can or should be using in your plan.

What Should You Measure?

Another important issue when looking at category trends is deciding which trends you should be measuring. Sales? Units? Volume? The answer to this may ultimately depend on the types of data you are able to obtain, but you need to keep in mind that what seems to be a trend when examining one number may disappear or be reversed if you turn to another. For example, while sales of your screwdrivers could be going up in dollar terms, you may actually be selling fewer units if sales are rising primarily due to price increases (i.e., you make more money on each unit sold, but sell fewer units as result). When looking at category trends in dollar terms, always remember to factor in the effects of inflation. What may seem to be a 7 per cent annual growth rate could turn out to be a 2 per cent to 3 per cent rate once inflation has been accounted for. Perhaps the category trend line shows that the number of units of shampoo sold is declining, but volume is holding steady. This might occur if the unit size has been enlarged, so the same total volume is being sold but in larger bottles. Again, ideally, you want to look at several trend lines using diverse measurements so that you can get an overall picture of what is going on in the category.

Brand Trends

When you turn your attention to individual brands, you perform analyses similar to those done at the category level. This time, however, you focus your attention on specific brand names. The use of the plural here is critical: You are not just looking at how your brand has been doing over the past several years, but even more importantly, you need to track how your brand's competitors have been faring during that same period. This requires finding the answers to the following questions:

- How many competitors are there?
- How many of these are major, and how many minor? In some categories, where there are just a few players, such as the airline industry, you should probably consider all of them, but in larger categories, such as fast-food restaurants, where myriad companies have offerings, you will do better to pay attention to the ones you believe are your most serious threats. In certain instances, it is a good idea to look at all of the competitors regardless of their size; you may find that the fourth-tier player of 3 years ago has gradually been gaining market share and is now a far bigger concern. Dell computers were for several years largely ignored by the likes of

IBM or Compaq. Today, however, Dell is the number-one seller of personal computers.

- How is the category characterized? Is it an oligopoly, where 3 or 4 brands define the category, or are there 20 or 30 brands each shouting to be heard?
- How aggressively do the brands in this category compete against one another? For example, is it advertising driven, or promotion driven, or does everyone rely heavily on direct mail? You can answer this either from your own experience in the category, or by looking at any available syndicated data on competitive media expenditures.

For each competitor (ideally for all of them, but at least for the major ones), you must also find out the following:

- What is the company's financial position? This can be found by looking at stock market information or Standard & Poors reports, where available, or by obtaining a recent issue of the company's annual report.
- How does the competitor position its brand? To determine this, you will have to use your own judgment. Examine the advertising for the brand and see what is being emphasized. Is it similar to your own current efforts, or not? If it is dissimilar, is that because there is an actual difference between the two brands, or do consumers just perceive a distinction between them? And who has the more favorable position?
- How does the competitor promote its brand? Which media are used? How much does the competitor spend to promote its brand? Where and when does it spend it money? The answers to these questions may come from several sources. Many large companies, and/or their agencies, subscribe to Competitive Media Reporting (CMR) or Nielsen Monitor Plus (NMP), the main providers of this type of syndicated data. Both show, on a weekly, monthly, quarterly, and annual basis, how much money was spent by a brand in each major media category. Smaller businesses may simply try to keep track of where their competitors'ads are appearing. This is not too difficult if you are dealing with a local product, but gets more complicated as the area that you or your competitors try to cover gets wider. You can also subscribe to a clipping service, which will do the tracking for you.

Share of Market.

Once you have looked at the trends for your brand and its competitors, you must then put that information together and see how your brand is faring in the marketplace. The percentage of total category sales that your brand enjoys is known as the market share. You should try to examine how this figure has changed over time. Have you been gaining or losing market share in the past few years? Again, be careful to avoid oversimplifying the picture. It could be that you have been losing market share, but so have your major competitors, because of the entry of several new brands into the category. We can see this in the media arena in television. Although 10 years ago the four broadcast networks commanded 90 per cent of the prime-time audience, today fewer than half of all viewers tune in to ABC, CBS, FOX, or NBC at that time, with the remainder watching cable networks.

Share of Requirements

One of the most useful pieces of information you can examine is the source of your brand's sales. This is known as the share of requirements. It is calculated by taking the percentage of total category volume accounted for by a particular brand's users. Quite simply, it tells you whether your brand is being bought primarily by your customers or by your various competitors'customers-and, conversely, how much of your competitors'sales are coming from your brand users. Looking at this figure, you will be able to determine what percentage of the volume that you sell is accounted for by your users, as opposed to people who usually buy another brand.

Let's say you are a manufacturer of a local brand of pretzels (Pioneer Pretzels), competing with other regional brands as well as a major national brand. As you can see in the table here, Pioneer Pretzels buyers account for 27 per cent of all the pretzels sold in the last 30 days. Of all the pretzels they purchase, 15 per cent of their usage is to your brand (Pioneer), and 12 per cent is to other brands. This means that 55 per cent (15 per cent/27 per cent) of their total category volume is given to your brand, which gives Pioneer a 55 per cent share of requirements. This is the lowest figure among all pretzel types, suggesting that Pioneer's users are not especially brand loyal, which could harm sales and future market share.

Where Is Your Brand Sold?

Once you have found out as much as possible about how your brand stacks up against the competition, you need to think about geographic and distribution considerations. Specifically, you must look at where your brand is selling well and where it is doing poorly both in terms of markets, regions, or states, and in terms of type of retail outlet.

This holds true whether your brand is available on a national, regional, or local basis. For unless your product is sold in just one store or location, there are likely to be some differences in sales according to geography and distribution outlet. What you discover by looking at the sales for your brand in these ways may lead you to develop a media plan with regional or local differences. Indeed, more and more marketers have adopted a regional approach to selling, realizing that people in Boise have different tastes, customs, and buying habits than people in Boston or Baton Rouge. So marketers are customizing their marketing and media plans (and, in some cases, their products) to meet the needs of specific areas of the country. Although some regional differences are obvious, such as higher snow blower sales in Maine than in Arizona, others might seem surprising (such as the fact that insecticides sell most heavily in the south). These types of differences occur not just at the product category level but also for individual brands. Dannon yogurt sells far better on the East coast than does Yoplait, which has traditionally been stronger out West.To understand geographic skews, the media specialist can turn to two pieces of information:

- Development indices.
- Market share.

DEVELOPMENT INDICS

You could, in theory, obtain sales data from every region or store in the country and look through them to find out your brand's sales picture. But a more efficient method for analyzing geographic strengths and weaknesses is to look at how the product category is doing across the United States and then how the brand is developing over time. Both of these are calculated by using developmental indices.

Category Development Index.

The category development index, or CDI, looks at product category sales in each potential region or market. A norm, or average, is calculated at 100, and then each area is assigned a value relative to that, expressed as a percentage. Numbers below 100 indicate the category has lower than average sales in a given region, whereas those above 100 suggest sales of the category are greater than the national average in a certain part of the country. If, on average, 30,000 tractors are sold per month per region across the United States, that might mean 25,000 units are sold in the East, 45,000 in the West, and 33,000 in the South. Eastern sales would index at 83 (25,000/30,000), meaning that sales in that area are 17 per cent below the national norm, whereas sales in the West would have a CDI of 150 (45,000/30,000), indicating that that region's sales are 50 per cent higher than average. Those in the South have a CDI of 110 (33,000/30,000), which shows that southern sales are 10 per cent higher than the norm. Based on such information, a company might decide to concentrate its marketing and media efforts in those regions with higher CDIs, as that is where there is greater potential for all tractor sales.

Brand Development Index.

You should not rely solely on the CDI in making geographic media decisions, however. You also need to look at how your brand stacks up against other brands in the category. One tool for this job is the brand development index, or BDI. The calculation is very similar to that of the CDI. You calculate a norm, or average, for all brands (or chief competitors) in the category, which is again set at 100, and then see how your own brand is doing in comparison. The John Deere tractor company might find its BDI for tractor sales is 10 per cent above average in the eastern region and 5 per cent below the norm in the West, suggesting that it is doing better than other brands in the category in the East, but slightly less well in comparison in the West.

When you look at the BDI, you need to keep the CDI in mind too. Once you have these two sets of data, you should compare your BDI to your CDI. In that way you will be able to find those markets where your brand is doing better than the category overall and, conversely, where your brand appears to be underperforming the category. For John Deere, its eastern BDI is greater than the CDI, so the brand is doing better than the category in that region. In the West, however, its BDI is below the CDI, so there is room for improvement here.

Armed with this information, you may choose to adopt one of three possible marketing and media strategies. You can focus your attention on those areas of the country where your brand is doing better than the category, playing to your strengths. Or you might choose to give more attention (and money) to the weaker markets where the category is doing well but your brand isn't, to try to bolster your sales there. Alternatively, you might decide to play it safe and concentrate on markets where both category and brand are successful. The one strategy you should probably avoid is pouring money into areas where both brand and category are doing poorly, as that suggests there is something about all the brands that is not liked or does not meet the needs of those consumers. To try and rectify that situation single-handedly is probably going to be more trouble (and cost) than it is worth.

MARKET SHARE

When looking at the development indices you can also find out how your competition is doing in each territory and calculate their BDIs. It is common to see that where your brand is doing well, your competitors are having a harder time, and vice versa. The exception here would be for a new or relaunched category where all brands are selling well, such as bottled water.

One way of investigating sales further in geographic terms is to look at your share of the market by region or locality. Is your brand number one in sales in the Central region but in third place in the South? Are you neck-and-neck in New York, but a distant second in Florida? Faced with these different scenarios you should explore some of the possible reasons behind the distinctions. And here you should go back to the other "P's" of the marketing process. Perhaps you have distribution problems in Florida that are harming sales. Maybe your brand is being undercut in price in the South by a local manufacturer. Or it could be that your chief competitor is flooding the local airwaves with promotional messages in New York and drowning out yours. By putting together the information you gather from the development indices with your market share figures, you will start to create a picture of how your brand is doing across the country. That will help you decide what marketing and media tactics might be needed in each situation.

The media plan will not be the miracle solution to all of the problems you might encounter, and you should not expect it to turn a floundering brand into a superstar. The better is your understanding of the marketing situation your brand is in, the more likely you are to come up with creative solutions to the problems. For example, if your problem is distribution, you might want to include extra trade promotions or incentives in your plan to encourage retailers or distributors to push your brand further. Pricing discrepancies might be alleviated by offering a coupon or on-pack premium to offset the lower priced competitors.

And if your consumers are being faced with a barrage of competitive messages in one medium, it might be wise to consider placing your own advertising in completely different media, or perhaps move to nontraditional media or special events to raise your own voice elsewhere. Finally, if possible, you should try to look at your brand's geographic strengths and weaknesses over time to see where the trends are going. Have you always been weaker in the Southwest, or does this seem to have started only in the past year? Is the overall category development index flattening out across the country, or moving to different areas? This is especially likely to be true for new product categories when they are first introduced, as was the case for palm pilots (PDAs) or sport utility vehicles (SUVs). As always, looking at several years of data will help you to avoid acting on "blips"in the numbers that might have disappeared without cause within a few months.

A Word About Budgets

One of the most important preplanning issues to look at is how much money you are likely to have to spend for media for the coming year. You may be given a specific amount up front, or you may have a range within which to work. In many situations, the media specialist is likely to come up with two or three alternative media plans at different spending levels, showing what could be achieved with $500,000, versus $1,000,000, versus $2000,000, for example. If possible, you should try to be flexible on the budget at this point, keeping in mind that if you lock yourself into a set figure from the very beginning you may limit your creativity later on when you put the plan together.

Timing and Other Issues

The last major area to explore in the preplanning phase is that of timing. This may include the month of the year, the week of the month, the day of the week, or the hour of the day. Although some timing considerations can be rationalized and justified, others may be out of your control. Some companies skew their messages toward pay periods, such as the 15th and 30th of the month, knowing that people are more likely to spend money when they have just been paid. Packaged-goods marketers may choose an end-of-week schedule to reflect the increase in grocery store shopping from Wednesday through Friday.

Other considerations may be out of your control. The CEO of the company that makes your brand of sports drink may demand that you purchase television time during the Wimbledon tennis tournament. He not only likes tennis but wants to get tickets to the event. The marketing manager may refuse to have the brand advertised in any magazine that accepts cigarette advertisements. Perhaps your candy company has been a sponsor of a local parade for the past 50 years and you cannot break with that tradition. There might also be key timing opportunities that you should consider. If you are going into a Summer or Winter Olympics year, you might want to look for some way to tie into that.

Although this sounds out of the league of any but the largest national advertisers, there may be an Olympic swim team member in your own town whom your brand of swim goggles could support in some way. Or if your city is celebrating its 200th anniversary and your pen factory has been around for almost as long, you could get involved in the preparations for related events. Or maybe next year has been designated the Year of the Child so you can look for opportunities to promote your diaper brand. Be alert and open to new ideas and opportunities such as these that might come along infrequently and sporadically but could greatly enhance your profile and sales locally, regionally, or even nationally.

DEVELOPING OPTIMAL MEDIA OBJECTIVES

Setting objectives is something we are all familiar with in our day-to-day lives. "I will get an'A'on this test"; "I'll lose 10 pounds by Christmas;""My goal is to become the CEO of the company by the time I reach 35."Whatever the objective may be, if you didn't have one it would be difficult to know what you've achieved! In the media planning context, you need to establish firm objectives for your plan in order to demonstrate how it will help your brand achieve its marketing goals. Although you may feel that in order to execute a media plan you must keep returning to your starting point, moving one step back for every two you go forward, it cannot be overemphasized that everything you do on the media planning side must be coordinated with the overall marketing strategy.

Therefore, in order to establish your media objectives-what you intend the media plan to achieve-you must first reaffirm and clarify the goals of your complete advertising programme to ensure that your media objectives fit in with the goals set in your brand's marketing objectives.

THE MARKETING OBJECTIVE LEADS TO THE MEDIA OBJECTIVE

The media specialist is likely to be presented with the marketing objective, rather than having to develop it on his or her own. It is usually stated in some quantifiable form, such as "sell x thousand more widgets in 2003 than in 2002, "or "increase awareness of Brand X to 75 per cent within calendar year 2003. "It may relate to any of the major marketing functions, such as increasing shelf space in the store, or increasing the number of distribution channels for your product. And frequently it is expressed in terms of specific volume and share goals, such as "within calendar year 2003, bring Brand Z's total volume sold to 25 per cent of the total category, raising its market share from 35 per cent to 38 per cent. "

If the marketing objective is vague or ill-defined, simply "increasing awareness"or "improving distribution, "then at the end of the year (or whatever time period has been set to achieve the goal) there is likely to be considerable debate over whether the plan was successful or not. It is also going to be more difficult for the media specialist to devise a plan that satisfies those objectives; even if awareness does improve, how much higher must it go in order for the media plan to be considered a success?

Along with understanding the marketing objective, the media specialist should also look at how that objective will be achieved, because that will affect what the media plan is supposed to do. Examples might be to increase product penetration among potential users by taking sales away from competitors or bringing new users into the marketplace. Alternatively, the strategy might be to encourage people to use your brand more frequently, perhaps offering new uses for it. In order to increase the sales of Ragu Spaghetti Sauce, the marketing objective might be to get current users to buy additional jars of the product for use in new and different ways besides just pouring it onto spaghetti. For the media plan, this could lead to an objective of increasing the frequency with which target users are exposed to the message to remind them of the various ways they can use the product.

For a hospital with the marketing objective of introducing some new health education programs to encourage more people in the community to choose the facility for their medical needs, the media objective could be to reach 75 per cent of people who live within a 10-mile radius to inform them of what is available. Clearly, the marketing objective has a major impact on how the media plan develops, affecting the target audience, communications used, and media selected.

MEDIA AND THE ADVERTISING OBJECTIVE

As we noted earlier, the marketing objective may relate to any of the four major areas of the marketing mix (product, promotion, distribution, or price). Therefore, before establishing specific media objectives it is also essential to focus on how the media affect your advertising goals. Although your ultimate marketing goal for most goods is to sell more product (or services or image), unless your audience finds out about the product through the media that you use, that goal is unlikely to be reached. You need to be aware, at the same time, of the other marketing mix elements.

If the product is no good, your media advertising will have little impact. Similarly, if you advertise your product heavily but it isn't available in most stores, sales will not improve. Frequently, the objective of your advertising is tied in to the stage at which the target audience is in the decision-making process. As we noted earlier, this process breaks down into three very broad areas: think, feel, and do. Once you have decided that you need a new TV set, you will think about what brands are available. Then, you will consider how you feel about each one of them. And finally, you will select a particular brand and take action (do) and buy it. This process can be better understood by revisiting the eight main stages of the consumer decision-making process:

- Need.
- Awareness.
- Preference.
- Search.
- Selection.
- Purchase.
- Use.
- Satisfaction.

NEED

Before you can hope to sell any more widgets, people have to have a reason to buy them. Contrary to what many advertising critics maintain, advertising cannot persuade people to buy something they do not want. Indeed, it is often easier to think of this first stage in the decision process as reflecting people's wants, for in today's industrial society most people are able to satisfy their basic needs, such as food and shelter.

Even when people buy products that seem pointless or silly, such as chia pets or hula hoops, they may feel they have a need to indulge in it just for fun. And although you might argue that no one really has a need for a $100,000 BMW, the person who chooses to purchase one clearly feels that he or she deserves this luxury automobile. Defining what the need might be for the product helps the marketer to understand the motivations behind why people might buy it, which in turn may provide some clues as to ways of reaching those people through the media. Although everyone buys toothpaste, if you can segment the target into different groups according to their motivation for use, you could reach each one through a variety of media forms. People who are most concerned with cavity protection are more likely to have children and therefore could be reached in parenting magazines. Those who want toothpaste with whitener tend to be younger, and reachable through fashion and beauty books. For the ones who use toothpaste several times a day to keep their breath fresh, health and fitness titles will be more appropriate. And all of that is just within magazines. Research may reveal that different segments have different media habits altogether, leading you, as planner, to determine what those media options should be.

AWARENESS

Once the consumer has determined that he or she needs a particular product, it is the job of marketing to make the person aware of the choices that are available. For the media specialist, this means reaching that consumer in the right place and often enough so that your brand's message is the most relevant and convincing. And it is not enough to simply make people aware of your brand; the real goal here is to make them aware of your brand's message. You might well be able to reach 95 per cent of all cat owners to make them aware of the new cat food that you sell, but unless they also learn that your product provides 100 per cent of a cat's daily nutritional requirement, which is more than any other competitor, your advertising is unlikely to increase sales. Of course, keep in mind that while you are promoting your message, every other cat-food company is also trying to boost awareness of its own brand.

Based on the various choices the consumer sees and hears, he or she will then develop specific brand preferences. Ideally, the marketer would like that consumer to develop brand loyalty to his brand so that every time Julie Smith needs to buy more running shoes, for example, she always picks Saucony. A media plan to enhance preference for your brand of mascara might include opportunities for the target audience to try your brand at home, perhaps by offering a free sample in magazines or via the Internet.

Once the target audience decides it might prefer your brand over others, the audience's next task is to find out where to purchase the item. Here, media advertising can be a big help, by notifying people of the places that sell your product. You have probably seen or heard this yourself in local or regional TV and radio ads that list which stores in your area stock the item. Billboards can be used, too, to display the retailer's or dealer's name. A web ad can link directly to a local seller of your product. If your audience cannot find the product when it wants to buy it, then not even the best advertising placed in the most appropriate media will increase sales.

SELECTION

Brand selection may seem like an easy stage for the consumer. If she has decided already that she prefers Cover Girl nail polish over others, and has learned that it is sold in Wal-Mart stores, then isn't it obvious that she will buy it? Not necessarily. Today's consumer is faced with so many different brands that, once in the store and standing in front of the shelf, she may decide to go with your competitor's offering, because it is on sale, or packaged more attractively, or comes in larger bottles. So the selection process is a crucial stage for the marketer and the media specialist to consider. From a media perspective, the nail-polish user may be encouraged by in-store vehicles such as in-pack premiums or point-of-purchase radio. Personal contacts can also be very important at this stage. Someone who has come into the store in order to buy a mid-range computer may be encouraged to select your more expensive model by being offered 1 year of free parts and service by the dealer.

Purchase and Use

Clearly, the ultimate goal of marketing and media plans is to persuade consumers to purchase the product. But if they buy it and never use it, then there is no reason for them to ever buy another one. No marketer can remain successful by continually targeting new product users.

Often, one marketing and media objective is that of encouraging consumers to use the brand. In media planning terms, this might involve increasing the message frequency so that users are reminded of the different ways in which the brand can be used. A good example of this, in past years, has been Bisquick baking mix, which often places recipes in its print ads to encourage people to use more of the product, and hence purchase it more frequently.

Satisfaction

The final stage in the consumer decision process is really a feedback loop into the earlier ones. If people use your private mail delivery service but are dissatisfied with the rate of delivery or quality of the staff, then their dissatisfaction will likely mean they won't use your service again. What is worse, they may tell their friends about their bad experience and decrease your potential sales even further.

So customer satisfaction is extremely important for future success. Satisfaction is generally not listed as the primary marketing or media objective of a plan, but should nonetheless be kept in mind when deciding where and when to place your advertising message. It is perhaps harder to achieve through the media, because it is ultimately up to the user to decide whether he or she is satisfied. But many advertisers promise "satisfaction guaranteed or your money back"as a way to reassure consumers that they will, indeed, be content if they buy your brand.

Advertising Objectives and the Consumer Decision Process

To see how advertising objectives might fit in with each stage of the consumer decision process, let's take an example. If your client is the Prudential

Health Maintenance Organization (HMO) offering employees a plan for managed healthcare, you would probably not have to create a "need"for your service. It is very likely, however, that you would want to increase awareness of Prudential's plans. So your advertising objective might be to boost awareness of the HMO from a baseline measure of 40 per cent to 70 per cent among employees at the companies that offer the Prudential plan.

It could be that most people know about your company, but are still choosing your main competitor as their healthcare provider. Here, your advertising objective would be to improve preference, so that instead of two out of five employees selecting your HMO over the other one, three out of five do so. Setting advertising objectives for the subsequent stages in the decision process is somewhat less common, because it is believed that advertising has a less direct role to play here. But you still might want to encourage consumers to use your HMO, setting as your advertising objective to boost member visits to your facilities from an average of two times per year to four by encouraging preventative care.

Media and the Consumer Decision Process

The advertising media will also affect each of these stages in the consumer decision process. To continue with the HMO example, you might boost awareness of Prudential through widespread local TV and radio ads or outdoor billboards in the communities where you have offices. Consumer preference could be encouraged by sending direct mail to potential members offering them a free check-up at one of Prudential's sites.

They could be helped in the search process by putting ads that provide maps to your office locations in local newspapers. Selection might be helped by having open houses for new members to visit the doctors'offices and meet the personnel. These special events could then be promoted in local media and perhaps receive additional publicity through press releases. Finally, to get current members to use the HMO more for preventative care, you might create a monthly newsletter that tells them about the numerous programs you have available.

Let's take another example. Say you are in the market for a new automobile. That puts you in the initial stages of needing a new car. You see some TV ads for various makes and models, increasing your awareness of what is available. Three of the cars that interest you are the Honda Accord, the Ford Taurus, and the Chevy Impala. You read several automotive magazines, check out their resale value on Edmunds.com, and pick up the Consumer Reports issue on new cars and decide that these models fit your needs. Now you have developed a preference for these particular models out of the hundreds that are available. Your next step would be to visit some car dealerships to search out the cars themselves. Here, your interaction with the salespeople is likely to play a major role in influencing your decision. You will also probably talk to friends and colleagues and return to the Internet to look in greater detail at each car's specifications. Faced with all of the information you have gathered, you select the Impala. You negotiate a deal and drive the car home; now you can use it, and based on your experiences, you will develop a degree of satisfaction with your new purchase. If you are happy with the car, you may well buy another Chevrolet the next time you are in the car market.

The media's role is important at several points in the process. Television advertising is frequently used to create or enhance awareness, informing people of the qualities of the brand and what it has to offer. Both TV and magazines can help develop consumer preference. Here, you might see ads that compare the Chevy Impala to other cars in the same class, or that cite the awards and rankings the car has received in automotive competitions. And as we noted above, personal contacts and the Internet may be critical too. Retail or local ads on spot radio and television and outdoor billboards help reach consumers who are searching for your brand; sometimes you will see a brief message from the local dealership tagged on to the end of a commercial. To encourage people to select your offering, the media may offer special discounts or added features, such as a 60,000-mile warranty or $1,000 cash back.

Getting people to use the product is also important. Although this is not an issue in the case of an automobile, it can be for other consumer products. Campbell's Soup, for instance, uses print ads that feature recipes that include its soups in order to encourage people to take the product off the shelf. As with the marketing objective, the more measurable the advertising objective is, the easier it will be to determine whether it has been achieved. This can be done either through specific testing after the ads have run for a while, or by setting up some kind of market test and determining the effect of advertising on sales.

ESTABLISHING MEDIA OBJECTIVES

Armed with clear and concise marketing and advertising objectives, you are now ready for the most important part of the media planning process-setting media objectives. As with the other goals, once you have a clearly defined course set for you, it becomes much easier to figure out how to get there. There are three main elements involved in the media objectives:

- Defining the target audience.
- Setting broad communication objectives.
- Considering creative requirements.

Definifg the Traget Audience

Although you haven't yet started to put a plan together, you are probably beginning to realise that much of the most important work needs to be done beforehand to establish the media objectives. Defining the target audience is one key step you must take in the objective-setting process, for only by knowing who you wish to reach through the media will you be able to put together a schedule that will convey your brand's message to the right people. Ideally, the target audience for your media plan should be identical to the audience for the overall marketing plan. Since most of a brand's sales are typically generated by its current users, the target audience definition is likely to include some product usage qualification. A marketing plan that is intended to increase sales of Finesse shampoo-conditioner combinations might have as its target audience "women 25 to 54 who currently use shampoo-conditioners, with an annual household income of more than $50,000. "Life stage can be a crucial factor too. A plan geared towards increasing awareness of your new Sony digital camcorder might have as its target "adults 18 to 49 who have had a child in the past year. "

Often, however, you will find that the media target may be both more and less precise than the marketing target. This is largely because the media themselves have traditionally been bought and sold on the basis of fairly basic demographics, such as age, sex, income, education, or race. For example, although your brand of Carr's crackers may be aiming to sell 20,000 more packets this year by expanding its user base and capturing more sales from "young adult gourmet lovers who enjoy entertaining and eating out, "when it comes to creating your media objectives, your target may be "adults 18 to 34 with college education and an annual household income of more than $40,000. "This is a more precise definition in that it specifies a particular age category as well as particular income and education levels, but it does not take into account (at least definitionally) the lifestyle variables (like eating out, entertaining, and fine foods).

Some advertising agencies have developed ways of examining people on the basis of these lifestyle or "psychographic"characteristics. The syndicated data sources of audience information are generally more limited in this respect. And if you are dealing with a nonconsumer target, such as retailers or dealers, you may find yourself without much syndicated information at all, relying more on your experience and judgment. You can assume, for example, that if you are trying to promote your refrigeration equipment to restaurants one place to put your message would be Restaurant News.

Another important consideration for defining your media target is whether it should be broad or narrow. Because everyone in the country uses laundry detergent, does that mean your media plan should be aimed at "all adults in the United States who use laundry detergent"? Increasingly, the answer will be "no. "Today's brands are becoming more and more segmented. So we don't just have one box of Tide on the store shelf, but powder or liquid Tide, Tide with Bleach, or Ultra (concentrated) Tide. There are 14 different sizes of Tide Liquid alone, aiming to suit the needs of diverse groups, from singles living alone to large families. Each of these groups is likely to have different media habits and preferences-and trying to create a media plan that would reach everyone would ignore the needs of different population groups both in terms of product benefits and media usage. There might be one plan aimed at mothers with young children, another for those with large families, another with an environmental slant, and a fourth promoting the smaller size for urban apartment dwellers. Each plan has a different target audience.

There is also the opposite danger, however. That is, you might define your target audience so narrowly that it would be almost impossible to reach them. You might, from previous research into who buys your personal digital assistants (PDAs), find that they are most likely to be men with a median age of 39 who work as salesmen traveling in the northeast region of the country taking on average three business trips per month, earning $80,000 or more a year, with a nonworking wife and three children, living in the suburbs, owning an American-made car, and enjoying computer games. But there may be only 50 of these!

There are two major problems to note here. First, most traditional media will not only present your message to your target, but also to many others for whom the product is probably irrelevant. This is a problem that can only be alleviated by careful consideration of exactly who your target should be and which media will best reach that audience.

A second consideration in establishing media objectives is the cost-effectiveness of the plan. It may well be the chief concern of you or of the top executives of your company. You could come up with an extremely elaborate and highly targeted media plan, with a clearly defined target audience and appropriate communication objectives, but if it is going to cost twice as much as is in the marketing budget, you are unlikely to be able to execute it. When defining the target audience, you must be sure that the audience will be reachable at an affordable cost. As the maker of Oral B toothbrushes, you cannot hope to reach everyone who brushes their teeth on a budget of $10 million.

Having defined your target audience, your next step should be to find out as much as possible about the individuals who make up that audience. Ideally, you should not only know their basic demographic characteristics (age, sex, education level, income, profession, etc.), but also learn more about the kinds of products they use and the media they tend to hear or see.

Again, depending on the target, you can often obtain this information from syndicated data services. Or you may have to rely on your own judgment and experience. So if your target for a hand-held computer is men 25 to 54 who take six or more plane trips per year, you should also know that they are also more likely to have a computer in their home, drink imported beer, own an American Express Gold Card, read photography magazines, listen to jazz radio stations, and watch pro football on TV.

COMMUNICATION OBJECTS

When it comes to writing down what you expect the advertising message to do for your brand, you will start to find that all of a sudden you are dealing with the art, rather than the science, of media planning. These objectives are measurable to some degree through communications tests with the target audience that find out what information the audience is taking away from the message. In addition, media calculations can be made to estimate what the plan should achieve.

But many of the criteria you need to use to establish what the goals should be are far more evaluative and rely on your judgment and subjective response to everything that you know about the brand, its advertising, and the marketplace. These objectives must also be in line with the overall marketing strategy for the brand. If you are trying to increase your market share of the athletic shoe category by 2 percentage points by increasing distribution into mass merchandise outlets, then your communication objective might involve increasing awareness of your brand among your target audience by 15 per cent within the first 3 months of the campaign.

Communication objectives will vary, depending on the kind of product you are promoting. For launching a new brand of cat litter, you probably want your advertising to generate awareness of the product. If you are advertising Maytag dishwashers, in contrast, which have been around forever, your message will more likely serve as a reminder to consumers of the reliability of the product. These differing objectives will also affect your reach and frequency goals. For a new product, you would want to establish some initial awareness levels and then sustain them (e.g., generate awareness of the product among 75 per cent of the target group within the first 3 months of the campaign).

Don't forget to consider your competition, too. You might set as your objective to achieve, within the first 6 months of your new campaign, awareness levels for your Cannondale mountain bike that are equal to or greater than those of your closest competitor. Geography is another factor. If your bike is the number-one brand in the category with the highest awareness levels in the Northeast and Pacific, but falls to number two or three in the South, then you might set different objectives in different parts of the country, broadening your reach in areas where awareness levels are currently lower. There are three main factors to consider when developing communication objectives: campaign timing, category and brand dynamics, and media reach and frequency.

Campaign Timing.

Here you should consider what stage your campaign is at are you launching a new product or changing the strategy for selling it, or is this the third or fourth year of an ongoing campaign? Also think about the specific timing of the campaign. Are you trying to communicate a seasonal message to warn young adults about drinking and driving during the holidays? Or maybe it's April and people are starting to think about summer vacation, so now is the perfect time to begin promoting your park district's swimming pool. Thinking of your communications objectives within a specific time frame will help to ensure that your media plan stays focused on that period.

Category and Brand Dynamics.

If you study the trends for your brand in particular as well as trends within the category overall, your communication objectives will be firmly fixed in reality. That is, if research shows that users of lawn-care products are extremely brand loyal, it makes little sense to say the objective for Scott's weed killer is to gain 15 market-share points from your competitors in the next 12 months. Related to loyalty, you should think also about what degree of consumer involvement with the category can be reasonably expected. It's hard to get people excited about staplers or canned tomatoes, no matter how wonderful your creative message or media plan.

Try to be objective about your brand's positioning, too. Is your advertising message really very different from competitors', or is it in fact just another version of the same idea? If you look at the advertising for most products, you'll see that the latter is far more common than the former. Almost all banks tout their low financing rates, whereas nearly all beers talk about great taste, and most garbage bags emphasize their strength. None of this should be too surprising; you wouldn't want to buy a beer that did not taste good, or a garbage bag that wasn't strong.

Reach and Frequency.

Having stated earlier that communication objectives tend to be more subjective than objective, more art than science, there is still a role for some numbers here. But they should only be included if you will have some way of measuring them. The two key concepts to consider here are reach and frequency. These are the two most commonly used media terms in the whole planning process. The reach of the plan refers to the number (or percentage) of the target audience that will be reached by the brand's advertising in the media.

That number is determined by calculating what percentage of the target audience will be exposed to the media in which your ad appears. Along with knowing how many people will have the opportunity to see or hear your ad, you also need to state how many times they need to do so in order for the message to have some effect. This is the concept of effective frequency. You should identify some reach and frequency goals as a way of measuring whether your communication objectives were achieved. If the communication goal is to "increase awareness of the brand by 10 per cent among the key consumer target, "then that can be measured by establishing what percentage of the target was actually reached with the message and how many times they heard it, and whether brand awareness levels did in fact go up.

Creative Requirements

The last area that should be considered in preplanning discussions is any special creative requirement that will affect the media selected. If you are introducing a new car and want to emphasize its solid engineering through long copy and details, you will have to think in terms of the media that can allow you to do that.

Or, if your task is to promote Chicago as a vacation destination for families, then the creative might consist of many different sights or sounds from that city to convey the desired image, and be placed in media such as print or the Internet, TV or radio. The message will, in part, determine where you choose to place it. Yet another example might be introducing a new Pillsbury cake mix. Your ads will showcase the delicious results of using the product, so the visual element is going to be particularly important. Immediately, this leads you in a certain direction when starting to consider your media-plan strategies and tactics.

3

Exploring the Media

We are all familiar with television, radio, the Internet, newspapers, or magazines from the consumer's standpoint. That is, we don't think twice about picking up the newspaper every morning, listening to the radio on the way to work, going online to look up a specific web site, watching TV when we get home at night, and leafing through a magazine in bed before going to sleep. For advertisers, each of those points of contact we make with the medium represents an opportunity to communicate with a potential target for their product or service.

So, for example, the local car dealer will place his ad for a GMC Envoy in the daily newspaper in the hope that you will see it in the morning and stop in at the dealership on the way home from work or at the weekend. The First National Bank might put an ad on the radio in the morning hours to reach commuters on their way to work to alert them to the bank's favorable interest rates on savings accounts. When you sit back and relax in the evening to watch television, a wide range of advertisers will remind you of their brand of beer, cookies, pet food, or coffee, hoping that when you next visit the grocery store theirs is the brand you will select. And finally, right before you fall asleep, advertisers in magazines will try to persuade you that their credit-card company will be there when you need it.

MEDIA VERSUS COMMUNICATIONS

The task of today's media planners has become much broader than in times past. Instead of just considering the traditional media (TV, radio, magazines, newspapers, outdoor), the planner now must evaluate all forms of'brand contact,'wherever or however they occur. Should Kraft Macaroni and Cheese sponsor the local Little League teams?

Can Columbia Sportswear be the official sponsor of an Olympic ski team? Would it make sense to put Powerbar ads along running trails? Or could Campbell's Soup ads pop up on the web site weather.com whenever the temperature falls below freezing in the location being viewed? The key with all of these communications is that they must be integrated with the traditional plan. That is, Powerbar's trails message should look and feel like its magazine ads, and should appear in the plan as another regular line item, scheduled in conjunction with all other media. And as with all media-planning elements, the selections must tie fully into the brand's marketing and media objectives.

Media Categories

Once you have clearly defined media objectives, the next step will be to decide which media types, and vehicles within those types, will best help you achieve your goals. Before exploring that further, we need to think about what the different media can offer you as an advertiser conveying an advertising message. Here, we consider the six major media categories: television, radio, Internet, magazines, newspapers, and out-of-home. Keep in mind, though, that there are many other alternatives available to you, such as direct mail, public relations, or promotions.

There are various ways of categorizing the media. We can contrast the print media of magazines, newspapers, and outdoor billboards with electronic media-radio, Internet, and TV. We can also make an important distinction between media that are predominantly local (newspapers, outdoor billboards, and radio) and those where most ads are placed on a national basis (TV, Internet, and magazines). Here, we look at the major characteristics of each media form.

A Television in Every Home

Almost every household in America has a television set, and two-thirds (75 per cent) have two or more. The average household owns 2.4 TV sets. More than 9 in 10 (94 per cent) homes operate their TV sets via remote control. Television is the largest mass medium available for advertisers. In 2000, about $59 billion was spent promoting goods and services this way. Households in the United States have their TV sets on, on average, 71/2 hours each day, which is one of the highest viewing figures of anywhere in the world. The average household can receive 75 channels, thanks to the presence of cable.

Broadcast television programming is usually divided up in two ways: by daypart and by format. The daypart refers to the time of day the programme airs. There are nine standard dayparts. Programme formats are also standardized into 12 main types. Again, it is worth emphasizing that these breakdowns are really only the concern of the programmers and advertisers; you don't choose to watch "situation comedies"or "reality-based programs, "but rather decide to watch "Wide World of Sports"on ABC on Sunday afternoon or "Survivor"on CBS on Thursday night.

The popularity of different programme genres changes over time. Typically, the two most popular types are dramas and situation comedies. In the mid-1990s, newsmagazines (such as ABC's 20/20 and NBC's Dateline) became extremely popular, in part as a result of networks realizing they were a relatively inexpensive form of TV programme to make. The average prime-time drama can cost more than a million dollars per episode, compared to a few hundred thousand for a newsmagazine. For example, in 2002, the six cast members of the very popular NBC sitcom "Friends"renegotiated their contracts so that each one would earn $1 million per episode for the following year of broadcasting.

More recently, reality programs such as "Who Wants to be a Millionaire"and CBS's "Survivor"took hold in the audience's favour, leading to a slew of copycat programs that created a glut of that programme type. Not surprisingly, viewers grew bored with seeing too much of the same format, and ratings for dramas and sitcoms rose again. The challenge for media planners and, particularly, media buyers is to predict which shows will be popular several months, or even 1 year from now, buying them at a less expensive cost and enjoying higher than predicted ratings.

There are four main types of television to consider: network, syndication, spot (local) and cable. Beginning in the mid-1990s, the ownership of these various entities became more and more consolidated so that today, just a handful of large media companies have majority control of all four types of TV, squeezing out the independents or mom-and-pop operations that flourished in the first 50 years of television. The viewer is not really aware of who owns what, and does not differentiate, for the most part, between network or cable or syndication. He or she chooses to watch a certain programme, regardless of how or where it airs, or who created it or owns it. So the distinctions we draw here are purely for media purposes.

Network Television

Network television consists of four major broadcast networks: ABC, CBS, NBC, and FOX. There are also three smaller networks: UPN (owned by CBS), WB, and Pax (owned by NBC). A "network"is actually made up of hundreds of local stations that become "affiliates"of the national organization. There are in total 1,276 network affiliate stations, about half of all TV stations on air (2,482). Each station receives a set amount of money every year from the network, in return for which they agree to air national programs for a given number of hours every week, although as the networks have looked for ways to cut their costs in recent years, they have attempted to cut or eliminate these payments. Network programs air at the same time in every market within a given time zone. So CBS's 60 Minutes appears at 7 p.m. on Sunday night in the Eastern zone, 6 p.m. in Central markets, and 5 p.m. in the Mountain zone. Programs in the Pacific time zone are shown at the same time locally as in the East.

Network shows come with several minutes of commercial time both within and between programs that are sold by the network. The local station is then able to sell an additional 1 to 3 minutes of commercial time in the hour to local or regional advertisers, depending on the daypart. Historically, local commercials always had to appear in the commercials that aired between programs, but in recent years that rule has been relaxed, allowing local or regional advertising within the programme too. The research findings on the relative effectiveness of ads appearing between or within programs has been mixed. The local station also decides what to air when it is not showing network programs. This might include locally produced shows, such as local news or current affairs programs, or programs purchased from independent producers, known as syndicated programming.

Stations not affiliated with a network are known as independents. Today, there are more than 800 such stations in the United States, most of them broadcasting on the lower-frequency, locally based UHF signal. Each one decides which programs to air throughout the broadcast day, and is responsible for selling its own commercial time.

Syndication

One of the major sources of programs for independent stations is syndicated programming. Here, an individual programme (or package of several programs) is sold on a station-by-station basis, regardless of that station's affiliation. It may be of any type or length. There are two main types original shows, and off-network fare. The former are filled with game shows, such as Wheel of Fortune, and talk shows such as Oprah. They are sold either by the program's producers or by syndication companies, such as Viacom's King World, that put together packages of properties.

The distinction between syndication and network shows is that syndicated programs can air at different times in different markets as well as on different networks. This leads to syndicated shows having to be "cleared"by each local station that chooses to buy them. The clearance figure refers to the percentage of markets across the country that can view that particular show. So, for example, if a syndicated talk show is "cleared"in 70 per cent of the United States, it means that broadcast TV stations seen by 70 per cent of all TV viewers have purchased that programme. Syndication clearances generally range anywhere from 70 per cent to 99 per cent.

It is worth noting, too, that some network programs do not have total (100 per cent) clearance because an affiliate station may refuse to air them, or will put them on at a different time than the rest of the network. For example, early on in its airing, ABC's police drama NYPD Blue received good ratings and won numerous awards, but could still not be seen by viewers of the ABC affiliates in several Texas markets because the affiliates felt the programme was too offensive. The goal of many network programs is to produce enough episodes to go into the syndicated marketplace (usually 100 episodes). This is known as off-network programming, and helps fill up the hours of airtime that stations have when network shows aren't running. Programs that have been popular on the networks can continue to air for many years in syndication. Hits from the 1970s and 1980s, such as MASH, Cheers, and Cosby can still be seen on TV during the early-evening or late-night hours in syndication.

Spot Television

Spot television is another way to purchase television time. Here, instead of contracting with the network to distribute a commercial to all of that network's affiliate stations across the country, an advertiser can pick and choose which programs and stations to use, placing the message in various "spots"across the country. As noted earlier, about half of all TV stations are not affiliated with a network, a proportion that will continue to diminish as networks (and their multimedia conglomerate owners) buy up independents as regulation is relaxed on station ownership. The spot TV buy could be as small as a single station in one market, to a couple of hundred stations across a region. Although the actual cost of placing spots on local stations is lower than a total network buy, once you start including a large number of markets it can become quite expensive.

Spot TV time is sold either by the individual station and/or by station representative firms, or rep firms. These firms put together packages of stations, known as unwired networks (because they are not physically linked together, or wired). Rep firms can usually customise buys for you, allowing you to pick only those stations that you are interested in in a given number of markets.

Cable Television

Cable television is sometimes thought of as a relatively new way to distribute programs and commercials, but in fact it has existed as a means of conveying television signals since 1948. Because it does not depend on over-the-air signals but comes into the home via wires laid underground (or sometimes on poles on the street), reception is much clearer in many areas. That was the original reason behind its growth-so that people in Eugene, Oregon, or Lancaster, Pennsylvania, could receive the signals of the broadcast networks more clearly.

Although the broadcast networks distribute their programs from a central location to each of their affiliates, cable programs are sent via satellite from the cable network to individual cable operators (franchises) within each market, which then distribute the signals to the subscribers'homes. There are more than 10,000 separate cable systems operating today, although the majority belong to one of the large multiple system operators (MSOs) that have cable systems in numerous markets. In 2001, the ownership stakes were changed again, with the purchase of the largest operator, AT&T Broadband, by the number three player, Comcast. This creates an MSO that serves 22 million cable subscribers and heavy concentrations in 17 of the top 20 markets.

Another difference between broadcast TV and cable TV, from the consumers'standpoint, is that consumers must pay a monthly subscription fee to receive cable service. The average monthly cost of cable in 2000 was approaching $40. For an additional monthly fee, consumers can receive one or more of the pay cable networks, such as Home Box Office (HBO), Showtime, or Cinemax, which do not show any advertising at all.

Cable TV is made up of a wide variety of different networks, many of which specialize in certain kinds of programs or appeal to certain types of people. This was originally called narrowcasting, in contrast to the more diverse or broad-based programming found on broadcast TV. CNN (Cable News Network) shows 24 hours of news and information programming, whereas ESPN airs sports all the time and Comedy Central has 24 hours of comedy. There are several cable networks, such as USA Network and TBS, that are more similar to the broadcast networks in their programming, airing a variety of different types of shows, from adventures to situation comedies to movies and dramas.

The number of networks available varies by system. Those that were built in the 1950s and 1960s typically have smaller channel capacities than do newer systems. Today, some franchises operate systems with 200+ channels on them. Large capacity is becoming increasingly common as the technology improves to allow for it. In particular, as cable signals are delivered digitally to the home, rather than via analog wires, this enables the operators to deliver far more'information'to viewers.

The development of cable TV as an advertising medium began in the early 1980s and has grown steadily ever since. Today, $2 billion of total TV advertising dollars go to cable television, representing 28 per cent of the total amount advertisers spend in television. Most of cable's ad dollars are purchased on a national basis, although the medium has been growing rapidly at the local level, too. If you manage a local restaurant or a bank, you can run your commercials throughout the area, or can confine your messages to a particular cable system's area. National advertisers can also use local cable, customizing their messages down to the neighborhood (system) level.

You can purchase time on several systems at once by going through a central sales office, known as an interconnect. This is similar to a rep firm-you select the cable systems on which your ad will appear. Most interconnects operate on a metropolitan or regional basis, such as Greater Chicago, or the Bay Area.

Satellite Television

Although listed here as a type of television, satellite TV is more of a means of distribution at this point. From being a way for rural inhabitants to receive any kind of signal via large C-band dishes, today's far smaller satellite dishes can be seen perched on the outside of houses all across the country, and are as common in urban markets as rural or suburban. By delivering digital TV signals directly from the satellite and eliminating the cables that have to be laid under the ground or above ground on poles, satellite services are able to offer a far larger number of channels to viewers. In 2001, one of the biggest satellite companies, EchoStar, which operates the DishTV network, agreed to buy another fairly large operator, DirecTV, formerly owned by the Hughes Corporation (part of General Motors). The antitrust issues that this raised were not fully resolved at the time of printing, but consolidation will clearly impact the satellite TV industry.

About 10 per cent of the country now receives television via satellite, and the battle between that form of distribution and cable is increasingly fierce. Without much of the high cost of transmission incurred by cable, satellite providers have been far quicker in offering new or high technology services to customers, such as two-way interaction with the TV set and the functionality of personal video recorders.

NEW FORMS OF TELEVISION

The development of new forms of television began in the early 1990s, but it was not until the latter part of that decade that technology began to catch up with the pipe dreams of the inventors. One of the first to be available was pay-per-view (PPV). Here, several channels are allocated to special programs, such as movies or sporting events, that are purchased by the cable subscriber on an individual basis.

They may cost as little as a few dollars, or as much as $50 for a special boxing match, for example. In order to be able to receive this form of programming, the cable linking the television to the cable system operator must be two-way, or addressable, allowing the operator to deliver the programme to individual households on demand. At present, more than half of all homes are addressable. The growth of digital cable, now in about 6 million homes, has greatly enhanced the ability of viewers to have more control over what and how they watch TV. All of the major cable system operators-such as Comcast, AOL-Time Warner, and Charter-have been rapidly upgrading their systems in recent years, seeing great potential in enhancing their revenues not only by offering more channels to viewers, but also by selling numerous ancillary services, from Internet access through the TV set to special channels featuring local news and weather.

With some of these enhancements, viewers can call up sports statistics as an overlay on the screen while viewing a football or baseball game. Beyond that, companies such as Wink Communications or Worldgate have been testing services that let consumers interact with their TV set, responding to promotional offers, for example, or getting more localized weather information. That information can be customized to individual households, so General Motors, for instance, could send an ad for a Cadillac to a more affluent and older home, and a GMC Envoy ad to households with children. Another way that television is being altered is through the video recorder.

The introduction of personal video recorders (PVRs) at the tail end of the 1990s promised to revolutionize the way people watched TV and, as a result, the advertising business for that medium. Although it has not yet done so, with fewer than 1 million homes owning them at the end of 2001, the concept and technology do, indeed, suggest a radically new way to view television. PVRs, offered by companies such as TiVo and Replay, put a large computer hard drive onto the video recorder, which allows it to digitize the programme as it is delivered to the TV set and therefore gives consumers the ability to fast-forward or pause programs as they air, and to skip commercials. At the same time, viewers can programme the device to find programs to record on a regular basis either by title (all new episodes of Law and Order, for example), or by actor/director (find anything with Brad Pitt). If these capabilities are taken to the extreme, we end up with every consumer creating his or her own schedule of programs, watching whatever programs he or she wants, whenever he or she chooses.

The implications for advertising are potentially huge. Television is planned to a large extent based on programme dayparts. What happens when there is no such thing as "prime-time"television anymore? And what if the viewership of a programme no longer occurs simultaneously because large numbers of people are recording the programme for viewing at a later date? What would the programme rating be based on? Last but not least, some of these PVR devices have a built-in mechanism to skip commercials, something that the manufacturers have realized is a double-edged sword, because the possible absence of ads will cut off an important revenue source for networks and programmers alike.

For now, these issues are not being directly addressed because penetration of PVRs is still less than 5 per cent. But the technology could easily be migrated to the digital cable box, at which point the implications for TV programmers and advertisers will become far more serious. Ultimately, instead of TV being a form of mass communication, the medium will become a means of one-to-one or personalized electronic marketing.

The use of the TV to connect to the Internet and the computer to view television has been happening only slowly. Despite promises that the two devices would become interchangeable by the 21st century, consumers have shown that they see them each as distinct and different from the other. TV viewing tends to be a more passive, "lean back"experience, in contrast to the active involvement required of the "lean forward"computer/Internet activity. Nevertheless, we are likely to continue to see new attempts to somehow merge the two media in the future.

Benefits of Television to Advertisers

Whichever type of television advertising you choose, you will enjoy a number of benefits unavailable from any other media. Among these benefits, television's ability to imitate real-life situations, its pervasiveness, and its broad reach are especially remarkable. The most obvious advantage of television advertising is the opportunity to use sight, sound, colour, and motion in commercials. This form of advertising is generally considered the most lifelike, re-creating scenes and showing people in situations with which we can all identify.

That does not mean we don't see cartoons or animated commercials, or fantasies on the screen; today's electronic wizardry lets TV ads show us everything imaginable. But of all the media available, TV comes closest to showing us products in our everyday lives. This is not only important for package goods advertisers-firms such as Pillsbury, Anheuser-Busch, or Unilever, who are able to show us what their products look like and how they are used or enjoyed-but also for service companies such as Marriott Hotels or American Express, which can offer us ways to use their amenities. As the Internet continues to expand, and bandwidth grows, many believe that TV-like ads will become more common there too.

THE MOST PERVASIVE MEDIUM

Television advertising is the most pervasive media form available. Several slogans from TV commercials have entered the mainstream of conversation, such as Bud Light's "Whassup?"or Wisk detergent's infamous "ring around the collar"line. Characters in commercials have also become part of our lives, such as the lonely Maytag repairman, or Tony the Tiger for Kellogg's Frosted Flakes.

Reaching the Masses

Another important advantage of television from an advertising perspective is the wide reach of people it offers at any one time. Even in programs with ratings of 8 or 10, you are reaching about 9 million individuals! Although there is generally a smaller audience for the commercials than for the programs themselves, nevertheless, television remains a truly mass medium. Moreover, by buying time on several different programs shown at different times and/or on different days, it is possible to reach a wide variety of individuals. And although an individual ad appears for a short time (usually 15 or 30 seconds), if it is repeated on several occasions more people are likely to be exposed to it, often more than once. This helps build brand awareness, which in turn may lead to the formation of favorable attitudes or intentions to purchase that brand.

Drawbacks of Television Advertising

Unfortunately, television advertising has unique drawbacks as well as the unique benefits we've just discussed. Four of the most commonly encountered drawbacks are cost, limited exposure time, cluttered airwaves, and poor placement of ads within or between programs.

Dollars and Sense

Perhaps the biggest disadvantage for advertising on TV, particularly at the national level, is the high cost. The average 30-second commercial during prime time in 2000 cost $300,000. An ad in the airing of the 2002 Superbowl, television's most expensive ad opportunity, cost about $2,000,000. For many advertisers this is way beyond their budget, leading them to cable or spot TV as cheaper alternatives.

Quick Cuts

Another drawback to this medium is its brief exposure time. Although many ads are seen several times within a short period of time, unless the commercial is particularly inventive or unusual it is likely the viewer will ignore it or be irritated by seeing it after the first few occasions and will deliberately try to avoid the message. Controversy remains over just how many times people can be exposed to spots without getting bored or annoyed, a phenomenon referred to as commercial wearout. In the future, this drawback may be avoided through interactive TV, where viewers select the kinds of messages they are more interested in, finding out more about a specific brand or product in detail. The key here is that this self-selected audience is more interested and involved in the message.

Cluttering the Airwaves

A related factor that is becoming an increasing concern for advertisers is the sheer number of ads appearing on TV. This leads to clutter of spots, again believed to reduce the effectiveness of individual commercials. There is evidence to support this fear. From 1990 to 2000 there was a 300 per cent increase in the number of spots shown on prime-time network TV. Part of the explanation for this is the increase in the number of broadcast networks (Fox, UPN, WB, PAX). But another major reason is the growth in the number of shorter length commercials.

For many years, the standard television spot lasted a full minute. Then, in the mid-1960s more and more advertisers started using 30-second commercials, finding them more cost-efficient and no less effective. As costs continued to increase during the 1970s and early 1980s, advertisers tried the same tactic, shifting to even smaller commercial lengths. Today, the 15-second spot accounts for 27 per cent of all network TV commercials. The result of clutter on consumers is questionable, but research suggests that it hinders the communication, sometimes considerably.

Placing Spots

Another area that has provoked a good deal of discussion is where commercials should be placed for optimal effectiveness. For network TV, you can buy time either within the programme (in-programme) or between two shows (break). Although some believe there is no difference in viewer attention between these two options, others feel that you are likely to lose more viewers during the breaks than within the programme itself. On spot TV the break position used to be the only timeslot available, although in recent years the "rules"have been relaxed, as commercial breaks have slid a few minutes into the programme rather than only at the top or bottom of each hour.

Related to this placement issue is where to position your commercial within the series, or pod, of spots being shown. Evidence suggests that the first ad to appear will receive the most attention, followed by the last one; those in the middle are likely to suffer from viewers switching channels, not looking at the screen, or leaving the room. The advertiser, however, does not routinely get the choice of where in the pod to air its ad. Some advertisers will pay a premium to ensure their ad appears first, but this is not always permitted.

RESEARCH ON TELEVISION

Much of the research literature on television has focused on two key issues: the impact of a lifelike message and the effects of programme environment. Buchholz and Smith found that the more "involved"consumers are in the medium, the stronger are their cognitive responses to ad messages. Kamins et al. examined how TV ads are evaluated depending on the mood created by the programme in which the ads appear. Other research articles are noted.

RADIO-THE "EVERYWHERE"MEDIUM

Radio is the oldest electronic advertising medium. It first became popular in America in the early 1920s and since that time has managed to hold its own against all other media forms. Although families no longer sit around their radios as they once did to listen to the most popular programs of the day, they still rely on this medium for both information and entertainment. Indeed, almost every home in America has at least one radio, and most have several of them. People listen to the radio, on average, for 3 hours 17 minutes every day. Most listening (84 per cent) occurs between 6 a.m. and 10 a.m. Increasingly, that listening occurs outside of the home. Almost all cars (95 per cent) are fitted with radios, and people can carry the medium with them wherever they go.

There are more than 13,000 radio stations across the country. Of those, 5,009 operate on the AM (amplitude modulation) wavelength, while 8,298 are FM, or frequency modulation, stations. The primary differences between them are in reception area and audience. AM stations can broadcast over a wider distance, but because the sound waves are impeded by any kind of obstruction (hills, tall buildings) the sound quality is inferior to FM stations, which broadcast in a narrower listening area. AM tends to be listened to more by older adults, reflecting the fact that more AM stations offer news and talk programs rather than the music formats that dominate the FM wavelength. Radio stations are either commercial, accepting advertising as their chief source of revenue, or noncommercial, funded by public monies and/or audience sponsorships. Commercial stations, on average, will air anywhere from 9 to 20 ads per hour, frequently concentrated in blocks of 3 minutes or more.

As with television, radio is classified by both daypart and format. The different formats that are available for the advertiser are not defined the same way by the listener. Radio dayparts and formats. Today, radio represents about 8 per cent of all advertising expenditures. The two main types of radio advertising are network (national) and spot (local). The way programs and ads are distributed is similar to that of network and spot broadcast TV.

Network Radio

Unlike television, network radio is less important than local radio is to advertisers. It currently receives 4 per cent of all radio dollars. Like TV, however, a message placed on network radio is distributed via satellite to each network's affiliate stations. These stations are paid an annual sum to take, or "clear, "the network's programs.

Perhaps surprisingly, almost two-thirds of all radio stations are affiliated with one network or another. The kinds of programs they receive from the network may be aired every day, such as the ABC newscast, or periodically, such as Casey Kasem's Weekly Top 40 show. There are presently four major radio networks, each of which has subdivisions based on the programming and the demographic makeup of their listeners. Altogether, there are 31 different net works. ABC Prime is aimed primarily at listeners from 25 to 54 years old through news and talk radio, whereas the stations that are part of ABC Genesis tend to be favored by younger adults, under 35, with contemporary hit radio and urban formats.

From an advertiser's perspective, one key benefit of using network radio is that you can go through a single source to place your ads across a region or across the country. The downside of this form of radio, however, is that you have less flexibility in choosing the stations you wish to be in. If you buy the CBS Spectrum Radio Network, you may get the number 1 station in Biloxi, Mississippi, but a distant fourth station in Little Rock, Arkansas.

Spot Radio

About 96 per cent of radio's advertising dollars are spent in spot markets, where you buy time on individual stations on a market-by-market basis. Here, if you were placing the advertising for Coldwell Banker realtors, you could buy time on individual stations in a market, regardless of which network they belong to, and choose which markets you wished to target. The advantage of purchasing radio in this way is that you can select the exact stations and/or markets in which you wish to advertise your product. This also allows you to customise the message to each location, so that, for example, Home Depot home improvement stores are able to mention the address or phone number of different locations in each market's ad. Some stations are linked together only for the purpose of selling advertising time. They constitute an "unwired"network, allowing you to select which stations within the group you wish to use based on your demographic or geographic preferences.

Typically, an advertiser buys time through a representative, or rep firm, rather than dealing with every station individually. So if you are trying to target teens with the Microsoft X-Box videogame, you could go to a rep firm that offers you stations that do well against that group. One example of unwired networks include the Wall Street Journal Radio Network, which offers classical music and performs well with adults over 25. Again, for the advertiser, using a network of this kind provides you with a single invoice for all of the stations. But, as with wired network radio, you may end up buying time on less attractive stations as part of the package deal.

Satellite Radio

We saw the arrival of satellite radio services. XM Radio and Sirius Radio both deliver about 100 different channels via national satellites. Consumers need special receivers in order to tune in to these services, and must also pay a monthly subscription (about $10/month) for the privilege. One incentive for them to pay is that about half of the stations air without commercials. XM has 71 channels of music and 29 entertainment/news/sports offerings. One-third of the total are without commercials. Sirius has 50 commercial-free music channels and 50 with other content. Even on those channels that include advertising, the amount will be far less than on regular radio stations-6 minutes per hour, compared to 15 to 20 minutes on terrestrial stations.

The content offered by satellite radio ranges from niche forms of music to college radio stations that let alumni keep up with their favourite college sports teams to syndicated talk show hosts such as Howard Stern or Rush Limbaugh. In addition, both companies have deals with the major U. S. auto manufacturers, who will be building satellite radio capability into several of their more upscale models going forward. The jury remains out, however, as to whether consumers will be willing to pay for something they are used to getting for free. Although they "learned"to do so for television back in the 1980s, the perceived value of the radio medium versus television may not be as high among most radio listeners.

Streaming Audio

As the Internet develops further, more and more people are listening to the radio via their computers through a technology generally known as streaming audio. Radio signals are digitized and then sent through the

Internet. Many traditional, land-based stations offer simultaneous signals on the Web, whereas other stations have been created solely online. Although still accounting for a small proportion of total listening, surveys suggest that nearly one-third (30 per cent) of the population has at some point tuned in to radio on the Web.

BENEFITS OF RADIO TO ADVERTISERS

As an advertiser, you cannot afford to ignore the many benefits of radio advertising. Although it does not offer the visual power of television advertising, it does provide the opportunity to reach targeted audiences frequently, at a reasonable cost.

LOCAL APPEALS

As we mentioned earlier, most advertising dollars in radio are spent at the local or regional level rather than on the networks. Radio is therefore listened to primarily as a local medium, allowing you the opportunity to tie in to local events, news, or celebrities.

REACHING THE RIGHT AUDIENCE

Because of the way radio stations are formatted, the medium provides you with targeted, specific audiences. If you run a local health club, you can reach women 25 to 54 by placing your message on light rock stations. Or, as the owner of a religious bookstore, you can promote your store by advertising on the local religious radio station.

Radio also offers good opportunities for reaching ethnic groups. In areas with sizable Black or Hispanic populations, you are likely to find at least one station that appeals to each of these minorities. It will generally have a very loyal following. For a baby-clothing manufacturer, for example, advertising to Hispanics may turn out to be very profitable because they tend to have larger families than non-Hispanic households.

Imagery Transfer

For many advertisers, radio is seen as a secondary medium, used in conjunction with a major print or television campaign. The good news here is that research has shown the power of radio ads to create a visual image in listeners'minds from the TV commercials they have seen for that same brand. This process, known as imagery transfer, gives radio ads offer far more impact than the auditory stimulus alone and therefore greater potential influence on consumer response.

Keeping Costs Down

Compared with television, radio is an extremely inexpensive ad medium. A 30-second spot in prime time on a broadcast TV network may run as high as $300,000, whereas the price for that same length commercial on a local radio station will be closer to $11,000. Of course, these costs are linked to the number of people you will be reaching.

Building Frequency

With a TV buy, you are usually looking for high reach numbers. In order to gain frequency, you need either a very large budget or inexpensive day parts. On radio, however, because the costs are so low, it makes sense to buy a lot of time and build up frequency against your target audience. It also makes sense to do this for strategic reasons; people tend to listen to a particular station for a fairly brief period of time, so you want to ensure you reach them while they are listening. You should keep in mind that listening habits are not seasonal, so frequency can be built up year round.

Radio and Purchasing

Research shows that the time between media exposure and purchase is shorter for radio than for any other traditional medium. This means that your potential consumers may well be listening while they are making their purchase decisions.

Flexible Messages

Compared to the high production costs and long lead times of television, radio is extremely flexible. If your ad is read live on the air, as is often done, you can change the message at very short notice without much difficulty. You can vary the message for different day parts or station formats, perhaps using different music backgrounds depending on the type of music played on that station. Radio also offers the flexibility of tie-ins to local retailers or other promotional opportunities, such as local contests or events.

DRAWBACKS OF RADIO ADVERTISING

In addition to the numerous benefits of radio advertising, there are a few drawbacks to keep in mind, as well. Each of these can be seen as a challenge; most can be overcome with some planning and creativity. When we listen to the radio, we are usually doing something else at the same time, making it a background medium. Ads on radio must therefore work a lot harder to grab and keep our attention.

Sound Only

Radio can only offer sound, rather than the sight and motion of television. However, the medium can still be used to great effect because it offers the possibility of inspiring the listener's imagination. You can hear the waves crashing against rocks, or breaking glass, or party chatter, and conjure up images in your mind of what the scene looks like. Radio advertisements also tend to feature humour fairly often both as a way to get attention and because the audience is less likely to be distracted by any visuals and can listen to the words. And as noted earlier, if radio is used in conjunction with similar TV commercials, listeners will often transfer the TV images to the radio spot.

Short Message Life

Because we listen to radio in the background, for the most part, ads on this medium have a very short message life. Like TV, and unlike newspapers and magazines, once the ad has aired, the opportunity for exposure has disappeared. This makes it all the more critical to grab the audience's attention right away with a message that is relevant, involving, and interesting.

Fragmentation

One of the drawbacks for radio is the fragmentation of the medium. We no longer just have "country"stations, but "hot country, ""young country, "and "traditional country"formats, among others. Each one appeals to slightly different kinds of people, so if you wanted to reach them all, you would have to buy each type of country station in a market. Audience shares, particularly in major markets, may be very small, which makes it hard to use the medium as a reach vehicle.

Research on Radio

Although radio is considered a "second cousin"to television in the realm of electronic ad media, research has been done to compare the two forms. In addition, the power of sound, and of music in particular, has been studied to see how that impacts radio ad effectiveness. Legal issues in the radio business are noted here, because the legal policies adopted by radio stations as far as which ads are accepted or not have a direct impact on the kinds of radio commercials that are broadcast.

NEWSPAPER ADVERTISING

Newspapers are one of the oldest media forms in this country. They were also one of the earliest media to accept advertising. In fact, the first advertising agencies were established to handle the purchase of space in this medium. Some of the earliest ads were for "medicinal"remedies, such as Lydia Pinkham's Compound.

In contrast to many other countries that have national newspapers, in the United States, the majority of newspapers are written for and distributed to a primarily local audience. As a result, most of the advertising is placed on a market-by-market basis. You can also choose which section of the paper to appear in, such as news (local, national or international), sports, entertainment, business, fashion, food, home, and travel, among others. There are currently 2,397 newspapers published in the U. S. This figure includes both weekday and Sunday editions. That number has remained relatively stable over time.

In 1970, for example, there were 2,349 papers published. Newspaper audiences are measured in terms of circulation, or the number of people who subscribe to or purchase the newspaper. The past decade has witnessed a decline in the percentage of the adult population that says they read a paper daily. Currently, about 57 per cent claim they do so, in contrast to the 78 per cent who read a paper back in 1970. What is even more worrying for the newspaper industry is that the readership figure is lower among younger people, who constitute the medium's future readers.

Another problem the industry faces is the demise of the two-newspaper town. Most large cities used to have at least two competing newspapers; today, due to the high costs of running a newspaper, that is the exception rather than the rule. Only in the largest cities (New York, Los Angeles, Chicago) are there still two or three daily papers. This not only harms the newspaper industry, it is not particularly good news for advertisers either. Without competition, the paper can set its advertising rates wherever it wants them, as long as it can still compete with other media alternatives. As major cities have dropped competing papers, some of the readership has moved to suburban or weekly newspapers.

The growth here is not too surprising, given population shifts from city to suburb in the past few decades. The focus of these titles is far more local, writing about high school sports scores or local ordinances rather than national or regional news. For advertisers, it offers the opportunity to bring the message down to the truly local level. National advertisers such as Gap Stores can announce the opening of a new store in Arlington Heights, Illinois, in the Arlington Heights Post, instead of a zoned or regional edition of the Chicago Tribune.

Newspaper Advertising Revenue

The largest part of newspaper advertising revenue (45 per cent) comes from retailers. This ranges from large companies, such as major national department stores like JC Penney and Sears, to regional banks like Fleet or Harris Bank, down to Joe's shoe repair shop around the corner. Second in importance as far as newspaper ad revenues are concerned is classified advertising (40 per cent). The most important classified sections are for real estate and automotive, which together account for the majority of classified ad dollars.

The third type of newspaper advertising is that which is placed on a national basis so that it appears in all (or most) papers across the country. This type of advertising represents only 15 per cent of total advertising revenues for the medium, despite the efforts of many newspapers to position themselves as valuable national vehicles in the face of increased competition with other local media, such as spot TV and radio, regional magazines, or billboards. The main problem that advertisers have with using newspapers on a national basis is the considerable premium that it costs to run their ads in all markets. Most are reluctant to pay that premium, which can cost up to 75 per cent more than a local or regional ad. Newspapers also offer a medium within a medium, in the form of free-standing inserts, or FSIs. These are preprinted sheets that are usually distributed within the Sunday paper. Most of them carry coupons. On Sunday, too, most newspapers carry a special magazine supplement, either produced by the paper itself or coming from one of the nationally syndicated Sunday supplements, Parade and USA Weekend.

At one point it seemed that newspaper classified advertising would be greatly diminished by the Internet. Automotive and real estate classified ad sites were very popular at first, and threatened to take revenues from the printed newspapers. It did not take long for newspapers to set up their own Internet-based advertising sites, either as part of their own individual newspaper sites or in concert with other newspapers (careercentral.com). In the hot economy of the late 1990s, the impact of the Internet on newspapers'classified business was minimal; how the industry fares in a less robust economy remains to be seen.

BENEFITS OF NEWSPAPERS TO ADVERTISERS

The top 10 newspapers in the United States reach nearly 10 million consumers every day. Add to that the circulations of the other, smaller, newspapers in the country, and you'll begin to see just what kind of exposure is possible with newspaper advertisements. But, in addition to reach, newspapers offer advertisers a number of important benefits.

Timeliness

The day after the stock market crashed in 1987, ads appeared in many newspapers reassuring consumers and stockholders that everything was still all right. Financial services companies reacted similarly after the terrorist attack on the World Trade Centre in 2001. And McDonald's quickly responded in newspaper ads when it discovered that someone at one of its agencies had stolen winning game cards to several of its "instant-win"promotions. The company immediately created newspaper and TV ads to apologize to the public, and then added a new game with daily prizes awarded randomly to customers in the store.

Unlike magazines or even television, newspapers are by their very nature filled with "news. "People turn to them for the latest information on products, prices, and availability. The role that newspaper advertisements play in purchase decisions may be critical. A survey found that 70 per cent of all newspaper readers agreed with the statement that "The paper helps me to decide where to shop and buy. "And 65 per cent felt that the newspaper was more important than television in making purchase decisions. In addition, electronic scanner devices in most supermarkets and retail stores are now able to assess the link between advertising and sales more directly and rapidly. Data suggest that newspaper ads can triple the sales volume for items that are advertised at reduced prices.

Desirable Audience

In the battle to attract advertisers, newspapers can offer highly desirable audiences. A newspaper reader is more likely to be better educated, have a higher income, and be more involved in upscale activities than nonreaders. People with a household income of $75,000 a year or more are more likely to be newspaper readers

In contrast to other media, readers spend a considerable amount of time with the newspaper. In 1999, the average length of time given to reading the daily paper was 45 minutes. And on average about two-thirds (67 per cent) of all newspaper pages are actually opened, a figure that depends in part on the number of pages in the issue. In thinner papers (10 to 32 pages), 78 per cent of all pages are opened, but when the paper becomes much bigger (81 to 204 pages), only 63 per cent are opened.

Another consequence of the time readers spend with the paper is that it offers the media specialist more opportunity to provide detailed information. If you are trying to sell a new home equity loan programme, you need the space to provide details on the terms of the deal, as well as on bank locations so interested consumers can find you. Although you might worry that so much fine print will be boring or encourage page-turning, those people who are in your target audience will probably be interested enough to read through the entire ad (assuming the copy is inviting and attention-getting).

Impact of Editorial

An obvious advantage of newspaper advertising is that you can choose which section of the paper your ad is placed in, putting food ads in the food section, or offering investment advice in the business pages, for example. This effectively narrows your reach to those consumers most likely to be interested in your product or service.

LOCAL AND REGIONAL POSSIBILITIES

Although advertisers are reluctant to use newspapers on a national basis, they rely on them heavily for local or regional marketing. If Procter & Gamble wishes to test a new detergent in Peoria, Illinois, it can advertise in the Peoria Journal Star and feel confident that the message will only reach those people able to buy the product, thereby creating awareness for the new item.

They might also test the effects of advertising on sales this way. For regional operators, such as Friendly Restaurants located only in the northeastern part of the country ads can be placed in newspapers in the selected markets where the restaurant is found. Even within a market, an advertiser can buy space in only those papers being sold in a certain area.

The Chicago Tribune, for example, offers six zoned editions of its daily paper within the Chicago area.

DRAWBACKS OF NEWSPAPER ADVERTISING

As with every medium, newspapers have their own drawbacks as well as benefits. The three most critical drawbacks of newspaper advertisements are short issue life, the challenge of grabbing the reader's attention, and the constraints of using a largely black and white medium.

Today or Never

Although magazines can often prolong their issue life and reach more people by being passed around or picked up on several occasions, at the end of each day the newspaper is usually discarded. If the reader misses your ad that day, you are not given a second chance. So although newspapers are available every day, their issue life is very short.

Active Readers

The issue life of the newspaper is closely linked to how people read it. Although more than half of all pages are likely to be opened, it is up to the reader to actively choose what to look at. If your headline doesn't attract Jane Doe's attention, she won't look at it at all; if the copy isn't intriguing and relevant to her, she can simply turn to another article or page. It is therefore crucial that newspaper advertisements get the reader's attention. When people sit in front of the television or listen to the radio, they are generally a "passive"audience with no choice but to attend to the ad (even if fleetingly) or turn off the radio or TV set.

Black and White

In the 1980s, it was rare to find a colour ad in a newspaper. Then along came the Gannett Corporation with its national newspaper USA Today, which offers full-colour capabilities. The quality of newspaper colour reproduction has been improving ever since, although it is still a long way from looking as sharp as magazine pages (due primarily to the poorer quality of the paper it is printed on). Even so, newspapers charge a premium for use of colour, generally about 17 per cent extra for a one-page four-colour ad. For many advertisers, particularly those who wish to show "lifelike"qualities such as food manufacturers, it remains more effective to use magazine or television ads.

RESEARCH ON NEWSPAPERS

Although the newspaper industry, through its trade association, Newspaper Association of America, conducts annual research on the size and strength of the industry, and periodic studies on the medium's effectiveness, academic research has been more limited in recent years. Some studies have been done on the impact of ad size on consumer responses, including work on different promotional formats for the ads.

MAGAZINES-AN EXPLOSION OF CHOICE

Although magazines have a long history in the United States, with the earliest publications appearing in the middle of the 18th century, they are also a medium that may be said to have had two very distinct life stages. Originally, most magazines catered to a very general audience, offering a mixture of news, stories, and features aimed either at the total population or, in the case of titles such as Ladies'Home Journal and Good Housekeeping, at women. The strength of publications such as Life,Look, and the Saturday Evening Post is reflected in the fact that an ad placed in those magazines in the 1950s would be likely to reach about 60 per cent of the total population.

But with the rise of television in the 1950s, general-interest magazines found they could not compete effectively either for advertising dollars or for readers. Rather than simply disappearing, magazines began to move toward greater specialization in their targeting and their editorial content. This trend continues today, with extremely narrowly focused magazines devoted to topics such as tropical fish (Tropical Fish Hobbyist), cross-stitching (Simply Cross Stitch!), or aircraft (Affordable Aircraft). And although there are still some general offerings, such as Atlantic Monthly or the New Yorker, their readership is considerably lower than the audience of their general-interest forebears. Because of this increased specialization, there are today more than 2,000 different magazines available. In 2000 alone, nearly 350 new titles were introduced.

Magazine Today

Despite this specialization, magazines as a medium reach a broad range of the population. Indeed, 94 per cent of all adults read magazines in any one year, buying about six different titles in that time period. The places they purchase them include supermarkets (accounting for 45 per cent of all magazines sold individually), discount stores, bookstores, and drugstores. Each magazine copy is looked at for an average of 45 minutes.

There are three main types of magazines available: consumer, farm, and business-to-business. Consumer magazines are usually categorized according to their editorial content, such as business, men's, women's, sports, news, and entertainment. This category includes titles enjoyed by all segments of the population, from Time to Sports Illustrated to Cosmopolitan. Farm magazines are geared toward that particular industry. Some may be crop specific, such as Cotton Farming, whereas others deal with the technical aspects of agriculture. The third type, business-to-business, covers all titles aimed at the industrial user, everything from Chemical Age to Offshore Drilling to Information Week.

Taken together, magazines account for 5 per cent of all ad dollars spent in the United States. Most magazines are considered as national vehicles for advertising, although city or regional publications are also classified within the consumer segment, such as Milwaukee or Southern Living.

More and more, however, national magazines offer geographic breakouts of their circulation, allowing an advertiser to place a message that will, for example, only reach Southerners, or people who live in the northeastern states, or in the Los Angeles metropolitan area. They are also developing more demographic "splits, "so that Fidelity Investments can advertise its mutual funds in the edition of Business Week that is read by people earning $75,000 or more per year. As with newspapers, magazines are assessed in terms of their circulation. Magazines are sold in one of two ways-at the newsstand or by subscription. For most titles, it is the latter that generates the most sales, typically accounting for 80 per cent of a title's circulation.

Benefits of Magazines to Advertisers

To an advertiser, three of the most attractive qualities of magazines are their high-end audiences, the enthusiasm of those audiences, and the long issue life of the medium.

Upscale Audiences

One of the incentives to using magazines for your advertising message is the favorable demographic profile of magazine readers. Similar to newspaper readers, the heaviest user of this medium is in the age range of 18 to 44 years, with a college education and household income over $50,000, and living in a household of three or more people.

Getting Attention

Another benefit of placing your ads in magazines is reader involvement. Although this concept is rather difficult to define (and even harder to measure), it generally refers to the interest that the reader has in the material, both editorial and advertising. Because most magazines today focus on a particular subject or interest, they can tie in more readily with the personal needs and lifestyles of the audience, enabling advertisers to do so as well. In this way, automakers can target car enthusiasts or prospective buyers in Car and Driver or Road and Track; detergent manufacturers can promote their new or improved products in magazines aimed at homemakers; and financial services companies can offer their mutual funds to interested investors in Fortune or Money.

Consumers also seem less resistant to seeing ads in magazines. One study conducted for the magazine industry in 2000 found that although 36 per cent of those surveyed said they usually ignored advertising on television, only 11 per cent felt similarly about magazines. Indeed, more than one-third of those surveyed said the advertising usually complements the content of the medium (compared to only 10 per cent who felt that way about the Internet). Nearly half (44 per cent) claimed they often purchase a product or service as a result of seeing the ad in a magazine, 10 points higher than the response to TV advertising, and fully 7 times more than those who said they made a purchase following exposure to an Internet ad. These findings are in part due to the fact that as a reader, you get to select what ads you read, whereas with television the ads are more or less forced on you (the remote control notwithstanding). Internet advertising is still in a nascent state and is seen, by most users, as mere "clutter"on the screen.

Reactions of readers to magazine ads also differ to their reactions to ads on television. Information seen in magazines tends to be retained longer because people can read up to five times faster than they take in the spoken word. They tend to trust magazine ads more, placing greater faith in the authority of the printed word. And in many instances, reading a magazine can be considered a pres hopping experience, allowing consumers the chance to compare products and services and learn new information about, say, the Sony DVD player prior to purchasing it.

Hanging Around

Another important and unique feature of magazines is their long issue life. The television programme is over in half an hour, and the newspaper is thrown out after one day, whereas you will probably keep a monthly magazine in your home for 4 weeks or longer. This not only gives you opportunities for additional or repeat exposures to the advertising, but it is also likely that other people, known as the secondary audience, may see the issue, too. The importance of this pass-along readership is shown by the fact that the average magazine is seen by four different readers, with each one spending about 61 minutes with the issue.

DRAWBACKS OF MAGAZINE ADVERTISING

Magazines, too, have their drawbacks. Among the most significant obstacles to keep in mind are the considerable lead time necessary and the relatively high cost of reaching your targeted audience.

Long Planning Cycle

For most publications, ads have to be completed and at the printer well in advance of their publishing date, a factor known as the lead time. This makes it difficult for advertisers to create particularly timely or newsworthy ads of the kind seen in newspapers. Moreover, despite the generally excellent colour reproduction quality, the magazine remains two-dimensional. This prevents the magazine ad from offering the truly lifelike qualities of a television spot.

Reacing Readers

The increasingly targeted nature of magazines means that the cost of reaching one thousand members of the audience is higher than that of a broader, mass medium such as television. Even some of a magazine's benefits can be viewed as potential disadvantages for you as a media specialist. The notion of readers'involvement with the magazine also means that, if they are not very interested in a particular product or ad, they can very easily ignore it by simply turning their attention to the next page.

RESEARCH ON MAGAZINES

Studies on magazines as a medium have focused on similar areas as broadcast research. The value of the context in which an ad is seen was found, by Norris and Colman, to impact consumer recall and recognition of the ad. 14 The same topic was explored further by Yi to see what happened when readers were given additional information prior to seeing the magazine ad in its context. Meanwhile, the magazine industry has itself sponsored several studies showing the impact of magazines on sales.

Whether you agree with that or not, outdoor billboards are certainly well established, having been around in this country since the 1800s. At that time, companies began leasing space on boards for bills to be pasted (hence the term billboard). There are two main types of billboard-poster panels and painted bulletins. Panels come in several sizes, named according to the number of sheets of paper originally needed to cover them, such as 8-sheets and 30-sheets. Posters are found mostly in populated areas, in or near cities and towns. Painted bulletins are larger boards situated along highways and major roads. Their name refers to the fact that they were originally painted by hand at the site.

Putting messages on outdoor boards used to be extremely labour-intensive. The sheets for poster panels were pasted onto the board while bulletins were hand-painted. Both were created either at the board site or at a central location within the market or region. Because this had to be done in each market, differences resulted in the look of the message from one market to another (and even one site to another within the market). Today, thanks to computer technology, poster panel messages are created electronically and then shipped either in one piece or in sections to the board site. Bulletins still tend to be hand painted, but computers are now used to make sure that the finished product looks identical across boards. Today, bulletins are often created using other materials, such as lithography or special stretch vinyl.

In the past 40 years the industry has come under increased criticism from environmentalists who claim that the boards are a blight on the scenery. Many cities and several states have introduced bans on putting up new boards and, in certain cases, demanded the removal of existing structures. So you won't see any billboards in Hawaii or Vermont, for example.

Unlike other media that have editorial material too, outdoor billboards exist solely for advertising messages. They are primarily a local medium, bought on a market-by-market basis, but are used by both national and local advertisers. The type of business using the medium has changed considerably in the past 20 years. For many years, the biggest category of advertiser was the tobacco industry, but in 1999, legislation was passed prohibiting the advertising of tobacco messages on any outdoor billboards. This not only had a significant impact on the tobacco industry, it freed up many high-profile and well-positioned billboards across the country for other advertisers who had never been able to buy that space because the tobacco companies had long term deals with the billboard companies. Today, you are far more likely to see billboards from local retailers, the travel industry, or health care providers than you would have even 5 years ago.

For many years, outdoor billboard audiences were calculated from manual traffic counts conducted by each system operator of how many cars passed by a given billboard, multiplied by government statistics that are updated periodically on how many people are present in the average car. That became the estimated audience viewing a billboard. In 2001, the outdoor industry's auditing organization, the Traffic Audit Bureau, introduced an automated system to count the traffic. It uses special software that looks at traffic counts by road segments within a market, and uses those to come up with the audience figures. This avoids inconsistent counting done by different operators within and across markets, as well as removing some of the human error involved in that process. The outdoor industry is far more expansive than it used to be. For example, outdoor messages are now quite commonly seen painted on the sides of buildings, on telephone kiosks and bus shelters, or in sports stadiums. More is said on this in a later section.

BENEFITS OF OUTDOOR BILLBOARDS TO ADVERTISERS

The advantages of billboard advertising have contributed to the medium's popularity over the past two centuries. Four of the most consistent and important benefits are size, mobility, effective reach, and cost.

Big Is Better

Simply the size of the poster panel or painted bulletin means that outdoor advertising gets noticed. In fact, at a typical busy location in the centre of a city, more than 10,000 people are likely to pass an 8-sheet poster panel within a given month. In addition, the message is there constantly, for 12 to 24 hours (and many posters are illuminated at night).

Mobility

Not only can painted billboards be moved around an area to expose more of the target to the message, but the outdoor messages can be designed for specific locations, audiences, or activities. So you could place ads for Samsonite luggage aimed at businesspeople at airports to catch them when they travel, or advertise Chiquita bananas near the A&P supermarket where your target audience shops.

Reaching Ethnic Groups

With outdoor billboards you can tailor your message to members of a particular ethnic group using their own language or culture yet still reach a mass audience within a specific market. You can buy space in areas with heavy concentrations of Hispanic people, for example, reaching them where they live, work, and shop. It is harder to reach a large portion of these groups with traditionally "Anglo"television or magazines. Furthermore, it is valuable to be able to reach nonnative English speakers in their first language, whatever language that might be.

Reinforcing the Message

Outdoor advertising is a good supplementary medium, helping to add reach and frequency to a media schedule at reasonable cost. A fairly typical outdoor buy could reach over 80 per cent of adults in a given area in a month. In addition, the fact that the billboard is there all the time means that frequency builds up and the message can be a constant reminder. Because many panels are situated in shopping areas, an advertiser can present a message very close to the point of purchase.

DRAWBACKS OF OUTDOOR BILLBOARD ADVERTISING

In considering what part of your advertising budget to commit to outdoor billboard advertising, you will need to keep in mind the two drawbacks of the medium: short exposure time, and the potential for criticism from environmentalists.

Brief Message Exposure

Because the average outdoor message is only seen for between 3 and 7 seconds, the copy needs to be extremely concise and compelling. For products that need a lot of explanation, outdoor is clearly not the right medium. One way to gauge whether there is too much copy on a billboard is to estimate how quickly people are going to pass by it. You can try the exercise yourself, and see how much of the message you can take in as you drive or walk by. Because most of the viewing is done at high speed, especially for bulletins situated along the highway, the advertisement must also be eye-catching and interesting enough to attract the driver's (or passenger's) attention.

Environmental Criticism

The outdoor industry, as noted earlier, has come under increasing criticism for cluttering up the environment. Advertisers might shy away from the medium to avoid legal or ethical disputes, especially in areas with a recent history of environmental controversies.

RESEARCH ON OUTDOOR ADVERTISING

The outdoor industry is one of the least researched of any mass medium. Studies have focused mostly on proving that the medium works, as shown by Bhargava et al. More information on how the medium has been researched can be found on the web site of the Outdoor Advertising Association of America.

THE INTERNET-THE ULTIMATE CHOICE

The rapid growth of the Internet as a consumer medium in the 1990s was unprecedented in the history of media. Internet penetration rose faster than any other medium (or appliance), reaching the critical mass of 50 million users in 5 short years (it took radio 36 years to get to that point). Today, with slightly more than half (54 per cent) of the country accessing the Internet from home, work, school, or some other location, the medium's capabilities continue to expand and develop.

The Internet was first devised as a means of communication for the academic community, more than 30 years ago. It was a fairly arcane and complex system, relying on a lot of computer language and processing. The hypertext markup language (HTML) that formed the basis of the Web is now seamlessly (and invisibly) connected to everything we do on the computer. That was not the case originally. It was not until the late 1990s that the Internet came to be seen as a genuine medium (as opposed to computer tool), and one that offered users far greater control than with any other existing medium.

Even more so than print media, the Internet lets you select exactly where you want to go, and what you want to see. You choose where to click, and how long to stay there. Although you can browse through a magazine or newspaper, you generally have to look at each page (or a table of contents) to find what you are most interested in. On the Web, you can type in a web address and be taken straight to that specific piece of information, without having to wade through other pages in which you have no interest. At the same time, the computer is keeping track of your every movement, capturing each site you visit, and each page within that site. This information proved invaluable in the development of the medium for advertising.

Indeed, as companies began setting up web sites (a fairly inexpensive proposition), they saw huge potential for advertising to help generate revenues. Analogies to the direct response industry are common. Companies were immediately able to track visits to their sites (by computer address only), and offer advertisers more information on who was not only visiting their sites, but also looking at the ads-and clicking through to the advertiser's site-than any other mass medium. They did so by placing special software known as cookies on a user's computer, to monitor the path that user takes in browsing different sites on the Internet. Internet ad revenues doubled each year for several years in a row in the late 1990s, surpassing total ad revenues for the out door and syndicated TV industries, to reach$7 billion in 2001.

At first, Internet ads consisted of banners-billboards on the Web-that did little more than offer a brand name or teaser, and a link to another site. Companies began to consider using web advertising for brand-building purposes, rather than simply to offer information. Before long, the ability to purchase via the Web became mainstream rather than exceptional. Today, 60 per cent of the online population has made a purchase over the Web. Before long, advertisers started to get more creative, changing the size of the ad message, and incorporating (as technology advanced) more sound, motion, and visual stimulation (animation, for example), a phenomenon known as rich media. Not surprisingly, the research findings showed that these kinds of ads had greater impact (recall, awareness) than the plain-vanilla banners. But it became more and more clear that as fast as advertisers moved to surprise consumers, those consumers became increasingly disenchanted with Web ads.

Today, when most consumers are asked about Web advertising, their response is primarily one of irritation. They talk about the "clutter"of Web sites, the irrelevance of most ads that appear, and their techniques for avoiding them. In particular, annoyance with ads that pop up, or pop under, a web site is considerable. At the same time, if an ad appears on the Web that is relevant and informative, consumers will click on it to find out more. For many, the line between the "editorial"material and the "advertising"is a narrow one on the Web, which is viewed by most people as an information cornucopia.

BENEFITS OF THE INTERNET TO ADVERTISERS

In many ways, the benefits of this emerging medium for advertisers are still being explored. Four of the current advantages are personalization, flexibility, reach, and measurability. Each is examined here.

Flexibility

There are many forms of Internet advertising. Unlike other mass media, where choices come down to 15- or 30-second commercials, or full-page versus half-page ads, on the Internet there really is little limit to the imagination. From traditional banner ads to pop-ups to buttons, ad messages can appear in numerous forms.

Beyond that, advertisers are increasingly trying to communicate with prospects via e-mail, asking people to opt in and be willing to receive messages that way, offering them cut-price travel deals on Travelocity, or the best-seller list on Amazon. Advertisers can also engage in affiliate marketing, where one site promotes another site's products or services in exchange for some commission on the sale.

Targeted Message

The Internet is the first mass medium able to offer a targeted, personal advertising message. Although direct response has been doing so for many years, it was not possible in TV, radio, newspapers, magazines, or billboards to talk to anything less than a sizable audience. With the Internet, however, advertisers are actually able to send messages to named individuals (via opt-in e-mail marketing). It is assumed that such messages, by being more relevant to that individual, are more likely to be accepted and absorbed.

Reach

Although the Internet does not offer as broad a reach as television, campaigns that appear on a range of web sites (particularly the gateway or portal sites many people have as their home pages, such as msn.com or yahoo.com) can indeed reach a high proportion of everyone on the Internet.

Portal sites are visited by at least 50 million people per month. Other sites such as cbs.com might expect 3 million visitors each month. In addition, the reach on the Internet can be given for specific advertising messages, not just the sites on which those messages appear (i.e., ad exposure, not just opportunity to see).

Measureability

For advertisers, the Internet's ability to measure who is doing what on the Web would seem to be answering one of the "holy grail"questions of the industry. But because the measurement is computer-based rather than person based, the measures are in fact not as precise and valuable as they might appear.

Having said that, Internet measurement is certainly far more detailed than for any other mass medium, where at best the media specialist can look at opportunities to be exposed to the ad, rather than actual viewer, reader, or listener behaviour. Initially, Web advertising was sold based on click-throughs, but it soon became clear that if Internet advertising was to be comparable to other ad media, the cost metric had to be the same. Today, most sites price their advertising based on cost per thousand (CPM). Web measurement services provide data on the demographics and lifestyles of web users, as well as web traffic to individual sites and/or ads.

DRAWBACKS OF INTERNET ADVERTISING

As new and exciting as the Internet is, it still cannot provide advertisers with everything they would want to reach their desired targets. Here is a summary of the downside to Internet advertising, in terms of consumer irritation, confusion, and nonstandard metrics.

Consumer Irrition

The plethora of advertising on the Internet is not always appreciated by consumers. Although users have the option to click on an ad to find out more information, there are more and more messages that pop up or "pop under"a site that the user has to actively remove if he or she does not want to look at it. Moreover, because people tend to use the Web to look for specific information (rather than passively consuming a TV programme or browsing a magazine's pages), the irritation level with the high number of ad messages on a web page (banners, buttons, sponsorships) can become overwhelming, detracting from the impact of any one particular message.

Confusion

Although this particular drawback reflects to a large extent the newness of the medium, many Internet users have only been online for a couple of years (at most). They are therefore fairly unsophisticated in how they use the Web, uncertain of what will happen if they click on an ad for example ("will I get back to the page that I really wanted to be on?").

There is also a more generalized confusion among many novice users about what in fact constitutes a web advertisement. Is it a company's web site (such as nike.com)? Or are the pages that pop up in moving from one page to another (so-called interstitials) ad messages or actual sites? Although some of this confusion may benefit advertisers (putting out messages that users see as information rather than advertising), the confusion is more likely to lead to avoidance than interaction.

Nonstandard Metrics

Again, as a new ad medium, the Internet has not yet developed fully standardized measurement metrics. Each measurement service uses slightly different methods (not always fully revealed) to measure a different list of websites.

Some sites try to sell advertising based on audience impressions, others on site visits, and yet others on actual sales. As the medium matures, it is likely that more standardization will be put in place, especially to make it more comparable to traditional mass media.

RESEARCH ON THE INTERNET

Given the relative newness of this medium, much of the research is outdated almost as soon as it is written or published.

Which Media Should You Use?

Now that you have some basic information on each major media category, we can start to consider why you might or might not wish to include them in your media plans. To make this process less cumbersome, we'll recap some of the most important advantages and disadvantages that each medium offers.

Alternative Forms of Communication

As the traditional media forms outlined above grow increasingly cluttered, advertisers are looking for new and different ways to present their messages to the target audience. Three of the most important means available are Yellow Pages, in-store advertising, and sponsorship.

Yellow Pages

Although placed under nontraditional media, Yellow Pages advertising has been in existence for almost as long as the telephone directory itself. Offering advertisers (and consumers) another type of classified advertising, the Yellow Pages generated $13.2 million in advertising revenues in 2001. There are more than 6,000 different Yellow Pages directories in the United States, which can make it harder for advertisers because of the lack of standardization in terms of ad sizes or guidelines.

People use the Yellow Pages to look up information and services. More than one-fifth of the time, the search is related to business needs. The top three categories that people turn to are food, dining out and entertainment, and automotive. The top three headings in Yellow Pages directories in terms of the number of listings are restaurants, physicians and surgeons, and auto parts.

According to Mediamark Research, Inc. (MRI), about one-quarter of the population has used the Yellow Pages in the past 7 days, while nearly two-thirds (63 per cent) have done so within the past 12 months. Within the past few years there have been some new developments in Yellow Pages advertising. First, the industry has attempted to attract more national advertisers, who accounted for just 16 per cent of total revenues in 2000. But for consumers, the Yellow Pages are usually considered a means of finding local information.

In many markets, you can see not only the name of the business or brand on the printed page, you can also hear about it on the phone or look up the web-site address included in the directory. Audiotext services are available that allow you to call a local phone number and obtain information on a wide variety of services or topics simply by entering a four-digit code. The advertiser sponsors an audio message that is played before you hear the information in which you are interested. If you call up to hear the weather forecast, you might first hear a message from Joe's Heating and Air Conditioning, reminding you to have your heating checked out before the cold weather arrives.

The availability of colour in the Yellow Pages has helped some advertisers gain additional attention from consumers. In a study conducted by Fernandez and Rosen, ads were seen as more informative and noticeable when colour was included.

In-Store Advertising

Just like Yellow Pages advertising, the notion of placing advertising messages inside stores is not especially new. Signs and promotions have been available in stores for more than 25 years. Today, however, more and more advertisers are including in-store media explicitly in the media plan, acknowledging this as advertising rather than simply a promotional expense. One of the main reasons for its increased popularity is that it is the most measurable of all media. Thanks to electronic scanning at the cash register, advertisers are able to see what happens at the checkout counter when their messages are in the store. Some of the most popular locations for in-store messages are on the shelves and in the aisles. In addition, messages or coupons can be generated at the checkout counter when people pay for their goods, tailored to the purchases that have just been made.

In-store advertising effectively eliminates the time between seeing the message and buying the item. Drawbacks include the possibility that the target misses the ad somehow, either by not paying attention or by its being covered up in some way. In addition, in-store advertising is not especially cheap. It tends to have its greatest affect among current brand users rather than persuading buyers of the competitor's brand to switch. The time for message exposure is very short, so messages tend to focus on price and be extremely brief.

Sponsorship

As advertisers have had to work harder to reach their target consumers, one of the nontraditional forms of communication they have turned to is sponsorship. This involves paying an organization a fee to put a company or brand name at the head of an event or as the key sponsor of that event. Examples include State Farm Insurance's sponsorship of an ice skating competition, and Visa's sponsorship of the U. S. Olympic team, as well as the renaming of sports stadiums after companies. The practice of sponsorship is now estimated to be worth $9.5 billion.

The majority of sponsorship spending (69 per cent) goes toward sports-related events, followed by entertainment tours and attractions (9 per cent), and festivals, fairs, and annual events (8 per cent). A rapidly growing area within the sponsorship area is cause-related marketing, where companies link up with nonprofit groups and become "sponsors"of their causes. Examples include Avon's support of an annual 3-day walk to raise funds for breast cancer research, and Tanqueray's sponsorship of a bike ride to raise money for AIDS. Even though sponsorship is generally considered to be undertaken to reach a national audience, there are often significant local opportunities too. Sponsorship of local sports teams can enhance a company's reputation in those particular markets, whereas companies that choose to sponsor a local annual festival often receive positive coverage in the local media. There are also significant benefits to be gained by sponsoring grass-roots or community festivals and fairs, especially among ethnic audiences. The reasons companies choose sponsorship instead of (or more likely in addition to) traditional advertising are many. They include the opportunity for heightened visibility for their brand name, thereby increasing the chances of shaping positive consumer attitudes. Sometimes sponsorship works well for smaller companies. Although they may have smaller ad budgets compared to bigger competitors, their sponsorship of a key event or attraction can make them seem an equal in consumers'eyes.

Coors Brewing Company spends far less on advertising than either Anheuser-Busch or Miller Beers, but when all three companies are sponsoring race cars at NASCAR events, the viewer or attendee does not see one company as a "better"or necessarily bigger sponsor than another. One of the potential downsides of sponsorship was seen in 2002 when the giant energy trading company Enron found itself bankrupt and subject to numerous criminal investigations for its financial practices. The company's earlier purchase of the naming rights for Houston's arena, now called the Enron Arena, no longer seems as smart a decision as before.

The media are getting more actively involved in creating sponsorships for advertisers. Cooking Light magazine created a "healthy"house filled with products of its sponsoring companies, such as Reebok (exercise equipment), Lennox Industries (air conditioning), and Whirlpool (appliances). The magazine promoted the house in its pages, and attracted thousands of visitors to its Birmingham, Alabama, location. After the promotion ended, the magazine was able to sell the home privately. Sponsorships are not only aimed at adults these days. The company that makes Barbie dolls, Mattel, took part in a shopping mall tour with Better Homes & Gardens magazine, sponsoring a girl's bedroom showcasing Barbie-themed products such as furniture and bedding.

4

The Structure of Media Organizations

The structure of media organizations has changed dramatically over the past decade with the globalization of mass media. The term big media has been redefinedas corporations such as Gannett and Multimedia have combined forces in billion-dollar mergers and buyouts. Within a 2-year period, Walt Disney acquired Capital Cities/ABC Inc. for $19 billion; Time Warner merged with Turner Broadcasting System in a $7.5 billion deal; News Corporation expanded Fox's reach with the $2.5 billion acquisition of New World Communications Group; and NBC merged with Microsoft in a $250 million exchange. Such ventures continue to underscore the reality in the world of corporate media that big begets bigger.

Regardless of size of the media organization, many people believe that in the right organizational structure, anyone should be able to perform well. In the 1980s, two assumptions guided behaviour in media organizations. One was that a firm's overall success could be achieved through the success of its unrelated parts. The second assumption was that profitability was to be obtained by serving mainly Americans. Today both of these assumptions have been broadly challenged. Non-American audiences have become key, and a firm's success depends on the interrelatedness of its personnel and divisional structures.

The scientific structure of media organizations defines the tasks, communication, and authority relationships within the organization, with organizational charts illustrating how the parts of an organization fit together. The humanistic structure analyzes ways in which managers and subordinates interact within an organization by looking at leadership behaviour, work cultures, and team-building. Taken together, scientific and humanistic organizational structures exist to order and coordinate the actions of employees to achieve key organizational goals.

SCIENTIFIC APPROACH

Classical approaches to studying organizational structure are based on a carefully developed chain of command and efficient division of labour. Although no longer strictly practiced, organizations still adhere to a number of principles drawn from classical literature. Early researchers believed that a firm's overall success was achieved through the success of its unrelated parts. In a formalized structure, positions were specified, roles were defined, and role relationships were prescribed independently of the personal characteristics of members.

Organizations were designed to attain specific preset goals and were less concerned with the selection of those goals than with their attainment. Formalization served to make the goals and relationships of an organization appear to be objective. The organizational structure was viewed as a means to an end that could be modified only to improve performance. Taylor (1947) believed it was possible to scientifically analyse tasks performed by workers and thereby discover procedures that would produce the maximum output with the minimum input of resources. He transformed the role of the manager from arbitrary decision-maker to one who makes decisions based on analytical, scientific procedures. For example, he believed workers would be scientifically selected to perform tasks for which they were best suited. Scientifically determined procedures would allow them to work at optimal efficiency for which they would receive top pay. The following list summarizes four prescribed techniques on ordering the workplace.

- For each task use a time and motion study to determine the best way of task performance that permits the largest average amount of production over 1 day.
- Provide the worker with a financial incentive to perform at a good pace in the best way.
- Use from four to eight specialized experts as functional foremen to instruct and supervise the workers on the different aspects of their work: methods, speeds, tools, task priorities, discipline, quality, and machine maintenance.
- Adhere absolutely to the principle that the standard production rate must not be arbitrarily changed.

Managers would devise appropriate work arrangements and salaries based on the prescribed techniques and workers would cooperate. Communication was to be formal and hierarchical. Its purpose was to increase productivity and efficiency. Overall, Taylor viewed communication as one-sided (from managers to subordinates) and task-oriented. Although many managers still adhere to some of Taylor's principles, this approach has many drawbacks. Employers questioned it because it undermined workers' good judgment. They saw the system as an unnecessary interference and an attempt to standardize every aspect of their performance. Workers also rejected incentive systems requiring them to perform continuously at optimal levels. Another scientific approach was the work of Weber, which has proven to be somewhat more useful for today's organizational structure. Weber developed the bureaucratic model of organizational design. He viewed a bureaucracy as a logical, rational, and efficient form of organization. He developed the model as a normative framework where organizations strive for one best way of administration. A simple list of these administrative characteristics present in bureaucratic forms is listed here.

- Fixed division of labour among participants--The duties of each office are clearly specified.
- Hierarchy of offices--Each office is subject to discipline from a superordinate office, but only in regard to the duties of the office. The private life of the official is free from organizational authority.
- Set of general rules that govern performance--Impersonality, as contrasted to personal relationships, regulates activity. The body of specific and general rules regarding dealings with subordinates, peers, rank and file members and clients are binding.
- Separation of personal from official property and rights--The officeholder is an employee. The"means of administration"are attached to the office, not the officeholder, and there are no ways whereby to gain personal rights to the office.
- Selection of personnel on the basis of technical qualifications--Hiring and promotion are governed by competence, as measured by certificated training or performance in office.
- Employment viewed as a career by participants--Membership in the bureaucracy constitutes a career with distinct ladders of career progression.

The bureaucratic model of organization has several strengths. Elements such as division of labour, reliance on rules, and hierarchy of authority may improve efficiency and are still used in organizations today. The model was also the starting point for later research about organizational design. The bureaucratic model also has several disadvantages. It tends to be rigid and inflexible. The human relations aspects of the organization are neglected. Some of Weber's assumptions about loyalty and impersonal relations are also unrealistic. However, the bureaucratic model of organization design was an important development of management theory and continues to shape definitions of the central elements of administrative systems. Principles that evolved and are still used today include unity of command, span of control, division of labour, and departmentation.

Unity of Command

The unity of command principle argues that a subordinate should have only one superior to whom he or she is directly responsible. To have more than one superior would create the possibility that subordinates would face conflicting priorities. However, in most newsroom situations, reporters are responsible to several supervisors. For example, television news directors judge overall job performance. Assignment editors evaluate coverage of a news story. Producers are concerned with story visualization and timing. Research suggests when unity of command has to be violated, as is the case in many newsrooms, there should be a clear separation of activities and a supervisor responsible for each. In today's media organizations, strict adherence to the principle of unity of command would create inflexibility and hinder performance; however employees should know to whom they are responsible for different tasks.

Span of Control

Span of control addresses the number of subordinates a manager can efficiently and effectively direct. Early researchers agreed that the number of people who directly report to a manager should become smaller at succeedingly higher levels of the organization. For example, the span for top executives should range somewhere between three and nine. The span for middle managers should be between 10 and 30.

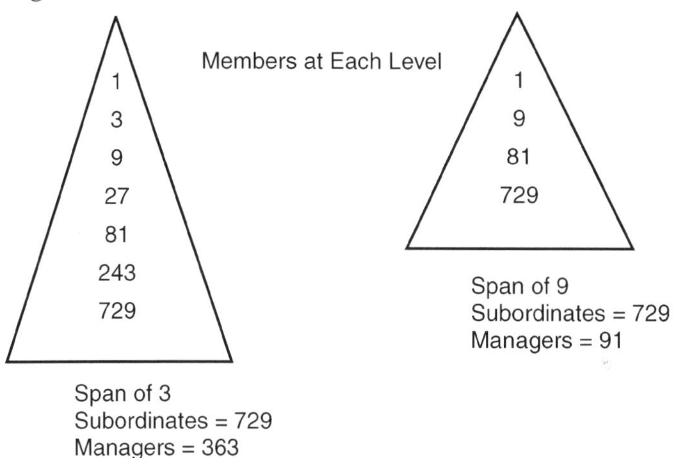

Fig. Contrasting Spans of Control.

The span of control is a major determinant of how many levels an organization has and the number of managers that are needed. Ideally, the wider or larger the span, the more efficient the organizations. For example, differing spans result in varying numbers of managers. If one media organization had a span of three and the other a span of nine, the wider span would have three fewer levels and 272 less managers. If the average manager earned $40,000 a year, the wider span would save more than $108 million a year in management salaries. However, questions remain as to whether wider spans are as effective.

Managers can give subordinates more attention when they have narrower spans of control; however, a number of contingency factors that could affect this relationship include the complexity of the work to be done and the amount of time managers spend with subordinates. Also, the degree of similarity of tasks being performed, the degree of standardization of work activities, the training and general capability of subordinates, and the amount of initiative these subordinates demonstrate all affect how the optimum span of control is determined. Because the early writers did not recognize these contingencies, research on span of control continues. The reality in most organizations today is a trend toward eliminating management positions and operating under wider spans of control.

DIVISION OF LABOUR

Division of labour is the extent to which jobs are broken down into a number of steps with the responsibility for each step being assigned to specific individuals. Instead of being responsible for an entire activity, employees specialize in doing part of an activity. For example, in unionized television stations, videotape editors are solely responsible for editing videotape. They perform this same standardized task over and over again. Division of labour is an efficient way of utilizing employees' specific skills. In media organizations, some tasks require highly developed skills. Others can be performed by untrained individuals.

However, if all employees were engaged in each step of producing a newscast, all would have to hold skills necessary for performing both the most demanding and the least demanding jobs. This would be an inefficient method of utilizing workers' skills. Other efficiencies are also achieved through division of labour. Performance skills increase through repetition of a task. Efficiency is also exhibited in reducing time spent in completing tasks as employees become more expert.

Training workers to perform specific and repetitive tasks is also less costly. Finally, division of labour increases efficiency and productivity by encouraging specialized creativity. Examples of division of labour of management positions within a television news organization include the assignment manager who is in charge of what news is covered each day. He or she creates a storyboard outlining which reporters and photographers will cover which news story. The newsroom producers stack the newscast. They are responsible for putting the newscast together, deciding the order of stories, timing the show, and making sure the show flows. They also write stories and edit videotape for the newscast.

Similar positions exist according to division of labour within newspaper organizations. The city editor is in charge of all reporters and coordinates all hard-news coverage. The news editor is in charge of the copy desk and is the chief person in charge of story selection and placement, copy editing and page design. The sports editor is in charge of producing the daily sports section. The television newsroom also has a similar sports director. The belief that organizations should be designed with a high degree of division of labour has been a widely accepted principle. However, this principle can be carried too far. The disadvantages are that too much division of labour causes boredom, fatigue, and stress, which may lead to inefficiency. In addition, with the computerization of media organizations, employees are expected to be able to handle many more aspects of production. For example, many copy editing positions have been eliminated at newspapers, with reporters and editors being responsible for proofing their own copy. Likewise, at many smaller and medium-sized television stations, new employees are expected to be a"one-man-band"with shooting, editing, and reporting capabilities. Although division of labour can be a valuable goal in planning performance in organizations, it is rarely strictly adhered to in most situations.

Departmentation

Division of labour creates a need for coordination of specialists. Departmentation describes how specialists are placed together in departments under the direction of a manager. The creation of departments is usually based on the work functions being performed, the target audience, or the geographic territory.

Function

Functional departmentation occurs when organization units are defined by the nature of the work. For example, newspapers are organized into departments of news--editorial, advertising, circulation, production, and business activities.

These departments, as well as departments of other media organizations, are engaged in distinct functions of preparing information, reproducing information, distributing information, promoting the product to readers and advertisers, and financing operations of the firm.Media conglomerates such as Gannett which owns newspapers as well as television stations, can be organized according to function as well as geography. The following job descriptions describe some of the functions of typical management positions in different departments at broadcast and print media organizations. Each of these managers has the responsibilities of hiring and firing personnel within a department.

Broadcast Organizations

- *The Chief Executive Officer (CEO)*: The chief executive officer is responsible for overall performance of the corporation. Primary responsibilities are for the media's relations with their perspective communities and audiences. The CEO must also coordinate the efforts of all units and oversee the allocation of resources to each.
- *General Manager*: The general manager is responsible for the overall management and operation of an individual station. He or she is concerned with matters such as income, expense, budgeting,

forecasting, and long- and short-term planning. General managers hire the managers of other departments within the station and oversee the activities of each department.

- *Chief Engineer*: The chief engineer is responsible for keeping the station signal on the air. This includes performing special tests required by Federal Communications Commission (FCC) regulation. This person is responsible for maintenance of technical equipment and for ordering new equipment.
  - *Sales Manager*: The sales manager is responsible for all sales activities of the station. He or she assigns account executives to particular areas or accounts and supervises their activities. He or she sets the rate for the sale of advertising time. He or she must be knowledgeable of market data, retail statistics, audience research, and all other marketing and advertising concerns.
  - *Programme Director*: The programme director is responsible for all local, network, and syndicated programming that is broadcast by the station. The programme director selects and schedules all programming. The programme director also must be knowledgeable of FCC regulations to ensure programming complies. This would be a position concerned with coordination and preparing information.
  - *News Director*: The news director dictates the style of the newscast and is responsible for all news operations. The news director supervises everyone in the newsroom including anchors, reporters, sports and weather announcers, producers, and assignment editors. He or she also has administrative duties such as budgeting and conducting staff meetings.

Print Organizations

- *Publisher*: The publisher is the on-site chief executive officer. This person is in charge of overall newspaper operations, as well as appointing or hiring key department managers.
- *Managing Editor*: This person is in charge of compiling the editorial functions of the newspaper into a quality product. This person schedules daily editorial meetings where story ideas are discussed and work assignments are made.
- *Advertising Director*: The advertising manager is in charge of selling and creating classified, display, and insert advertising. This person is also responsible for setting advertising rates.
- *Business Manager*: The business manager is responsible for handling administrative and general business operations. These may include payroll and personnel matters, accounting procedures, and billing.
- *Circulation Manager*: The circulation manager is responsible for selling

and delivering newspapers to readers. These duties include marketing and promoting the product, distributing the paper in a timely manner, and collecting subscription fees.

- *Production Manager*: The production manager is responsible for procedures that take place once the newspaper content has left the editorial and advertising departments. These duties may include printing, platemaking, and the addition of colour and words to newsprint.

The primary advantage of organizing departments according to these functions is that it allows for specialization. It also provides for efficient use of equipment and resources. The disadvantages may be that members of a functional group may develop more loyalty for the group's goals than the organization's goals. Furthermore, in today's computerized media organizations, many functions have been combined. Employees need to be adaptable and be able to assume various functions. Also, all departments must understand the mission of the organization and support and strive for mutually accepted goals. Conflict will arise when different departments strive for different goals.

Target Audience

Audience departmentation is based on division by the type of customers served. One example would be a newspaper organization that has one department to handle home deliveries and another to handle industrial customers.

This type of departmentation has the same advantages and disadvantages as product departmentation. For example, if the home deliveries group becomes too competitive with the industrial customers group, cooperation between the two departments will diminish and the organization's overall performance could decrease.

Geographic Territory

Geographic departmentation occurs in organizations that maintain physically scattered and independent operations or offices. Departmentation by territories permits the use of local workers and/or salespeople. For example, media conglomerates such as Gannett own television stations and newspapers across the country. In addition, their large-market newspapers have branch offices to serve suburban editions of their newspapers. Such departmentation creates customer goodwill and an awareness of local issues. It also provides a high level of service.

Different geographic territories become easier to track as media utilize more online services. New versions of media content are being created daily as newspapers, magazines, radio, and television stations go online with their products. Most job openings in these fields require computer-minded people who can provide quality content different from the print or broadcast version. Internet users want a quick product that is updated as often as possible. Because the new technology cuts across all media, corporations will depend on employees who are able to adapt to continuous changes. Print journalists will have to be broadcast journalists who will have to be online journalists. This scenario has already taken place at a Tribune-owned venture, Chicagoland TV or CLTV, where print reporters are housed with news staffers of the 24-hour cable channel.

Both groups provide each other with content. In addition, the newspaper, The Chicago Tribune, and the cable product are available online. This type of creativity and openness to new technology will be necessary for all corporations to compete in the future. Distinctions between different departments and even different media will continue to blur as more services are offered online.

HUMANISTIC APPROACH

With rapid change taking place in the structure of media organizations, the need for good human relations increases. The humanistic approach is based on the assumption that work is accomplished through people. It emphasizes cooperation, participation, satisfaction, and interpersonal skills. One word that has been increasingly used to describe the optimal balance of the organizational mix is synergy. Synergy is the coordination of company parts so that the whole is worth more than the sum of its parts acting alone. A company may have a formal structure intact, but without a willing, satisfied, and competent work force, goals will not be achieved.

The Hawthorne Effect

Mayo was one of the first to document the importance of human interaction and morale for productivity. He studied individual characteristics such as fatigue to determine the optimum length and spacing of rest periods for maximum levels of productivity. The Chicago Hawthorne plant of the Western Electric Company was the site of the research. Management at the Hawthorne plant was aware that severe dissatisfaction existed among workers. Mayo and colleagues began to experiment with changing physical conditions to determine which condition would increase productivity.

They worked with variables such as lighting, noise, incentive pay, and heating. They found little support for the expected relationship between improved working conditions and improved productivity. Mayo summarized these surprising results: The conditions of scientific experiment had apparently been fulfilled--experimental room, control room; changes introduced one at a time; all other conditions held steady. And the results were perplexing.... Lighting improved in the experimental room, production went up; but it rose also in the control room. The opposite of this: lighting diminished from 10 to 3 foot-candles in the experimental room and the production again went up; simultaneously in the control room, with illumination constant, production also rose.

Mayo observed that work output increased no matter how the physical variables were changed. As a result, he realized it was the attention the researchers were paying to the workers that resulted in increased productivity. The workers were so pleased to be singled out for special attention that they tried to do the best they could for the researchers and the company. This effect became known as the Hawthorne effect. As a result of the Hawthome studies, productivity could no longer be viewed as solely dependent on formal organizational structure.

Cooperative System

Barnard's ideas also contributed to human relations approaches. Barnard was not a researcher but an executive of a telephone company. He stressed that organizations are basically cooperative systems that integrate the contributions of their individual participants. Barnard defined an organization as an entity where cooperation is conscious, deliberate, and purposeful. Barnard believed that goals were imposed from the top down, whereas their attainment depended on the willingness to comply from the bottom up. However, Barnard did not believe that authority always came down from above, noting situations where leaders claim authority but fail to win compliance. Rather, he believed that authority depended on subordinates' approval.

Barnard was one of the first theorists to signify the importance of human motivation as crucial to productivity. Material rewards or economic motives were sometimes viewed as weak incentives that must be supported by other types of social and psychological motivations. The most critical ingredient to successful organizations was the formation of a collective purpose. Overall, Barnard (1938) believed that when formal organizations came into operation, they created and required informal organizations. Informal structures facilitated communication and maintained cohesiveness.

Theory X and Theory Y

These attitudes were termed Theory X and Theory Y. A Theory X manager believes the average person dislikes work and will avoid responsible labour whenever possible. These managers must respond to this attitude with controls such as punishments if employees fail to produce. Theory X managers also assume that employees prefer to be directed in order to avoid responsibility. Theory X managers were based on the scientific approach to management theory. Theory Y managers, on the other hand, believe that employees find work as enjoyable as play. They are self-motivated and self-directed. Because employees are committed to organizational goals, they do not need the threat of punishment to be productive. Theory Y workers seek responsibility and are creative in solving organizational problems. Although the beliefs of Theory X and Theory Y managers are quite opposite, McGregor assumes these to be a range of behaviors. Managers can draw on both sets of ideas depending on the situation.

Theory Z

Theory Z makes assumptions about the culture of organizations, whereas Theory X and Y made assumptions about individuals. Theory Z also contrasts U.S. organizations (Type A) with Japanese organizations (Type J). Type A organizations are characterized by short-term employment, specialized career paths, rapid promotion, formal control, and individual responsibility. They value individuality over group membership. Social needs are provided by institutions such as churches, neighborhoods, and schools rather than the formal work group.

Type J organizations, in contrast, are characterized by lifetime employment, slow advancement, informal control, consensus decision making, and generalized career paths. Loyalty to groups is of primary concern and more important than individual achievement. Japanese companies reduce incentives to leave the organization and do not rapidly advance employees. The Theory Z organization attempts to blend the best of both worlds by retaining individual achievement and advancement but also by providing a continuing sense of organizational community. Theory Z is important because it draws attention to the human relations approach to management. It also sets the stage for team-building, which is the basis of many decision-making structures in media organizations today.

Team-building

In today's media organizations, group productivity is often more important than individual task accomplishment. Therefore, managers are needed who can promote teamwork for problem solving and work improvement. According to Blanchard, Carew, and Parisi-Carew (1990), managers who build high performing teams within the structure of their media organizations must understand stages of group development. When task groups initially meet, they are in Stage 1, the orientation stage.

During this period, team members usually have high expectations and are eager about working. However, they are more dependent on authority and need to establish their place in the group. As team members become more familiar with each other and begin working on the tasks at hand, they move into Stage 2, the dissatisfaction stage. Here they begin experiencing a discrepancy between hopes and reality. Some members react negatively toward authority and become frustrated with tasks and plans. In this stage, members experience a discrepancy between early hopes and later realities.

During Stage 3, the resolution stage, the team experiences more satisfaction in working together. Members start to share responsibility and control. They also develop trust and respect. The final stage that most teams experience is Stage 4, the production stage. Here, team members show high confidence in accomplishing tasks, as well as feel positive about task successes. It is at this level the performance is highest.

Managers who work with teams realize that they must adapt their leadership behaviors according to the stages of group development. In the orientation stage, a more authoritative or directing leader is needed. During the dissatisfaction stage, a coaching leader who is concerned with relationships and tasks is needed to help the group work through conflict. As the team moves toward the resolution stage, the leader can exhibit less directive behaviour and become more supporting or relationship-oriented. Finally, in the production stage, the leader functions best as a delegator or just as one of the team members.

Each of these approaches to informal structure is only as useful as the situation in which it is employed. Only when managers consider all situational variables that affect corporate efficiency and productivity can any single structure be successfully used. As a result, contingency theories have been developed that incorporate both scientific and humanistic approaches to management study.

THE CONTINGENCY APPROACH

Different combinations of situational elements require different organizational structures and management behaviors. According to Path-Goal Theory, three important interdependent factors that organizations must consider are forces involving the manager; the subordinates; and the situations. Forces acting on the manager include his or her value system and personal leadership styles such as task-oriented or relationship-oriented. Relationship-oriented behaviour is the extent to which the behaviour of the manager promotes friendship, mutual trust and respect, and good human relations between the manager and group. Task-oriented behaviour is the extent to which the behaviour of managers tends toward organizing and defining the relationships between himself and the group, in defining interactions among group members, establishing ways of getting the job done, scheduling, criticizing, and so forth.

Forces that act on the subordinates include ability, experience, and need for independence. People who perceive that they are lacking in ability may prefer directive managers to help them understand path-goal relationships. However, subordinates who perceive their abilities as high may resent directive managers. Personal characteristics also include education, experience, and age. Effective management behaviour varies in conjunction with the personal characteristics of subordinates. As employees' maturity level, age, and experience increase, management behaviour should be characterized by a decreasing emphasis on task behaviors and an increasing emphasis on relationship behaviors. Forces that act on the situation include type of organization, time pressure, demands from upper levels of management, and demands from government, unions, or society. These so-called environmental characteristics are usually outside the subordinate's control. If tasks are straightforward, attempts to direct by the leader will be redundant and seen by subordinates as unnecessary.

The higher the degree of formality, the less directive management behaviour will be accepted by subordinates. Furthermore, when the work group provides the individual with social support and satisfaction, relationship-oriented management behaviour is less critical. However, research indicates that relationship-oriented management behaviour has the strongest positive impact on satisfaction and productivity for those subordinates who work on stressful or frustrating tasks.

The model divides factors affecting job satisfaction into four groups: individual factors, market factors, organizational factors, and leadership. According to the model, these four types of factors influence journalists' perceptions of how successful their organizations are at attaining goals such as profit, good human relations, and quality news. If journalists believe their organizations are successful at attaining these goals, their level of job satisfaction increases.

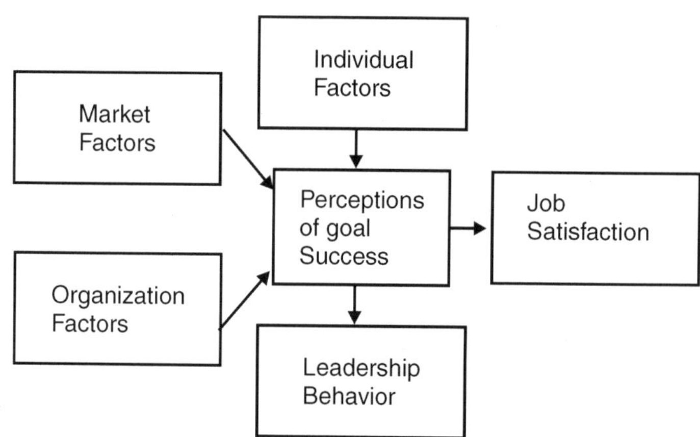

Fig. Model of Job Satisfaction for Local Television News Departments.

A negative relationship between market size and perceptions of good human relations suggested that local television journalists in large newsrooms perceived news managers to be more task-oriented than those in newsrooms located in smaller markets. A negative relationship was also found between the organizational factor of group ownership and profit success. Local television journalists at group-owned stations perceived no more success at making a profit than did those at independently owned stations. The most important result of the study for predicting job satisfaction among local television journalists was the relationship behaviour of the news directors. Employees were more satisfied with relationship-oriented managers than with management that was task-oriented. Also, job satisfaction related to participation. This implies that news directors should include journalists in the decision-making process if they want satisfied employees who will stay.

Minorities in the Decision-Making Process

When employees feel like they are part of the group and know that what they suggest will be heard and probably implemented, productivity and loyalty increases and stress is reduced. However, knowing how to include employees in the structure and decision-making process becomes increasingly complex as the work force becomes more diverse.

More women and minorities are employed by media organizations today than ever before, although many still reach the glass ceiling when it comes to upper management positions. Nevertheless, the popularity of contingency approaches and Japanese management theories has lead to what advocates say is a"feminine"model of sharing information and encouraging participation in organizations. Rosener (1990) found that men were more likely than women to describe themselves as task-oriented. They view job performance as exchanging rewards for services rendered or punishment for inadequate performance. The men were also more likely to use formal authority and power that comes from their organizations.

Women, on the other hand, described themselves as being relationship-oriented. They were able to get subordinates to transform their own self-interest into the interest of the group through concern for a broader goal. They credited their power to personal characteristics such as charisma, interpersonal skills, hard work, or personal contacts rather than to organizational stature. Women were found to make their interactions with subordinates positive for everyone involved. Women also encouraged participation, shared power and information, enhanced other people's self-worth, and excited people about their work.

Not all men or all women lead in a particular manner, and leadership styles are not mutually exclusive. Women are capable of managing organizations by adhering to the traditional, task-oriented model; some men are relationship-oriented. The larger issue concerns the need for organizations to be willing to question whether traditional command-and-control management is the only way to ensure results. As the work force continues to demand participation and the economic environment increasingly requires rapid change, relationship-oriented behaviour may emerge as the management style of choice for many organizations. Inclusion of minorities in media organizations continues to challenge most media organizations. Because the minority population in the United States is rapidly increasing, the need for skilled minority employees to represent the population has greatly increased as well. Forward-looking media managers must cast a wider net for skilled minority applicants and, more importantly, produce a more hospitably diverse workplace, just to compete for the most talented workers.

One way managers can do this is by valuing diversity in the workplace. Managers can diminish prejudices by acknowledging the problem, addressing negative behaviour, and obtaining feedback. According to Brown (1990), successful companies have open and frequent internal communications because minorities translate silence as lack of concern. However, many staffers are uncomfortable in pointing out things that offend them because they fear being perceived as"the minority person"who has no other interests or expertise. Minorities, women, as well as all people from varying cultures need to be comfortable in discussing concerns about the work environment. Valuing diversity in the workplace means recognizing the worth and dignity of others and treating people with respect.

Recognizing Contingencies in Media Organizations

The structure of media organizations affects many aspects of productivity and performance and is contingent on a mix of scientific and humanistic principles. For example, the size of a newspaper may affect how employees express themselves in their writing. Newspapers that were part of a large chain such as Gannett were more likely to advocate activist positions in their editorials and be more critical of mainstream institutions because they perceive themselves to be in powerful positions. Other examples of structure's influence on conduct are findings that indicate managers of chain newspapers emphasize profits at the expense of quality when compared to independently owned newspapers.

Large corporations encouraged the flow of communication and that extensive communication existed; however, much of it was written in the form of reports, memos, and newsletters. Annual evaluation of management performance was required, as were weekly and monthly reviews of station departments. The structure of the newspaper also affects human relations within the organization. Johnstone (1976) found that in newspaper organizations, face-to-face communication declines as organizations increase in size. He also found that communication in large news organizations flows primarily down the organizational ladder.

The management behaviour of higher level executives set the tone for communication at lower levels of the organization. For example, a news director who initially had a hands-on approach or participative management style felt obliged to exhibit a more authoritarian behaviour when that was what was coming from corporate headquarters. Consultants are sometimes needed to change the overall management environment if a company wants to foster more participation within the entire organization. Newspaper managers evaluated employees on a regular basis and interpersonal communication was the preferred and most often used means of communication. They also found that the perceived atmosphere of the newsroom was related to the amount of participation in which reporters were involved on matters of importance to reporters. The atmosphere was better when reporters participated in decision making. Likewise, Adams and Fish surveyed television news directors, general managers, and sales managers and found that participative, or democratic, leadership behaviour related to higher levels of job satisfaction. Additional research also has indicated that work dissatisfaction exists when management makes most decisions. An increase in centralization and bureaucratization fosters job dissatisfaction because of diminished autonomy.

These studies indicate media personnel are likely to be satisfied when they have more autonomy and are involved in the decision making process. Job satisfaction also increases with additional feedback from supervisors and with opportunities for advancement. In Argyris' (1974) study of the organizational structure of a major newspaper, one reporter commented,"Reporters are an irrational bunch. And the ego is high. You need to hear you're doing well".

STRUCTURAL ANALYSIS

To find out whether or not departments or media organizations as a whole are doing well, effective managers make time for strategic planning. Strategic planning covers a relatively long period of time. It affects many parts of the organization, and it includes the formulation of objectives and the selection of the means by which the objectives are to be obtained. Tactical planning, on the other hand, involves short-range planning such as production schedules and day-to-day procedures. Porter (1980) suggests that managers should periodically analyse the structure of their organizations by conducting a structural analysis. The framework provides a company with a way to understand its own position in the environment. In addition, Porter suggests conducting a competitor analysis to develop a profile of the nature and success of the likely strategy each competitor might take and the environmental shifts that might occur.

There are four diagnostic components to a structural analysis that can also be used for a competitor analysis. These include looking at assumptions of the firm (or the background of the firm and industry), current strategies (how the business is currently competing), capabilities of the firm (both strengths and weaknesses), future goals, and making recommendations. In this process, managers are basically trying to obtain as much information on the formal and informal structure of the organization as possible to identify potential problems, the effect of new technology, the cutback or addition of staff, the opening or closing of divisions, or whatever else is relevant. Compiling the data for a sophisticated structural or competitor analysis requires much work. There are many sources for field data or published data, much of which is available on the Internet. Top management can stimulate the completion of such analysis by making someone responsible for the effort and by requiring sophisticated profiles as part of the planning process.

Learning About the Bottom from the Top

Easternhouse Broadcasting Corporation owns 12 television stations, 12 AM radio stations, and 12 FM radio stations in the eastern United States. The corporation is divided into two geographic divisions; the Midwest Division has five television stations, six FM stations, and seven AM stations and is headquartered in Chicago. The remaining stations are in the Atlantic Division, with headquarters in Philadelphia. Each division has a president and two division vice presidents, one for television and one for radio. Answering to the regional vice presidents in charge of radio and television are the individual station general managers. Easternhouse also has a corporate headquarters in Washington, DC, with corporate heads for both radio and television.

The Case of the New Editor

The Bloomington Mercury-News rapidly was becoming one of the best suburban dailies in the Midwest when its editor, Jim Westley, took a job as a business writer for the Detroit News. The news staff of eight reporters and two assistant editors at the Mercury-News had been together for about 18 months. During that time, the staff had developed a spirit of teamwork that had made them friends and improved the newspaper. The Mercury-News had been named the best daily newspaper under 25,000 circulation a month earlier by the Michigan Press Association (MPA). The circulation of the paper had gone from 14,000 to 17,000 during Westley's 2-year tenure as editor. The advertising linage also had increased 35 per cent. Publisher Janet Gaylord attributed much of the financial improvement to the work of the editorial staff. At the MPA awards banquet, she mentioned that Westley not only brought skills as an editor, but his ability to work with people had resulted in the longest period of staff stability in the paper's 25-year history.

The Mercury-News staff was saddened by Westley's leaving, but they knew it was a big break for him. They felt they would continue to remain a close-knit staff. The natural curiosity of the staff about their new editor was answered when Gaylord announced Steve Smith, a former assistant city editor for the Dallas Morning News, would be the new editor. Smith seemed to be a nice guy. He had worked in newspapers for about 6 years--the last 3 in Dallas. He had a degree in history from the University of Michigan. He explained to one staff member that he took the new job to get back to his native state. Relations between Smith and the existing staff went well for a week. On the

Thursday afternoon of the second week, reporter Leslie Bridges came into the newsroom and pounded her desk. When asked what was bothering her, she said,"Our new leader butchered my story to the point that it is unintelligible. I'll be surprised if we don't get sued by someone."

The story involved a lawsuit filed against the local school board by a parents' group over teaching handicapped children. The group contended the board was violating federal law by not providing adequate facilities for their children. The board argued in turn that it did not have the facilities to teach some of the more severely handicapped students. Bridges had written a 30-column-inch review of the case to run the day the court hearing was scheduled to start. Almost half of the story had not made the newspaper.

When Bridges asked Smith about it, he mentioned almost casually that he had miscounted the inches in laying out the story. He said the Mercury-News five-column format had thrown him off. Smith told her to rework the story and he would run it on Sunday.Relations did not improve the next week. During the staff's informal weekly lunch gathering, Dave Simmons, who works general assignment, told the other staff members about what had happened the day before. He had been following a controversy involving 60 homeowners in Bloomington and the builder of their homes. The homeowners said they had been sold houses that were not complete and that had many serious structural problems.

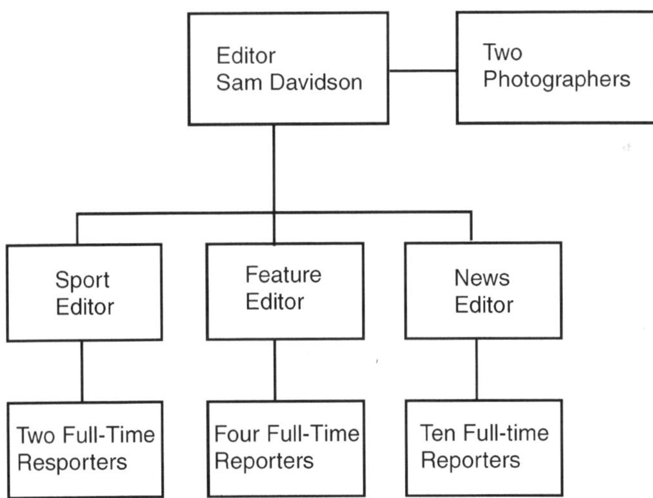

Fig. Newsroom Organizaional Chart of the Brighton Light.

The builder said the houses were fine when the deals were closed. Simmons had wanted to attend the homeowners' demonstration, which would be in front of the builder's offices. Smith, however, said no one was really interested in that sort of thing and assigned Simmons to cover the Chamber of Commerce luncheon, where the Chamber was about to reveal its new promotion campaign for a better Bloomington. Simmons had suggested another reporter be assigned, but Smith said rather sharply that he wanted Simmons to do it.The next 4 weeks saw similar conflicts arise between the new editor and other members of the staff. The weekly luncheons, which had been attended by the old editor but were not attended by Smith, had become gripe sessions. Each staff member tried to outdo the others with a horror story about Smith. Susan Moore, one of the assistant editors, told the group about the day Smith was writing one of his weekly columns."He turned to me and asked,'How do you spell Negaunee?' I said I didn't know and told him to look on the map. He just shrugged, said'Never mind,' and kept typing. He ended up misspelling Negaunee in the paper."Five days after the luncheon, the publisher called Moore and the other assistant editor into her office and showed them an unsigned letter complaining about Smith. It said he had undermined staff morale, had shown sloppy work habits, and had shown poor news judgment. The letter went on to say several of the staff had decided to find other jobs.

The Case of How Much Work in the News Bureau

This was her first job after finishing her journalism degree at MU. She had done well in school, with a B+ average and a newspaper internship at a metropolitan daily. So far, she felt the job had gone well. John Silverstein, the head of the News Bureau, had dropped her a note saying he liked the story she wrote about the new telescope acquired by the astronomy department. The note had complimented her on her ability to make the technical aspects of a large telescope easy to understand.

Megan had been trying to produce about four stories a day, with one of them being a longer personality feature. Her"beat"covered some of the less prestigious departments at MU, but as one of her journalism instructors had told her,"Everything and everyone has a story, it is up to the journalists to find it and make it interesting." As lunchtime approached, Megan started thinking about her three colleagues who had asked her out to eat. They seemed so much older, all in their 40s, that she was a little nervous.

But her concern passed quickly as they got to the restaurant and settled into eat. Bob Hammer was the oldest of the group at age 49. He had been at the News Bureau for 5 years, after working 12 years at the local daily newspaper as a staff writer. Joan Collars had been at the News Bureau longest of all the staff, having started right out of college 23 years ago. The final member of the lunch group was Beverly Thomas, who had been a staff writer for the News Bureau for 8 years. Conversation was cordial as the four ate their lunch. As they sat drinking coffee after finishing lunch, Joan started talking about Megan's work.

"We have been amazed at your work, Megan. Your copy is clean and your story ideas are fresh,"Joan said."We're delighted to have you on staff, but we're curious about how you like being part of our little group."

“The job is just great,"Megan said."The work is interesting, and I've got all sorts of ideas I want to work on.”

“We're glad to see your youthful enthusiasm, dear,"Beverly said, joining the conversation,"but we are a bit concerned about your work pace. Four stories a day is an awful lot of work. I would hate to see you burn out from too much work. Maybe you should try to pace yourself.”

“Oh, I enjoy writing,"Megan said, as a feeling of uneasiness crept over her."I don't think I'll burn out.”

"That's how everyone feels at first,"Joan said."But you've been here less than I month. After several years, it's a little different. You get a better understanding of what management wants.""I think what Joan's trying to say is that you don't quite know the lay of the land yet, Megan,"Bob added."The seven of us who have been here a while know the setup pretty well, and we have to be careful with the way we work. MU is one giant bureaucracy you know. Once you set up work patterns, they will continue to expect you to work at that level. “Bob's right, dear”, Beverly said. “We're concerned that you not put yourself in a bad situation in the future. We hope that you hang around for a while, so we're just trying to help out.” Generally, we aim at 10 to 12 stories a week, including one nice personality piece, “Bob said.” Take it from an old newspaper man, the news media won't use even that many stories. We'd be wasting paper by writing too many press releases."Megan was taken back by all of this. She managed to say she understood and thanked the three for their concern and interest. She left the lunch with a sense of uneasiness, of being on trial. That evening all she could do was think about the conversation at lunch. She wasn't really sure what was going on, or what it all meant to her future. About 9 pm, she decided it would help to talk with someone, so she called her old school roommate, who was working on a newspaper in another city. As her friend said hello, Megan blurted out,"I think I've got some problems here and I need your advice."

The Case of Paper Glut at the Herald-Telegraph

Henry Peterson, publisher of the Herald-Telegraph, had figured the monthly department heads' meeting would be a quick one. No major problems had come across his desk during the past few weeks. The meeting started at 3:30 pm and he had a 5 pm tee time for golf. He never reached the golf course. These meetings had been held every Monday of the month for the past 3 years at the 200,000 circulation newspaper. As usual, the first 45 minutes had been somewhat dull. Marie Laraby, the editor, discussed the need for replacing two assistant editors who recently quit. Lynn Madison, the circulation manager, told the other heads about the district manager who had left town with a week's worth of receipts. Robert Atkins, production manager, told the others about the recent problems in colour registration.

5

Media Regulation and Self-Regulation

Media managers must be aware that the law changes constantly. Laws affecting media firms have changed and instances when legal advice should be sought. The practices and principles that all media managers must apply in order to avoid legal problems. Some online as well as traditional resources for media managers are identified. It does, however, highlight areas of contemporary interest, and focus on the prevention and response to legal actions. Readers interested in more detail should review the appropriate legal resources referred to throughout.

PREVENTING LEGAL PROBLEMS

There are general principles and procedures managers at all kinds of media organizations can institute to minimize legal problems. First-time managers must learn and understand the goals of the organization to direct, coordinate and involve the people they supervise. Then, organizational goals must be communicated and implemented by establishing timetables, which can be tied to performance evaluations. Performance evaluations allow managers to quantify performance to promote or fire employees fairly, avoiding wrongful-termination lawsuits.

Performance Assessment and Termination

One of the first things a new manager must do is to ask employees whether they know how their performance is measured. If the performance evaluation process is not spelled out, ask employees for their ideas about performance assessment and how to improve it. Then managers should work with supervisors to develop an equitable and understandable employee performance review process.

Employees should be given a personnel manual including job descriptions and duties, organizational employment policies, performance assessment documents and procedures, the company's progressive discipline process, human resources information, and other related materials.It is especially important to be specific about standards, deadlines, and other appropriate performance measures. All employees should be notified ahead of time when evaluations occur and how to prepare for them. Managers and employees should discuss written goals, performance measurements, and deadlines of evaluations. Rewards for exceptional performance should be clear.

New managers can develop ideas for appropriate performance evaluation forms and criteria by obtaining copies of such forms from their own supervisors, or talking to a former teacher or managers at other media organizations.For example, a reporter's performance evaluation might include ratings of:

- Story accuracy;
- Ability to meet deadlines;
- News gathering skills;
- Ability to suggest and develop story ideas;
- Ability to develop sources;
- Level of awareness and knowledge of the reporter's assigned beat and community;
- Breadth of coverage, including coverage of minorities and minority viewpoints;
- Wskills, including story organization, importance, style, and word selection;
- Ability to communicate and work with the public, supervisors and other staff members;
- Ability to respond to constructive criticism or feedback

Occasionally, performance reviews will be unsatisfactory. So managers must be familiar with appropriate procedures for disciplining, and if necessary, firing employees. Again, employee handbooks including job descriptions, performance evaluation documents, procedures, and the company's progressive discipline system must be developed and distributed. If termination policies are spelled out in handbooks, and progressive discipline policies and procedures are followed and documented, the company should be protected from wrongful termination suits.

The first time job performance does not meet minimum standards the employee should be notified in writing. The document should explain why performance was unsatisfactory, suggest how to improve, and outline the consequences of failing to improve. For non probationary workers, the disciplinary time period for improvement may vary from 30 days for a poor performer's work, to 60 days for an underachieving sales person, or up to 90 days for a tardiness or absenteeism problem.The employee must be given an opportunity to respond verbally and in writing.

The same type of document is used for any employee making a similar infraction to ensure consistency of discipline. If one employee received a reprimand or discipline for a particular infraction, all employees making the same infraction should receive the same discipline. Falcone suggested using a step system of due process to discipline employees. The purpose of progressive discipline is to rehabilitate, so employees and employers need a system fair to all. Here are the steps to follow:

Step 1. Clearly state the problem in writing and explain how and why the employee's conduct or performance damaged the company.

Step 2. State a clear and unambiguous warning that failure to improve will result in discipline, up to and including termination.

Step 3. Through progressive written disciplinary actions, demonstrate that the employee's performance did not improve despite repeated written and verbal warnings.

Step 4. Demonstrate that any worker would expect to be fired under similar circumstances because discip-line was meted out in a fair and consistent way.

Thus, a wrongful termination lawsuit may be avoided by demonstrating in writing that consistent, predictable steps were taken within the organization to rehabilitate an employee. When an employee is disciplined, discuss the unsatisfactory performance in private and provide a written warning. Place a warning copy in the employee's personnel file and give one to a union representative, if appropriate. Only other employees who need to know about the warning, like an immediate supervisor, should be informed and directed to keep it confidential. That way, the employee's privacy is protected and the company does not risk defamation charges. Falcone provided examples of how to write up progressive disciplinary actions, in this case for excessive tardiness.

Although it is difficult to fire someone without due process, on-the-spot firings are appropriate for employees who break the law, engage in illegal conduct, endanger other employees, or are insubordinate, negligent, intoxicated, or use illegal substances on company property. If there is any doubt, a manager can suspend an employee until an investigation of the conduct is completed. This allows time to speak to an attorney versed in labour law. Previous disciplinary actions may also be examined to ensure disciplinary actions are fair. Whether or not a firm uses a termination review process, all managers can ask themselves the following questions to ensure that a termination is fair. What is the employee's overall record? Are there any mitigating factors that might explain or excuse the employee's misconduct or unsatisfactory performance?

Are any statutory problems involved? Were any job security representations made to the employee? If yes, is the termination consistent with those representations? Are there any public policy concerns? Has the employee received progressive discipline? Is the termination justified? Does it fit the offense? Employers also need to be conscious of how they fire employees and consider ways to minimize the employee's frustration, anger, and embarrassment. Employees should be told privately and as candidly as possible why they are being fired. The supervisor should do so firmly, yet compassionately, without being apologetic. An apologetic demeanor suggests guilty feelings exist and implies wrongdoing to the fired employee. Employers should limit the amount of information provided to prospective employers calling for reference checks on fired employees. Only the fact and dates of employment and the positions held should be provided. Avoid providing negative information, as the former employee may sue if such information is publicized.

Contracts and Agreements

Managers should establish written procedures for dealing with all sorts of potential legal problems, not just progressive discipline and termination. Instruct employees to document their dealings with interviewees, news sources, business contacts, advertisers, and freelance writers, photographers, and artists. That way, a written record exists if any problems arise later. Managers and their legal counsel should review important transactions to identify which potential pitfalls should be explained in clauses. Then, clauses spelling out details of possible concern can be included in all contracts. For example, agreements with freelancers should be in writing and signed by both parties. Fees and expenses should be included, as well as what the work's appropriate subject matter is and what its finished form should be.

Due to recent court cases, newspaper managers should ensure that contracts for carriers include appropriate language. For example, if publishers do not wish to provide benefits to carriers, contracts must include language specifically stating that no benefits are provided. Contracts should also state that the plan administrator has the discretion to decide who is entitled to benefits. Contracts might also include an express waiver of benefits. All types of media firms should spell out all benefits, expectations, agreements, and rights in all contracts. Documentation of communications with persons outside of the organization is recommended too. Media organizations should establish procedures for dealing with complaints.

Irate advertisers, public or private persons who are the subject of stories, readers, listeners, and/or viewers contact such companies regularly. Employees should be trained to treat all complaints seriously. Employees should be as polite and conciliatory as possible, even if they believe the complaint is baseless because courteous treatment often defuses a situation. Train employees to tell a telephone complainant that they are writing down the facts for internal investigation and then do so, without admitting anything, interrupting, or passing blame. All employees should bring complaints to the appropriate supervisor's attention immediately, to ensure complaints are dealt with consistently. This also prevents a defensive employee from complicating the situation. The supervisor should determine whether the complaint has merit and then send a letter to the complainant, that day, that confirms the call, provides an explanation, proposes a solution, or provides a deadline by which the complainant will be contacted. The same general procedure can be used for written complaints. Different rules apply in the event of a serious complaint, when a lawsuit is threatened, and when the complainant is an attorney. Instruct employees not to admit anything and immediately refer the matter to top management, along with all available documentation. Top management must then contact an attorney before responding and allow the attorney to handle the problem, when necessary. In any event, employees must feel comfortable about reporting complaints to supervisors, especially complaints caused by employee error or misconduct. If a retraction or letter of apology is needed, an attorney must review it before dissemination. A retraction could repeat the offense and be viewed as an admission of wrongdoing.

Finally, media organizations should publicize their policies internally and have training sessions regarding appropriate procedures and behaviour. Never assume that employees have the judgment and experience to deal with legal and ethical dilemmas; even experienced employees can make mistakes. The best way to prevent legal and ethical problems is to anticipate and prepare for them. The media provide information to the public; such organizations must never forget the legal and ethical responsibilities that accompany this role.

GENERAL AREAS OF LEGAL CONCERN

Employee Health and Safety

Employment health and safety are other important management concerns that change often. One recent concern has been establishing and implementing drug-testing policies fairly, primarily because a lack of adequate preemployment screening for drug use and other factors could open up a media firm to liability charges. Firms must avoid hiring employees who may harm or endanger others on the job.

The New York Times Regional Newspaper Group has a drug-and-alcohol free workplace programme demonstrating how such policies might be set up. Prospective employees are required to take a urinalysis drug test. Pending completion of the test, applicants accepted for a job must sign forms stating they understand the policy and allow the company to perform the urinalysis and a blood test. The blood test consent is filed and used only when medical treatment is needed for a work-related accident possibly involving the use of drugs or alcohol. Employees hired before the drug policy's implementation sign consent forms allowing the company to test them if job-related accidents occur.

To avoid lawsuits, tests are completed at a federally certified lab that meets stringent guidelines. Chain-of-custody forms identifying the specimen and donor by number are completed to ensure the testing procedure's confidentiality and integrity. The chain-of-custody form, as well as the blood and urinalysis consent forms, are kept on file until a job-related accident occurs or a worker's compensation claim is filed. Employees who refuse to complete forms are notified that refusal is grounds for termination.

Employers can take steps to minimize the likelihood of drug-testing suits. If an applicant tests positive, conduct another, more sophisticated test as a check and give the applicant a chance to explain the result. Sometimes a medical statement can clear up a potential misunderstanding over a positive test. Employees who test positive should be referred to only licensed treatment centers and sign releases so information may be shared with appropriate parties like insurance companies.

Managers should require employees to sign a reentry agreement, covering a specific period such as 2 years, after completing treatment. Other suggested provisions include requiring the employee to: abstain from mood-altering drugs or alcohol; agree to random drug testing; agree to continue in follow-up treatment for a specified time; agree to submit a record of all such meetings attended for the employer to verify; and agree that the aftercare treatment is the employee's and/or insurance company's expense.

Managers face a much larger variety of health and safety concerns on the job than discussed here. For example, managers must consider how to deal with employee concerns about tobacco or smoke-free work environments, AIDS, and other health problems. The importance of keeping up with regulations in the trade press and consulting with the appropriate legal expert for advice cannot be overemphasized.

Business Recovery, Disaster, or Crisis Plans

Business recovery, disaster, or crisis plans are developed to ensure employees know how to respond in case of a technical problem, natural disaster, sabotage, crime, or an environmental incident. Although loss of market share, possible harm to public image or credibility, and excessive down-time are concerns, legal and regulatory compliance issues are a primary reason for developing a business recovery plan. Although a disaster plan may not be followed exactly in a real-life situation, it focuses employees' efforts because all know what goals are and what each should do.

A sudden crisis disrupts company operations without warning and is likely to generate news coverage, which may adversely affect employees, offices, revenues, business assets, or the company's reputation. Examples of sudden crises include accidents resulting in significant property damage to company facilities, a natural disaster that disrupts operations or endangers employees, unexpected job actions or labour disruptions, and workplace violence. A smoldering crisis is a serious business problem that is generally unknown without or within the company that could generate negative publicity when revealed and could result in fines, penalties, legal awards, or other unbudgeted expenses over a certain amount. Examples of smoldering crises include customer allegations of improper conduct, action by a disgruntled employee like serious threats or whistle-blowing, or disclosure of serious internal company problems to employees, investors, or customers.

A crisis plan should clearly identify the types of situations in which the plans are in effect. Media outlets in areas where natural disasters like hurricanes, tornadoes, or floods often hit are especially advised to develop such plans. Emergency management and operations groups should be identified so employees know who is expected to try to come to work and when. Disaster preparedness guides should be developed explaining to employees production or broadcast details such as a list of emergency organizations and agencies, the number of editions to run, whether to print colour or black-and-white, and departmental checklists.

The St. Petersburg Times, located in a hurricane-prone area, developed a colour-coding system identifying certain employee groups who should report to work in an emergency. For example, red and blue teams of production, circulation, and news employees must report to work if the paper expects to produce emergency editions. Yellow and green teams include other employees who report after the storm passes to relieve red and blue team members. Members of each team receive a card identifying their colour codes and telephone numbers to call in the event of a disaster situation. An outline for developing a disaster plan including:

- Identifying sudden and smoldering crises that are likely to or may occur;
- Evaluating critical individuals and departments and identifying those essential for maintaining operations in a crisis situation;
- Determining in-house expertise;
- Determining critical in-house software and equipment;
- Deciding whether and when to use outside consultants (e.g., to aid with a smoldering crisis);
- Determining the availability of or purchasing appropriate backup software and/or equipment;
- And establishing a contingency budget and example schedule for the major types of crises.

By planning ahead, media outlets can minimize the occurrence of employee injury and provide coverage to warn local residents of impending danger.

Antitrust

Antitrust is another major legal area of interest to media managers. The Supreme Court affirmed in Associated Press v. United States (1945) that antitrust laws apply to the media. The Newspaper Preservation Act (NPA) of 1970 gives certain daily newspapers a limited exemption from antitrust laws.

Two newspapers within a market may form a joint operating agreement (JOA) when one is in probable danger of financial failure. Under a JOA, the newspapers' advertising, circulation, production, and administra tive departments are merged, whereas their editorial departments are kept separate.

Proposed JOAs must be approved by the US Attorney General, although administrative hearings often are held before a decision is made. Readers interested in additional information on antitrust, the NPA, and JOAs might read. A recent antitrust case underscores how rules regarding the practices of media firms can change overnight. In a November 1997 case with implications for newspapers, the US Supreme Court overturned its rule barring manufacturers from fixing the maximum price at which independent dealers and distributors can sell goods to consumers. Newspaper publishers may now establish a maximum price at which independent distributors sell newspapers to the public without automatically violating federal antitrust laws.

In future antitrust maximum pricing cases, plaintiffs will have to prove that the maximum pricing has an anticompetitive effect. Maximum resale pricing should be evaluated using the rule of reason under which a fact finder decides whether the questioned practice imposes an unreasonable competitive restraint. Various factors are taken into account including the relevant business' condition before and after the restraint was imposed, as well as the nature, history, and effect of the restraint. Publishers should seek an antitrust attorney's advice before making any pricing decisions or changes based on this case.

The major causes of libel suits are"carelessness, misunderstanding of the law of libel, limitations of the defence of privilege (including the First Amendment privilege) and the extent to which developments may be reported in arrests". Surprisingly, many libel suits result from fact errors in minor stories, court and police news, birth notices, and engagements. At least one newsroom editor or manager must be knowledgeable about state and federal libel developments. Advise reporters and editors when they research and write stories that the plaintiff in a libel case,"has the right to try to prove the press was reckless or even knew that what it was publishing was a lie".

Instruct employees to keep careful notes and memos, obtain more than one source for potentially libelous accusations, obtain supporting documents for controversial statements, and obtain the appropriate court documents (such as complaints, cease-and-desist orders, and judgments) when allegations are made. These materials are to be kept in files demonstrating the care taken to ensure stories are accurate. Potentially libelous stories should be reviewed by a legal expert before publication. Any post publication contact with a person claiming to be libeled should be handled carefully, as the response is an important factor in a decision to sue. Judges and potential jurors in a libel-related survey described journalists as irresponsible, lacking decency/courtesy/

ethics, invaders of privacy, and arrogant. Journalists should consider how the average person will react when weighing the use of hidden cameras or other potentially controversial news gathering techniques. And editors might consider whether other techniques could be used that would not open a media outlet to libel. The ABC/Food Lion Case, where a Prime Time Live story reporting that Food Lion sold spoiled meat products and encouraged employees to work unpaid overtime, was a suit based on secretive news gathering techniques, not libel as sometimes reported.

Although Food Lion's actual damages were assessed at $1,402, the jury awarded the company $5.5 million, which was later reduced to $315,000. The large punitive jury award may have occurred because ABC employees appeared arrogant. Some journalists reported the case as a libel suit, based on releases from Food Lion's lawyers. One juror who favored a high punitive award said,"The people who wrote the Articles I have read did not understand the case". The ABC/Food Lion case underscores how important it is for managers, editors, and journalists to conduct themselves with the utmost professionalism.

However, media managers must avoid self-censorship that does not serve the public. Lawyers may evaluate how much a lawsuit would cost rather than whether it could succeed. Small papers, and presumably other small media organizations, have become especially careful about what they publish for fear of surviving a costly libel battle. Although prudence and care always make good sense, a manager must always consider whether the potential suit is meant to intimidate and whether the public interest would be served by publication or broadcast.

Privacy

The right of privacy encompasses"the right to be let alone"or to live one's private life free from publicity. Privacy entitles an individual to prevent the use of, or interference with, personal and intimate aspects of life. Such invasions presumably have a negative effect on a person's psychological well being. Journalists may read more about privacy in the most recent AP Broadcast News Handbook and AP Stylebook and Libel Manual which states that once an individual is volun-tarily or involuntarily involved in a news event, the right to privacy is forfeited. A journalist should be protected when writing about an individual involved in a matter of legitimate public interest, even if it is not a bona fide spot news event. But publication of a story or picture that"dredges up the sordid details of a person's past and has no current newsworthiness" may not be protected.

The increasing use of computerized records and Internet access appears likely to intensify the conflict between open access to records and individual privacy. Ten years ago, in developing a story to explain why three children were run over by school bus drivers, a Providence Journal reporter compared the roster of school bus drivers with Rhode Island state driver's license and criminal records. The results revealed that some had bad driving records and drug convictions, which led to stronger requirements for bus driver background checks. Today, because of the federal Driver's Privacy Protection Act of 1994, drivers in Rhode Island can choose to close their records to the public and news media.

The same story could not be done as effectively now. The Driver's Privacy Protection Act"closes personal information records including names, addresses, telephone numbers, Social Security numbers, photographs, driver identification numbers and medical or disability information". Media groups have two options to mitigate the Act:

- States can pass opt-out laws allowing consumers the option of keeping personal information confidential, making some but not all records open,
- Media exemptions established by law or administra-tive rule allowing journalists continued access to personal information. Managers need to discover whether either option has been pursued in their states, and if not, which action is appropriate to take. Thus far, opt-out laws have been the prevalent choice because national press groups have traditionally opposed special treatment for the news media.

Firms are also feeling the public backlash regarding privacy. America Online (AOL) had to cancel a plan to sell subscriber phone numbers for telemarketing. Lexis-Nexis changed its Internet-based people finder P-TRAK due to vehement public objection to the display of Social Security numbers. Privacy advocates also cite concerns with aggressive marketers annoying consumers, identity theft, and stalkers and radicals gaining access to information through new technologies.

Poll results document the level of public concern over privacy. According to a Pew Research Centre For The People & The Press poll conducted in February 1997, 64 per cent of U.S. adults believe TV news programs invade personal privacy unnecessarily, whereas 57 per cent believe newspapers do the same. In a 1996 Louis Harris/Centre for Media and Public Affairs poll, 80 per cent of respondents said the news media often invade people's privacy. Protecting privacy takes on special concerns for marketers or others targeting children on the Internet.

The Council of Better Business Bureau's Children's Advertising Review Unit (CARU) developed self-regulatory guidelines for marketers to children. Online advertisers should make reasonable efforts to ensure that the person paying for the child's online transaction controls it, either by written consent or the ability to cancel an order. Advertisers should have children ask their parents for permission to answer questions, discourage them from using their full names on the Net, and tell them to get their parent's permission before giving out their e-mail addresses to anyone. A publication or broadcast station can apply these same principles when adding a children's section to its home page. As with libel, some journalists believe that the press has not explained its legitimate need for access sufficiently. Journalists must help the public understand why access to government is an issue the public should be concerned with, not just journalists.

Free Press/Fair Trial Issues

Managers and journalists must begin to carefully consider how to publicize the importance of free press/fair trial issues and cover high-profile trials professionally to avoid damaging the image of the profession further. Public and judicial perceptions of the media after the highly-publicized"... the news media will be better off saving its litigation energies for technical strikes where the law already is essentially on its side or choosing very carefully when to push the law in unresolved areas, such as access to documents. Today's climate does not seem likely to produce any broad new rights for the coverage of criminal trials.".

Because of the perceived success of the Timothy McVeigh/ Oklahoma City Bombing trial (e.g., no major delays or disasters), journalists can expect that other judges will copy presiding Judge Richard Matsch's tactics. Matsch took numerous measures to ensure the jurors's privacy and protect the defendant's rights.

He"... issued gag orders limiting press contact for lawyers in the case, denied McVeigh's request to give on-camera interviews, withheld personal information about jurors, and even ordered the construction of a wall in his courtroom between the jury box and the gallery". The case may establish a perception in the judicial community that,"secrecy and security should trump openness and access"in high-profile cases.

Access to Government Information

Media organizations may obtain government information using The Freedom of Information Act, which established a process for requesting information from federal agencies. The Act allows citizens to request any records from the federal executive branch, but does not cover Congress, the federal courts, or state or local governments. Records include documents, papers, letters, reports, films, photographs, audio recordings, and computer tapes. Managers and employees should be familiar with state laws concerning access.

Copyright

Media managers can expect to deal with copyright protection, which extends to almost anything authored, created, performed, or produced in a tangible or permanent way. Electronic publishing is a new area of copyright concern. A federal judge recently ruled that newspapers and electronic publishers did not improperly exploit the work of freelance writers by publishing electronic versions of their Articles on the Internet. Yet managers must be sure to specify which media are covered in all copyright contracts. Some publications offer additional pay for using Articles online.

Unless a newspaper or firm has a written agreement to the contrary, freelancers retain the copyrights to their works. For example, if a freelance Article or photograph about tomatoes is printed without a written agreement by a newspaper and then displayed on its web site or the Nexis database, the use is allowed.

But if the Webmaster were"to feature, separate from the archive, a special tomato button linking browsers to electronic resources on tomatoes, one of which happened to be the freelancer's Article,"the use would not be protected. So, managers should obtain written agreements from all freelancers which give the company all rights to their work.

Media firms that use or set up web sites for themselves or clients must consider several copyright and publishing liability issues. Unless protected by fair use, uploading and downloading copyrighted works without authorization is an infringement of the copyright holder's rights. Under fair use, portions of copyrighted materials may be copied, but only if it does not undercut the copyright holder's ability to profit. Establish copyright ownership by having all web design firms or employees who worked on the site sign contracts ensuring a complete and perpetual assignment of copyright ownership to the firm. Under the work-for-hire doctrine, web or other materials developed by an employee within the scope of employment belongs to the employer.

Before including preexisting material on a web site, determine what rights the authors may have been granted. For example, if an advertising agency's nonprofit client wanted to post past issues of a newsletter on the web, the agency must determine who wrote the Articles. If Articles were always written by employees, the nonprofit organization should own the copyright. However, if volunteers wrote Articles, because the volunteer gave the right to publish originally does not mean that such a right grants permission to put that same Article online. Before uploading preexisting material, the original written contract should be reviewed to see what the parties intended at the time. Vague contract language that does not clearly delineate future uses will not be considered a grant of rights. Contract language that clearly states that the work can be published in,"technologies now known or hereinafter invented"covers all future uses.

Online copyright infringement liability is determined without regard for the intent of the infringer. Anyone who infringes the rights of the copyright holder without authorization is liable, although,"innocent"infringements allow a reduction in damages. A distinction is usually made between a"publisher"and"distributor"when determining liability, unless the distributor knew that the distributed material was illegal or libelous. Thus, management should evaluate a firm's level of involvement in reviewing, editing and passing along website material to determine its liability for online publications on its site.

Deception in Advertising

Advertising managers, publishers, broadcast sales managers, and general managers may need to clear or review an ad to determine whether it is deceptive or appropriate to broadcast or print.The current FTC deception definition is composed of three elements:

- There must be a representation, omission or practice that is likely to mislead the consumer;
- The representation, omission or practice is examined from the perspective of a consumer acting reasonably in the circumstances, to the consumer's detriment;
- The representation, omission or practice must be a material one."Regulable deceptiveness results only if purchase behaviour of a substantial number of people is likely to be affected".

Practices found deceptive include false verbal or written statements, misleading price claims, selling dangerous or defective products without adequate disclosures, not delivering promised services, and failing to meet warranty obligations.

Although all claims made in an ad are technically true, if the general impression of the ad is false, it still may be deceptive. That is because the FTC considers whether the entire ad is likely to mislead consumers acting reasonably; it is not necessary for the ad actually to deceive. Nor is it necessary to prove that the advertiser intended the deception. The FTC stated that certain practices are not likely to deceive reasonable consumers, such as misrepresentations regarding inexpensive products that are evaluated easily and purchased frequently by consumers. Such advertisers are less likely to deceive consumers intentionally because they depend on repeat sales for survival.

And as long as consumers understand the sources and limitations of such ads, the FTC usually does not pursue cases based on correctly stated and honestly held opinions about a product, or puffery, which is obvious exaggerations about the product or its qualities.

SELF-REGULATION OF AND BY MEDIA COMPANIES

Many media outlets, advertisers, and advertising agencies screen ads before airing or publication to ensure that they are not deceptive nor offensive. Media managers should take clearance and other legal and ethical concerns seriously for both moral and professional reasons. An industry that provides information to society bears a special responsibility to assure its accuracy and fairness. A responsible manager turns the gaze of honest, critical scrutiny to one's own organization or medium because employees look to managers for behavioral cues.

Each media profession develops codes and standards of behaviour to help guide ethical behaviour. Many questionable practices are not technically illegal; they are simply"wrong"by generally accepted moral standards.. Codes of conduct and self-regulatory bodies are useful to managers seeking advice on fair and ethical conduct.

However, critics argue that codes are developed to prevent government regulation. Critics assert industry members are not critical enough of their colleagues and often have ethical standards that are different than the public they are supposed to serve. Critics also complain that ethical violations typically result in a minor"slap on the wrist"; thus, such codes and bodies do not represent a meaningful front against unethical behaviour. Finally, critics assert that if self-regulatory codes were truly effective, would the public have such negative opinions about media firms and their practices?

Developing A Performance Evaluation System

Depending on your interests, contact a newspaper, magazine, radio station, television station, cable channel or system, advertising agency, or public relations firm. Ask to review their performance evaluation system, or develop a system for them. Start out by asking for a copy of the company's overall mission, as well as mission statements developed by the individual departments. If available, review the appropriate performance evaluations forms to see if they are consistent with the firm's mission statement(s). Next, interview a few employees in various positions regarding the performance evaluation system. See if they know what the major evaluation criteria are and when evaluations occur. You might also ask whether and how the evaluation system could be improved.

THE CASE OF THE POORLY PERFORMING SALESPERSON

Elaine Miller, sales manager at WCTV, was considering how to handle a problem with one of her salespersons, Rick Folsom. Elaine had been promoted to sales manager 3 months ago, after working at WCTV for 2 years. She earned her promotion by exceeding sales goals every month after her first on the job. She developed a research report using secondary data like MRI and the SRDS Lifestyle Market Analyst, to analyse the market. Her former boss praised the report, gave a copy to all salespersons, and included a summary of it in the rate card. When her former boss left for a new job in a larger market, he had recommended Elaine as his replacement. Rick had been a salesperson at WCTV for 2 years. For over a year and a half, his sales performance had been average to slightly above average. However, for the past 6 months, he had not met sales quotas. After her second month as sales manager, Elaine talked to Rick about his performance. He attributed his below average performance to the closing of a major advertiser, Anthony's Fashions. This local clothing store closed because several major retailers, including J.C. Penney's and Dillard's, had opened at the local mall.

Elaine listened to Rick's explanation, then suggested ways to obtain new clients for the station. She asked Rick whether he had set personal sales goals, set up a prospect file of new and inactive advertisers as well as existing businesses that were potential clients, kept up with research and data on the market to use in presentations and reports to clients, came up with new ideas or opportunities to advertise for clients, or asked his clients about their needs and goals. Rick said no, he simply telephoned or visited his clients regularly to see if they wanted to run ads.

Elaine also asked Rick why several of his clients had not paid their bills. She explained that it is a salesperson's obligation to check out a client's ability to pay before running a schedule. Rick replied that he was not aware of that fact; no one had ever really trained him to sell. He had sold time for a radio station before, but that was all the sales training he had. Elaine's predecessor had just hired him and,"cut him loose." She gave Rick a memo after their first meeting a month ago asking him to focus on sales training for the next month. First, he should read Shaver, Making the sale! How to sell media with marketing.

She gave him a copy, told him to read it, and asked him to contact her if he had any questions after reading the book. He should establish written personal sales goals, begin to develop a prospect file and develop three ideas for new advertising opportunities for existing clients. In the memo, Elaine told Rick that she would not hold him to sales performance standards that month. She wanted him to focus on doing the background work she assigned to help him improve his future sales performance. At the meeting a month later Elaine found out that Rick had made a half-hearted attempt at training. For example, he had not developed a prospect file, telling her he had no idea how to do it. She asked him why he had not contacted her to set up a meeting to discuss questions he had about the book or completing her assignments, as noted in her memo. He said he had forgotten.

When she asked him specific questions about Shaver's sales book, he was unable to respond, suggesting he had not read it. Elaine asked him to read the book again, and she scheduled a meeting with Rick to discuss the book. Elaine instructed him to have a written memo ready for the next meeting that identified the assistance or training he needed to accomplish the tasks she had set for him, the previous month."Base your needs assessment memo on the Shaver book, and be prepared to discuss the book fully,"she told him. She said she would be sending him a memo about their meeting outlining what she had asked him verbally to do during the next month, as well as the consequences of not completing these tasks."Rick, if you do not start to make a serious effort in participating in your training, and ultimately improving your sales performance, your job here could be in jeopardy.

"Elaine's"gut feeling"was that Rick was either lazy or unqualified for his sales job. She was surprised that an employee would respond so half-heartedly to a written notice of unsatisfactory job performance. She wondered if there was another reason why he was not responding to her attempts to help him. She wanted to give him a fair chance to improve, but she knew she would have to fire him if he did not take his training seriously and improve his performance. She wondered how to be fair to him yet protect the station at the same time. She had never faced this kind of problem before."Welcome to management,"she told herself.

Developing an Arbitration System

Depending on your interests, contact a newspaper, magazine, radio station, television station, cable channel or system, advertising agency, or public relations firm. Find an organization that does not have a formalized arbitration system for handling disputes between employees and management, such as sexual harassment, discrimination, discipline, productivity, promotion, demotion, and job termination.

Surf the American Arbitration Association's (AAA). The AAA provides assistance for resolving disputes and has developed specialized rules and procedures to ensure that the dispute resolution process is fair to all involved. Review the guides, rules, and explanations of alternative dispute resolution included to help you figure out how to develop an alternative dispute resolution system or process for your chosen firm.

Here's a basic explanation of dispute resolution to help you get started. Alternative dispute resolution techniques include mediation where a skilled facilitator helps disputing parties reach a voluntary settlement. The mediator serves as an advisor who helps the parties explore issues, discovers each party's needs, and suggests ways to resolve a dispute. However, the disputing parties must resolve the dispute themselves. Under arbitration, a dispute is referred to one or more impartial experts for final and binding determination. Disputing parties agree to present their case to a mutually agreed on and disinterested neutral mediator for a legally binding ruling.

According to the AAA, mediators or arbiters should be people committed to impartiality who have at least 8 to 10 years of experience in the field. A fair and judicious temperament is needed; arbiters and mediators must be patient and courteous. Dispute management skills are a must, as well as a strong academic background and respected professional credentials. Good choices are typically business persons or attorneys with expertise in the particular field. With both methods, the parties involved control the process. Other advantages are that expensive and lengthy lawsuits can be avoided; arbitration is quicker and often much less costly. Unlike court cases, all information is kept private, preventing embarrassing disclosures for the company or employee. More important, maintaining privacy makes it more likely that the parties can continue to work together after the dispute is solved. The person who assists with or decides the case is impartial and an expert in the field. For example, parties to a newspaper industry dispute might select an independent and impartial journalist, publisher or attorney who specializes in press law to serve as mediator or arbitrator, depending on case specifics. Many trade or professional organizations use the AAA to resolve disputes. Also, in the less formal setting, participants can tell completely their sides of the story.

Relevant evidence cannot be excluded by technicalities, as it often is in courtrooms. The appropriate rules, techniques, and clauses that might be included in a dispute resolution handbook for your firm of choice. Then select two managers and two employees in various departments to interview. The idea is to get as many viewpoints as possible on how disputes have been handled in the organization and how the process could be improved.If you cannot get an organization to participate, interview managers and employees in various firms in your community.

Evaluating a Home Page for Copyright Problems

Surf the home page of a media firm, media outlet, or professional media organization of interest. Artwork, hot links to other sites and other information or material included in the site. If possible, interview whoever developed the web site. Ask if the employee or person developed all site materials or obtained materials from other sources or persons. Ask the employee or person whether copyright protection was secured or considered when developing the web site.

Monitoring Broadcast Advertising for Children

Many critics of television and advertising have expressed concern about television advertising for children. As a result, the FCC treats children as a special group of viewers with special rules about advertising. These rules limit the number of minutes per hour of advertising and the connection between programme and advertising content. The purpose of this assignment is to examine advertising content aimed at children to see if it meets these standards.

6

Planning

If a manager wants to make effective decisions, he or she must plan. If a manager wants to plan adequately, he or she must make effective decisions. Many of the steps are the same. Despite the similarities, planning and decision making do differ, although these differences tend to be more practical than theoretical.

The planning process differs from the decision-making process because planning is so concrete. Although the decision wheel can be applied to most any decision, business planning takes three forms: strategic planning, intermediate planning, and short-run planning. Strategic planning involves allocating resources to achieve the long-term goals of an organization. These plans can cover I to 10 years, but they usually are developed for a 3 to 5 year period.

Intermediate planning usually covers 6 months to 2 years and provides reinforcement or correction data for the long-term goals. Short-run planning involves plans for a few weeks or at most I year. This type of plan is meant to allocate resources on a day-to-day or month-to-month basis. The strategic plan fulfills the firm's mission and overall general goals. The intermediate plan involves the general way in which the strategic plan will be pursued, and the short-run plan is how the strategic plan will work on a day-to-day basis.

COMMON CHARACTERISTICS OF PLANNING

All three types of planning have commonalities although the time period, responsible parties, and actual steps vary. Companies have general organizational goals which are fairly abstract statements of what a firm hopes to achieve within given areas of performance.

These goals are derived from the organization's mission. Smith, Arnold, and Bizzell (1985) defined an organization's mission as its business domain. About the firm's role outside its primary business markets. For example a newspaper's mission might be to provide its readers with a complete and accurate report on the events and issues of concern to its community. The goals associated with this might include:

- Covering all important issues confronting civic organizations, such as the city council, police and fire departments, and school board;
- Covering noncivic issues that relate to individual readers' health and welfare; and
- Covering events and issues that relate to the community's culture and social background.

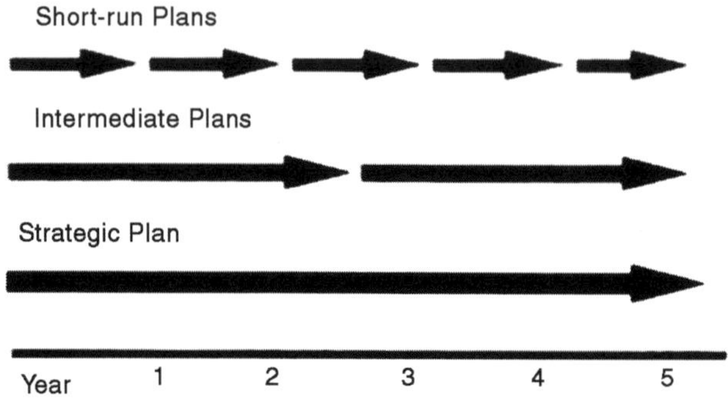

Fig. Relationship Among Strategic, Intermediate, and Short-run Planning.

Planning goals help an organization achieve its mission, which should reflect the expertise within an organization. For instance, it would make little sense for a television network news department to pursue a goal of developing an inexpensive but powerful computer because news staff would not ordinarily possess the background or resources to accomplish this. In order to assess progress, an organization must have operational definitions for measurement. For example, the goal of increasing viewership among long-term residents of the community could be operationalized as increasing ratings by two points during the next 6 months among audience members who have lived in the area of dominant influence (ADI) for more than 10 years. The operational definition must specify in measurable terms the group to be affected (people who have lived in the ADI for more than 10 years), a time period during which the change is expected (next 6 months), and a measurable level of performance that is being sought ('two ratings points).

STRATEGIC PTANNING

Strategic planning is the long-term process by which an organization pursues its mission and hopes to reach its goals. If a media organization participates in two or more of the three markets--information, advertising, and intellectual--the strategic plan must address explicitly these markets and explain the relationship among them. A television station cannot make plans for the advertising market without including the information market where it will attract viewers. A newspaper cannot plan for the information market without examining the role it will play in the intellectual market.

Smith et al. (1985) used the term strategic management in lieu of strategic planning because the traditional concept of strategic planning did not include control of the plan as it was implemented. They said strategic management includes:

- Analyzing the environment,
- Determining objectives,
- Analyzing strategic alternatives,
- Selecting strategy alternatives;
- Implementing the strategies, and
- Evaluating and controlling performance.

Combining these approaches with the decision wheel and adding control to planning results in a more refined approach to strategic planning that includes the following steps:

- Examine the business environment and past performance.
- Evaluate available resources.
- Identify, select, prioritize, and operationalize planning goals.
- Identify alternative approaches for obtaining goals.
- Select from the alternative approaches.
- Implement the plan.
- Monitor implementation.
- Evaluate plan's progress and adjust the plan.

As with decision making, the collection and analysis of information is a part of all eight steps in strategic planning. Plans for the future must be grounded in experience and an understanding of current market conditions. The market analysis is the primary method of evaluating the business environment.

The internal examination involves how well the firm accomplished its goals in the past and why. Failure to reach goals could have resulted from any number of problems inside the firm, including inappropriate goals, goals set too high, poor analysis of data, inadequate resources, and poor performance.

Evaluate Available Resources

In order to make sure the planning goals can be met, a manager must evaluate at-hand resources. At hand resources include the company's name and reputation, personnel, plant and equipment, and finances. At hand means the resources either are held currently by the firm or can be borrowed easily. Thus, financial resources also include an organization's credit.

Evaluating available resources is important because resources determine whether goals can be achieved, and although resources can be changed from one form to another, the process does not occur as quickly as management would like. If a large metropolitan newspaper needs an experienced award-winning columnist, it will take time to recruit such a writer. The uncertainty of time necessitates good resource planning based on accurate evaluation of which journalists might be good prospects. As the strategic plan develops, evaluations of available resources reveal whether the resources needed to achieve the plan's goals are currently available in the form necessary.

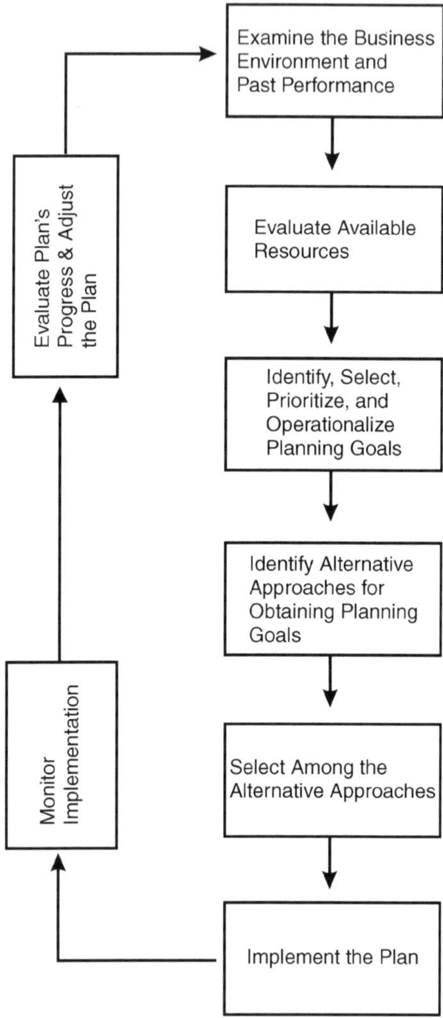

Fig. Steps in Stregic Planning.

When the organization does not have the resources needed by the plan in the appropriate form, the plan must include ways of getting or converting these resources. If the needed resources are not and cannot be made available, then the goals associated with those resources should be reconsidered or not pursued. No guidelines exist for how many goals a firm needs to identify or select, but all of the selected goals should be obtainable and consistent with the general goals and mission of the firm. Each goal requires resources that are relatively fixed. The more goals a firm pursues, the more competition will exist within the organization for resources. For example, a smaller newspaper group might select the following goals:

- Add daily newspapers until the group has papers in markets that make up 20 per cent of the circulation in Ohio (information market goal).
- Increase significantly the penetration of existing markets (information market goal).
- Increase revenue from national advertising (advertising market goal).
- Increase the column inches of display advertising that are run in the paper (advertising market goal).
- Increase the column inches and percentage of the news hole devoted to letters to the editor and guest columns (intellectual market goal).

The goals listed for the information and advertising markets conceivably could compete for resources. The acquisition of newspapers will cost money, as will efforts to increase penetration. The penetration goal will involve additional spending for the circulation and news departments, as well as money for promoting the changes from the increased spending. All five goals will consume resources and initially would compete. However, as the plan is placed into effect, the achievement of some of the goals will generate revenue, which then can be applied toward meeting other goals. Timing is important to consider because not all goals have to be reached at the same time. Some can be set for the second or third year of the plan, and some can be made contingent on reaching others.

Identify Alternative Approaches for Obtaining Goals

Almost all long-term goals can be reached with more than one approach, and they often require multiple approaches. For example, a radio station that wants to increase its share of listeners can do so by altering its music format and promoting itself in a number of ways. The aim is to select the most efficient and effective way of reaching or surpassing the goals. The ability to select the"best"approach depends on how exhaustive the analysis procedure is. Often management settles for a less than optimal plan for achieving a goal because not all ideas were identified in the decision-making stage. Brainstorming is a commonly used technique for generating ideas. It accepts two basic principles of creative thinking techniques: A positive attitude is established, which means criticism is withheld until after ideas are developed; and unusual ideas are encouraged, even if they seem impractical.

Assessing alternatives includes eliminating the ones that are impractical or improbable. Improbability and impracticality can be based on any number of characteristics, including approaches with high risk, high environmental uncertainty, and high resource needs. The list of approaches should be pared to a manageable number of good alternatives for achieving the goals. This usually would range from 3 to 6 methods. Comparison of alternative plans can be as formal or informal as management likes. Formal methods for comparison and include cost-benefit analysis, decision trees, and utility theory. From these comparisons efficiency and effectiveness can be determined. Efficiency is measured by the amount of resources needed to reach a given goal, and the most efficient approach is the one that will achieve the goal with the smallest expenditure of resources. Effectiveness is the probability that the approaches will achieve the goals of the plan.

INTERMEDIATE PLANNING

Intermediate planning requires a marketing plan, a financial plan, and a human resources plan. The three must be coordinated with each other as well as with the overall strategic plan. The main difference between strategic and intermediate planning is the plan itself A marketing plan must deal with the market mix, which includes product, place, price, and promotion (the four Ps). The marketing mix is applicable to the information, advertising, and intellectual markets. Although they are interrelated, each should have a marketing plan of its own.

The product is simply the thing that is sold or given to a consumer in exchange for time or money. In the information and intellectual markets, the product is information and ideas, with their various subdivisions. In the advertising market, it is the potential attention of consumers to advertising information. The value of the advertising attention depends on the number of viewers, readers, or listeners and the types of people paying the attention.In most organizations, the product decision is based on the location of older products in their life cycle.

Five stages of a product's life cycle:

- Infancy is when a product enters the market. Sales are low.
- Growth occurs when the product matures as to who and where it will sell. Sales grow rapidly if the product finds its niche in the marketplace.
- Approaching maturity is when the established product begins to battle competitors over market share. Sales continue to grow, but at a slower rate than in the growth stage.
- Maturity occurs when a product finds its place in its segment. Competition continues and sales grow much more slowly than earlier stages.
- Decline is the final stage when consumers lose interest in the product for whatever reason and sales begin to decline.

With most media products, place is an important part of product. News commodities, such as newspapers and newscasts, are aimed at specific geographic areas. The content reflects this aim. The size, geography, social aspects, cultural characteristic, and political nature of a society affect the places for which news products are designed. Place is also related to price in the United States. Some parts of the country have higher and lower standards of living than others. The same book for example, would face a lower demand due to price in one region than in anòther.

Place also affects the process and cost of distributing the media product. The cost of delivering a newspaper increases as one moves away from the production site. The cost of distributing a broadcast television programme is basically the same within the range of the signal. If the station wants to distribute the programme elsewhere satellite transmission would increase costs.

Price will affect demand, but it also determines how much revenue is taken in by the firm. Pricing is a difficult process for many media firms because the joint commodity nature of most media commodities creates extreme uncertainty. Managers are afraid to overprice in one type of market because it will reduce demand in another.

Increasing the subscription price for a magazine will reduce circulation, which can affect the price charged to advertisers. Research indicates that newspaper managers often charge less for their advertising and circulation than they could.

The traditional way of pricing existing products is to look at inflation, examine competitors' prices, add on additional expenses that have developed, estimate the impact of price on demand, and state the price with a profit goal in mind. The traditional way of pricing new products is to calculate the costs of production and distribution and add a desired profit margin. The final P in the marketing mix is promotion, which involves persuading people to use the product. Promotion includes advertising, public relations, and promotional activities.

SHORT-RUN PLANNING

Just as the intermediate plans are maps of reaching the goals of the strategic plan, short-run plans are ways of meeting the goals of the intermediate plans. There types of short-run planning are important: budgets, employee planning, and management by objective (MBO).

Budgets are the yearly plan of the organization. They cover the expected sources of money and how to spend that money. The budget must reflect the priorities of the intermediate and strategic plans or the mission of the organization will not be accomplished. Employee planning involves the development of the talents, skills, and aspirations of people within an organization. MBO is where the budget and employee planning intersect. It is an explicit way of setting up objectives, evaluating employees' contribution to those objectives, and allocating resources such as time and money to the successful completion of the objectives.

PLANNING FOR INTERNATIONAL MARKETS

When a media company's long-term strategic plan includes moving into international markets, new issues arise that must be carefully considered within the context of the overall planning process just discussed. The need to plan for international operations is becoming increasingly important for media corporations. Although there have been a handful of multinational media corporations over the years and media products such as films and television programs have been exported to foreign audiences, during the 1980s and 1990s the internationalization of the media industry grew dramatically.

Although the degree to which media and communication companies have internationalized is difficult to measure precisely, the U.S. Department of Commerce (1993) noted that in 1990, 10 per cent of the U.S. work force employed in the motion picture and television production industries was working for the U.S. affiliates of foreign-owned companies. That was twice the rate of employment by foreign-owned companies for the U.S. work force as a whole.

During the same period that foreign companies were investing in the U.S. media industry, U.S. media and communication companies were buying or starting companies overseas. The economics of media production make global operations desirable because once a company has created a media product such as a television programme, film, or magazine, it costs almost nothing to distribute it to more people (U.S. Department of Commerce, 1993). Moreover, each additional person who sees the programme or magazine spreads the costs of producing that item more widely and thereby increases the media company's profit.

But despite these economics, media companies interested in international expansion face significant barriers. First, most nations--including the United States--have had laws limiting or forbidding foreign ownership of media companies in order to protect domestic media industries from foreign competition and because of concerns that foreign owners might influence content and public opinion in times of war or national crisis. Restrictions on foreign ownership generally have been most stringent for telephone systems, and television and radio stations. Magazine companies and book publishers have tended to be less regulated and, therefore, foreign ownership has been more common in those media sectors.

Many countries not only restrict foreign media ownership but also imports. Europe and Canada, for example, have strict quotas on the importation of U.S.-produced films and television programming. Critics of imported media fear the sheer volume of relatively inexpensive U.S. film and television products will inhibit domestic activity. They also fear the values shown in foreign films and television may undermine national cultures and values--a process known as cultural imperialism. In the 1980s and early 1990s, however, a number of factors came together to encourage Western countries to open media markets to foreign investment. Improved communication and transportation technologies made it easier for corporations to expand into new markets, and companies in many industries around the world began to globalize their operations.

In order to run expanded operations multinational companies need access to highly developed information transfer systems such as computer networks, sophisticated telephone systems, and databases. That need put pressure on governments to deregulate their domestic telecommunications industries so that consumers and businesses could have access to the latest telecommunications technologies and services-regardless of whether they were provided by domestic or foreign-owned providers. At the same time, there was a general movement to reduce the number of trade barriers between nations in the belief that free international trade would create greater economic efficiencies, help business, and provide consumers with more choices of products for lower prices.

These two factors--the need for access to the best communication technology and services and the desire to reduce trade barriers in general--led many developed nations to reevaluate their limitations on media ownership. A number of trade agreements signed during the period, including the European Union agreement among European nations and the North American Free Trade Agreement (NAFTA) among the United States, Canada, and Mexico, included specific provisions to encourage the opening of media markets to foreign trade and investment.

Whereas changes in the international economy and business environment were pressuring developed countries to make it easier for media companies to operate internationally, changes within the media industry were encouraging media companies to actually take that step. The growth of the global economy encouraged many media companies to expand by buying media operations in foreign countries. The Canadian company Thomson Newspapers heavily invested in U.S. newspapers during the 1980s as part of its strategic plan for corporate growth, for example. Other companies pursued a similar plan but bought different types of media, becoming multimedia international conglomerates. News Corporation Ltd., Rupert Murdoch's company, started out as an Australian newspaper company but expanded by buying newspapers and television operations in Great Britain and the United States.

The convergence of media technologies also encouraged media companies to expand internationally by eroding the distinctions among the telephone, computer, television, radio, newspaper, magazine, and book industries. Increased competition in many media sectors combined with reduced revenues and profits pressured companies to look for new ways to grow. Media companies developed profitable synergies across media products, distributing the same content or concepts through different media. A story idea, for example, could be cross marketed by a multimedia conglomerate through its book publishing and film studios, whereas the soundtrack from the movie could be sold through its record company. Media corporations began realizing these synergies through the acquisition of other, often foreign, companies.

Convergence also encouraged media companies to invest in new lines of business overseas in order to gain experience in those areas. Many of the Regional Bell operating companies, for example, invested in cable systems in Great Britain and other nations to prepare for the day U. S. cable and phone industries were deregulated.

Another motivation for overseas investment was media technology manufacturers' desire to gain control of popular content such as films or music to ensure that those entertainment features were distributed in formats compatible with the manufacturers' media technologies. Japan's Sony Corp., for example, bought Columbia Pictures to make sure films would be distributed using its home entertainment technologies--a strategy it developed after consumers abandoned Sony's Betamax VCR because not enough movies were available in Beta format.

Finally, media companies recognized that investing overseas or setting up joint ventures with foreign partners was a means for getting around the limitations some nations placed on the foreign import of media products. Thus, overseas investment became a way to maintain and increase foreign exports. As globalization of media continues, it will become increasingly likely that, at some point in their careers, media professionals--whether in broadcasting, publishing, or new technologies--will find themselves working for a company that either has overseas holdings or is itself owned by a foreign company. Thus, ambitious media managers should be prepared to meet the challenges of managing across cultures and across borders.

Examine the Business Environment and Past Performance

As with strategic planning for domestic companies, strategic planning for international media operations begins with examining the business environment and past performances of the country or countries in which a company is considering investing. The questions raised during this process, however, are somewhat different than those a manager faces when looking only at the home market and company. There are a number of factors that influence a decision about where to invest, including the strength of the local economy, the regulatory environment for media, and language and cultural differences that may affect how media are received and what advertising might be sold to support the media product. These factors also affect which media product(s) will be developed.

Media products are generally luxury items. If most residents of a country are living a subsistence existence with little to no disposable income, the market for media products generally is not strong. Advertisers are not interested in reaching markets where consumers have little potential buying power. However, countries with strong economies also generally have highly developed media markets which means stiff advertising competition. Thus, a manager engaged in international strategic planning must balance the analysis of the economic conditions in the country against what is known about the competition for the type of media the company produces.

Sometimes, as in the case of the opening of Eastern Europe, media managers can spot countries that do not necessarily have a strong economy or media industry but show signs of growth in both areas. For example, media corporations from Europe and North America invested heavily in countries after the collapse of the Eastern Bloc in 1989 to the point where the ownership of large segments of Eastern Europe's print media passed into the hands of foreign companies.

Other opportunities may arise when developed countries deregulate or privatize a media sector. Until 1984, for example, Germany had only two television networks, which were publicly operated. In 1984, Germany decided to permit commercial broadcasting, which expanded rapidly. Today, although commercial television in Germany is largely controlled by German companies, some foreign media enterprises--including Murdoch's News Corporation Ltd. and the Walt Disney Co. have holdings in German television.

Media managers also need to evaluate carefully national regulatory environments. Media companies can face requirements that foreign media be owned partially by domestic partners, or media content and copyright regulations can be troublesome. Copyright is of particular concern in the international media environment. Some countries have not yet signed international copyright agreements, whereas others do not enforce international copyright laws. If a media company were to enter such a market, it might have difficulty protecting its publications or programs from illegal copying or pirating. Such pirating already is widespread in the recording and software industries. If a country has not signed international copyright agreements, then the products a media corporation produces or distributes within that country may be particularly vulnerable.

These economic and regulatory decisions greatly impact the question of what media products a media company should attempt to produce and/or sell overseas. If, for example, the economy of a market is relatively weak and the potential audience does not have a great deal of disposable income, the media manager might want to focus on developing publications or programs that give audiences information that can be used--such as home repair programs or sewing publications--rather than fashion and gossip publications or programs that may not be seen as"necessities"by financially strapped readers and viewers. Similarly, content regulations in another country could affect a media manager's choice of what to produce there. Many nations have strict laws regarding what media may publish, and content that is routinely published or broadcast in the United States would be censored elsewhere. Great Britain, for example, has more restrictions than the United States on what media can report about criminal justice proceedings and official secrets, whereas some photographs and advertisements depicting women in U.S. magazines would be deemed pornography in some Middle Eastern countries. Such regulations can make it more difficult for a media company not only to produce content for its overseas operations, but also to sell advertising for its foreign editions or programs.

Other elements that affect product and market choices are educational, cultural and language differences. If, for example, the media company is a publishing company, then the manager must examine literacy rates. Only if a major segment of a country's population can read will there be a thriving market for magazines, books, and newspapers. Similarly, if only a small percentage of the population is computer literate or has access to computers, online media services are not likely to be successful.

Cultural differences also are critical in making international media planning decisions. Media content is, by its very nature, something that mirrors and influences the culture in which it is created and sold. That is why so many countries have been concerned about cultural imperialism from foreign-produced media.

For a media manager, it is important to thoroughly understand the local culture of the country where a company is planning to invest. Cultural differences influence how media content and advertisers are received. For example, humour often is culturally based, playing off subtle situations or plays on words that are familiar to people in one culture but often not to their neighbors over the border. Thus, humorous content does not tend to travel well. Similarly, Carveth (1992) noted that Dallas was not well received by television audiences in Japan because the television series was based around family conflicts--which violated Japanese cultural values.

Finally, language must be considered. Media content is language-based, regardless of the form it takes. In order to reach an overseas audience, media content must be available in the local language. For films and video, this often means dubbing or subtitles. Publications must be either translated--which is often difficult and fraught with a high risk of error--or produced locally by native speakers in the overseas market. Advertising campaigns or product names that are successful in one language sometimes do not translate well into others.

For electronic media, the issues are even more complex. English has become the dominant language of the new electronic media. But that, by definition, means that non-English speakers cannot access English-based electronic media content and advertisements. Although there is a great deal of non-English content available and people and companies from around the world have web pages available, language remains an issue in the new media.

Moreover, some countries are concerned that the growing importance of new media and its domination by English will undermine their local languages. As a result, some governments, such as the French government, require electronic content and media products offered locally to be in their national language. Thus, media companies and their advertisers who wish to make their content available to French audiences must arrange for it to be translated or dubbed.

Evaluate Available Resources

When evaluating the resources available to support international expansion, several important issues surface. First, the manager must decide what the company's primary goal is for internationalizing its operations. The answer to that question influences the answers to the other key decisions that must be made when evaluating the available resources for investing overseas.

The issues the manager faces include how the company should enter the foreign market--by taking its products into the new market or by acquiring existing media companies in that market. The manager also must decide how the new venture will be financed and how much financial risk the company wants to incur. Those issues raise questions of whether the investment should be managed through a wholly owned subsidiary, a partnership, a strategic alliance, licensing, or through some other ownership structure. The manager will then have to decide how the new venture will be organized and managed and how the human resources necessary for success will be found.

The first issue to be considered is, of course, the company's primary goal for overseas operations. The answer to that question usually influences how a foreign investment is structured and managed. Four primary models used by companies to manage cross-border operations and the goals that drive those models. One model is called International. This defines companies that are primarily interested in using overseas operations to distribute their domestic products in foreign markets.

As a result, the overseas operation is seen as secondary to the company's main purpose. Control of the foreign office stays with company headquarters, as does almost all of the knowledge needed to produce the product. Information flows one-way from company headquarters to the subsidiary and the overseas operation is expected to return little to the parent company besides profits. Television companies that establish overseas joint ventures in order to get around import quotas on their domestically produced programming would be an example of the international model.

A second model is the multinational company, which places more emphasis on its foreign operations. The multinational corporation uses its foreign subsidiaries to develop products for different markets and modifies its strategies and management practices to maximize its efficiency in each of the countries in which it has operations. The emphasis is on producing products that are specifically tailored to local markets. In multinational, companies, managers often are hired locally and operate with a fair amount of independence from company headquarters in making daily decisions. A multinational company might be seen as a series of semi-independent but affiliated national companies with similar but distinct product lines. This strategy maximizes the relevance of the company's products to its local audience, but lessens the company's ability to capture economies of scale. Canada's Thomson Newspapers, which owns many U.S. small and medium circulation newspapers, would be an example of this model.

Each of its newspapers is produced for a very local audience. Only some of the copy from any given newspaper can be shared with Thomson's other U.S. papers, and even less would be of interest to Thomson's Canadian newspapers. Global companies--of which Japanese industries provide the best example--think of the entire world as their market and produce products that are designed to be sold universally. Global companies maximize their production efficiencies, and they assume that consumers want basically the same things, no matter where they live.

In global companies, most management planning and decision making is made in worldwide headquarters although production may be scattered around the globe. Magazine publishers often take this approach to publishing. Magazines are frequently reproduced by a single company in multiple countries with only minor adjustments to content and translation. Germany's Aenne Burda publishing company, for example, distributes its fashion and sewing magazine Burda Moden in many different European countries. The U. S. film and television industries also have taken traditionally a global approach to film production. In recent decades, the large budgets required to make films have made it necessary for Hollywood producers to take foreign film markets into account because overseas audiences can make the difference in profit margins.

For this reason, foreign audiences have something more than a secondary market for Hollywood studios and films have been produced with global popularity in mind. European audiences are increasingly interested in film with European content, which may eventually move the film industry to adopt the last of the four models of operation--the transnational model. The transnational corporation, which is the model of international management that began emerging in the mid-1980s and 1990s, tries to merge the best of these other approaches while becoming more responsive to consumers' increasing demands that products be somewhat localized.

In the transnational corporation, the company is neither centralized in the home market or global headquarters, nor decentralized in all of its outlying operations. Instead, different subsidiaries are assigned different specialties and given the resources and responsibilities to produce them. This approach is designed to make the company both flexible and responsive in meeting local needs, while still being able to combine the efforts of its different overseas operations to gain efficiencies in production and economies of scale. Corporate managers share planning data with overseas subsidiaries, but those operations also are constantly scanning their local environments for new product ideas, new markets and new efficiencies that they can share with corporate operations around the globe. This two-way learning process is one of the key distinguishing elements of the transnational model.

The truly transnational manager recognizes that one of the main benefits of operating in markets around the world is the ability to learn from the people in those markets, gaining new ideas for better products and better ways of doing business. Germany's Bertelsmann corporation, one of the world's largest multimedia companies, fits the transnational model in many ways. The company operates multiple units with responsibility for different media businesses in countries throughout the world. The corporation uses a decentralized model of management, giving its division managers a great deal of responsibility and authority to develop new products and specialties, while maintaining control through the principle of"leadership from the centre".

The recording industry also could fit in the transnational model. A handful of multinational media companies control the worldwide recording industry--up to 80 per cent of the market in some countries--research has shown that at the same time consolidation in the industry increased, so did the number of new artists and diversity of music available to consumers. Burnett argues that this phenomenon is due to the multinationals' strategy of affiliating with small semi-independent recording labels worldwide, which then search their local music scenes for new talent. Thus the small labels are constantly bringing new music and new artists to the market locally and regionally, which the multinationals then distribute widely if they believe the sound may have appeal.

Once a media company has decided what it wants to accomplish through international expansion, it must decide how it will enter its chosen foreign market. There are two basic approaches. The first is to start its own overseas operations. The second is to acquire an existing media company in that country. If a company's primary goal is to be an international company--that is, to use its overseas operations as a secondary market for its existing products--then it probably would not enter a foreign market by buying another company and its product line. However, multinational, global, or transnational operations might be accomplished through either start-ups or acquisitions. Acquisitions allow the buyer to enter the new market with an already established product, thus reducing the risk of the investment. Much of the globalization of the media industry that took place during the 1980s and 1990s was accomplished through mergers and acquisitions. A third element of overseas operations that must be planned is the new venture's ownership structure. As with domestic operations, a company's ownership structure directly affects its available sources of capital. The simplest approach to ownership is to set up the overseas operation as a wholly owned subsidiary--that is a company that the parent company owns and operates entirely on its own. This certainly makes some aspects of operating overseas easier. It simplifies decision making and leaves little room for misunderstandings among co-owners from different countries.

However, running a wholly owned subsidiary also means that the parent company cannot learn about the new market from a local co-owner or another company that already has expertise in that market. It means that the company must shoulder all of the financial burden of the foreign investment--which can be considerable as operating a foreign subsidiary means additional costs in terms of travel, shipping, and communication between the subsidiary and headquarters. As a result, it usually takes several years for a foreign investment to become profitable.

Another option is to set up a joint venture or strategic alliance with one or more partners. In this arrangement, partners share the risks and costs of the foreign investment and the decision making for it. When the investment becomes profitable, success also is shared. Many countries require that foreign-owned media companies operating within their borders have at least one local partner.

In other instances, strategic alliances with local producers are a means for foreign media companies to gain access to restricted media markets. Having a local partner for a cross-border investment can be particularly valuable because the partner can provide contacts with government, industry, and clients, advise on the development of culturally appropriate and attractive content, and help the new venture avoid the mistakes that are inevitable when doing business in a new environment.

But even when the partner in a strategic alliance is not a local company, there are significant advantages to the joint venture arrangement. Particularly in technology-intensive media specialties, strategic alliances can help companies share knowledge, tap new innovations, and share the costs of technology development. Joint ventures have pitfalls, however. Disagreements can arise over strategies for the partnership and authority over decision making. When the partners come from different countries, there can be culturally based misunderstandings. There also is the risk that a company will use an alliance to gain proprietary knowledge of the dominant partner's product line, later dissolving the joint venture and using that knowledge to compete against its former partner.

Finally, if one partner is financially weaker than the other, problems can arise if the new subsidiary does not perform as expected and it becomes necessary to subsidize the venture for longer than planned. A third approach to overseas investment is licensing. In this arrangement, a media company sells to another company the rights to produce one of its specific media products in a foreign market. The company that buys the rights assumes all the risks of making a successful entry into the new market. Usually, the parent company supplies the concept, graphics, and design elements for the product, and the company that buys the license is responsible for translation, production, and distribution. Television programs such as Wheel of Fortune and America's Funniest Home Videos have been licensed to European media companies. Magazines also are sometimes licensed to publishers in overseas markets.

For the media company that sells the license, this arrangement allows it to widen the distribution of its publication or programming with minimal risk and financial investment. The licensee, in turn, gains the rights to a proven and successful media product, which makes it easier to find an audience and advertisers.

The downside of licensing is that license fees greatly reduce the direct gain the company that created the original publication or programming receives from having its product in a new overseas market. Additionally, the licensor loses control over the production of its publication or programme, making it difficult to ensure that its own high standards of quality are maintained. Finally, if the licensee fails in the new market, it can make it difficult for the company that created the media concept to reenter that market with that publication or programme with a different licensee or under some other arrangement.

A final, crucial area of planning for the media company evaluating the resources available for an overseas investment is in the area of human resources. Unlike more routine product manufacturing where an initial good idea is mass produced in a routinized manufacturing process, each individual media product--magazine edition, television programme, web page, advertisement--is unique and requires the creativity, insight, and specific effort of one or more people to bring into existence. Personnel management across borders is complex. When a media company enters an overseas market, it must conform to local personnel laws. In Germany, for example, most companies are required by law to have a"Betriebsrat,"or worker's council, that has significant authority over the company's decisions to hire, promote, and terminate employees, as well as to rearrange work schedules, reassign individuals, and set other work rules and conditions.

One German newspaper, for example, tried without success for almost I year to rearrange the work schedules of three of its print shop employees to cover vacancies left by retirements. However, management's proposed rescheduling of the remaining employees would have disrupted a car pool shared by two of them, and the newspaper's workers council refused to permit the change. As a consequence, one shift in the print shop was over-staffed, whereas the later shift was severely short-handed. Such a situation would be almost unimaginable to U.S. media managers.

More importantly for media companies, however, is the issue of employee training. Local employees must have adequate management, creative and production skills to meet corporate goals as well as comparable values in terms of the quality and production. Once a company has evaluated the business environment and performance of a potential overseas market and the resources available for its expansion, the planning process becomes more similar to strategic planning for domestic operations.

The company needs to further refine and operationalize its planning goals, identify and select alternative approaches to meeting those goals, and then implement, monitor, evaluate, and adjust the plan. Each of those steps, however, will be carried out in the context of the company's original goals for internationalization, its analysis of the business environment of its target country, the decisions it made about how its foreign operations will be structured, and the effects those structures will have on available resources. When the company enters the intermediate planning process for its overseas operations, however, managers face additional issues that are specific to transborder media management.

Intermediate Planning for International Operations

During the intermediate planning process for a cross-border media investment, particular attention must be paid to the product aspect of the marketing plan. As already noted, the economy, regulatory environment and culture will affect a media company's choice of what publications, programs, or other media services to distribute. But even after a media company has decided to distribute a particular product, cultural factors must be carefully analyzed. Often differences are so subtle they may be difficult for a nonnative manager to recognize. But in the culturally based world of media, those differences can signal success or failure for the new foreign venture.

If, for example, a magazine or television programme features recipes or cooking tips, the producers of that publication or programme must make sure the recipes have been adapted for local tastes and the ingredients required to make the food are available. Home repair and other how-to publications or programs must take into account local needs and available products and tools. A programme or magazine that teaches people how to build decks and patios, for example, would be useless in a country where the majority of the population live in apartments in cities--as is the case in many European nations.

Advertisements must be screened to ensure that they do not offend local mores or insult readers and viewers. One German publisher, for example, received complaints from female readers in Russia about advertisements for Western cosmetics and fashions after the collapse of the Soviet Union in 1991. Readers told the publisher that the upscale products it advertised were unavailable to most Russian women at that time, and that they would be unable to afford the products even if they were available. Readers said the advertisements were depressing and a subtle form of Western elitism. Even the colors used in publication layout and design, company logos, or programme set designs must be carefully reevaluated with the foreign market in mind as colour is very culturally significant and can signal different things in different countries. White, for example, is the colour of mourning in the Middle East.

Place also is an issue in overseas markets. The transportation and communication infrastructures of many countries are less developed than they are in the United States. The media manager considering a cross-border investment must examine the infrastructure of the target country to see how easy it will be to distribute its products outside of urban areas and whether the costs of widespread distribution will be acceptable. The promotion process also may change when a company moves overseas. Promotional slogans and even the name of a publication or programme may not translate well into other languages. Promotional strategies common in the U.S. such as event sponsorship, live broadcasts, and other techniques for increasing audiences may not be possible or acceptable. Similarly, in many countries, it is difficult if not impossible to collect ratings and readership data, which makes it very hard to do target marketing. Before entering an overseas market, the media manager must carefully research the promotional strategies that are possible within that country and develop an appropriate marketing plan within that framework.

As with domestic operations, the human resources plan concerns the acquisition and development of people needed to manage the operation and produce the media content. For the global media company the question is where it will find that personnel. One possibility is to send existing managers or key personnel to oversee the new cross-border operation. This ensures that staff are familiar with the goals of the company. Such managers, however, do not know the new market or have contacts in the new environment. For U.S. media companies, it also can be difficult to find Americans who are prepared to go overseas to work. The percentage of Americans who speak a second language and have lived or traveled extensively in other countries is lower than might be found in some other regions of the world.

Another option is to hire people locally for the new foreign office or to leave existing management and personnel in place. The advantages and disadvantages of this strategy are the opposite of those of the first approach. The foreign managers and employees would have local contacts, but they would need training and time to assimilate corporate expectations. In addition, a large measure of corporate control would be forfeited with this arrangement. Among transnational companies, there is a third approach to personnel management. This approach is to seek the best personnel wherever they are found. Under this approach, a New Zealand executive might manage a U.S. office for a German parent company, or a Japanese national might run a subsidiary in India for a British corporation. Companies using this approach make long-term commitments to these multifaceted, international managers and groom them carefully for top leadership positions where their international outlook, expertise, and experience can be used to guide the transnational organization. For ambitious future managers, this means increased competition for top jobs as companies look throughout the world for the most talented, capable, and adaptable individuals.

When planning market entry into a new overseas operation, most financial planning will be done during the initial strategic planning process. Details of how the new venture will be capitalized during its first few years will be worked out as the venture is set up and the ownership structure is established. The initial financial plan may need to be reconsidered if unexpected difficulties are encountered. Overseas operations, in general, are expensive to run because of higher travel and communication costs.

New start-up media ventures usually require several years before they become profitable under the best of circumstances and, when investing in a foreign market, it can take even longer. Economic downturns are harder for the parent company to anticipate and are likely to throw off initial financial plans if they occur. Hiring a local staff may create greater than expected training costs because the entire staff will need to learn new ways of working even if the parent company buys an existing media company. A media operation may need new equipment and legal expenses may soar as the parent company negotiates with an unfamiliar legal and regulatory environment. Cultural differences between the parent company and the new target audience increase the likelihood that aspects of the media content produced will not be accepted and will need adjustment. Any or all of these factors may affect intermediate financial projections and require emergency funding to support the new venture.

Finally, during the intermediate planning process, managers must establish a benchmark against which to measure their new venture's financial success. Some media companies will consider a new venture successful if, during the intermediate planning period, it is able to generate enough revenue to cover its own operating expenses. Others will not consider the venture profitable until it also is covering the parent company's additional overhead--travel, communi-cation, training, management oversight--for the overseas operation.

Some managers will not consider a new venture to be profitable until after it has repaid all of the parent company's initial investment and start-up expenses in addition to covering its own operating costs and management overhead. Probably the most difficult situation for a media manager occurs if the new venture fails to meet the financial benchmarks the parent company established during the intermediate planning process. At that point, the manager must decide whether the long-term potential benefits of global investment justify maintaining a media operation that is not profitable. The manager also will need to rethink the way the overseas investment has been structured, the way it is being managed, and the publications or programs it is producing. Sometimes a struggling media venture can be rescued by changing partners, managers, the product mix, or by launching an established publication or programme with changes. In some cases, however, the only viable decision is to abandon a particular market and focus the company's efforts on other products or other countries.

Adding a New Product

The Daily Sentinel newspaper is a profitable stable business with no direct competitive threats (from other media) to its future. Although there are local and state-wide radio and television stations servicing the area, there are no other newspapers. There is a free circulation paper that takes some classified advertising revenue from the Sentinel market, but the publisher, Mal McAuley, does not consider the losses significant. The owner's son, Harry, who joined the newspaper after graduating from college, has been trying to interest his father in developing a web site. Mal thinks the idea has potential but sees no reason to rush into development of a web page. He asks Harry to put together a solid strategic plan for consideration. He says the plan must show how the web page would be supportive of the newspaper's mission, which is to provide useful and entertaining information for all the readers in Cheyenne County who are primarily ranchers, small business owners, and government workers."I want to know in specific terms how this web page is going to help my readers and who is going to pay for it,"Mal tells his son. Harry has I month to develop the plan and make a presentation to his father, the news editor, the advertising director, and the circulation manager.

Harry sets up a meeting with the advertising department and learns some of the salespeople are worried a web site might impact current customers' commitments to the traditional newspaper. They say they would not like to see customers drop newspaper ads for web advertising. They also want to know if new staff will be hired to handle the accounts because they do not feel current staff can handle accounts for both media. The younger members of the staff are the most enthusiastic and mention the possibility of adding new or different customers to the web site because they have been asked by potential advertisers when or if the newspaper will have a web site. They mention that some ranchers use the Internet regularly to do research for their businesses, and the medical staff members at the local hospital use web pages and the Internet to keep current in their field. Harry suspects that the government employees also use the Internet and web pages to communicate with their central offices, which in some cases are located in Washington, DC. There is disagreement among staff members as to whether there is a local advertising market for a web site.

The news editor tells Harry she is worried that some of her staff will be asked to provide news for the web site. She does not think she has enough current reporters to write"fresh"copy for both the web site and the Sentinel.

"And what's the point of just repeating the news online?"she asks Harry. She also challenges Harry to explain why readers would want to have a newspaper web site."It's a toy for people with too much time on their hands, and I don't think any readers out there care to read local news on a web site,"she bluntly tells Harry.

The circulation department tells Harry they do not care what he does because the idea does not seem to have anything to do with delivery of newspapers. Harry suggests that an online newspaper might affect circulation figures, but the manager argues that nothing will replace the newspaper and how it is currently delivered (by truck and local subcontractors).After his discussions, Harry realizes that the staff members in the three departments do not know much about web newspapers. In fact, he learns that although all the staff use e-mail at work, none use it at home and only five of the younger staff members (in their 20s) know much about this emerging technology. No one is familiar with web pages except a photographer who has a software programme he has downloaded from the company computer to produce his private home page.

The Transnational Tightrope

European Magazines Inc. (EMI) publishes a group of magazines that cover the consumer electronics market. EMI publications report on, test, and review new products and developments in consumer electronics. Many of the magazines offer readers classified advertising where new and used consumer electronics items can be bought and sold. The company also publishes catalogs of consumer electronics products and an annual book offers a year-in-review perspective of the industry as well as a forecast of the coming year. EMI is based in Germany, a Western European country with a generally strong economy. The market for consumer electronics in Germany is among the strongest in Europe, so there is solid demand for information about consumer electronics products. EMI has established itself as the leader in that publishing niche in its home country.

Over the past 20 years, EMI also has branched out to sell editions of its magazines in neighboring Western European countries. There is considerable competition in those markets, however, because Western European countries, in general, have strong publishing industries. In each neighboring market EMI entered, there was already a strong domestic magazine covering consumer electronics. So, although EMI's international operations have been successful, they provide a relatively small percentage of the company's total revenues. EMI's bread and butter is still its home country market. And for a growth-oriented company, that is not entirely good news. In Germany, the magazine industry is fully mature. Although, the industry's total circulation, revenues, and number of advertising pages have been climbing in the last decade, so has the number of magazine titles being published and, therefore, the competition for readers' attention. More importantly, the magazine industry's real share of the national advertising market has been slipping during the 1990s as television and emerging media syphon off advertising dollars.

In short, EMI cannot expect to enjoy strong or rapid growth in its publishing niche in either Germany or other Western European markets in the foreseeable future. For EMI's growth-oriented management, that means that the company will have to look outside its Western European region for new opportunities. Because most countries that have economies strong enough to generate a large market for consumer electronics products also already have established magazines serving readers in that niche, the best opportunities for EMI to expand are likely to be in countries with emerging economies, that is, countries where a significant percentage of the people are starting to have some extra income that they can afford to spend on items that are not strictly necessary for survival.

From a management standpoint, investing in a country with an emerging economy entails significant risk. Such countries may require foreign investors to have local partners in order to do business, but local capital to fund initial investments and start-up expenses is often in short supply. Meanwhile, the requirement that investors work with local partners means that company management must be prepared to deal with language, cultural and financial differences even in its internal decision-making processes as it manages the new enterprise.

Perhaps most importantly, if the economy of the new country does not develop as expected, there may be no market for the product the investor produces. In the case of EMI, for example, if it moved into a new country and the economy there did not grow enough for people to have the money to buy consumer electronics, there would be no market for its magazines. For media companies, the risk can be even greater than for other types of businesses because media products are, by definition, language and culture-based products. For example, a lightbulb can be shipped to another country as long as the electrical currents and light sockets are the same in the new market as in the old and some minor adjustments are made to packaging. However, a magazine publisher has to be sure that every element in the publication's content is appropriate for the new market. Success hinges on getting all of the details right in every single published edition.

Articles must be relevant and of interest to readers in the new market. Items that are advertised or described in stories must be available in that country. Generally, it is most cost efficient for the start-up publication to draw some of its content from material that already has been produced for the company's flagship home market editions. But if the publisher shares content between publications, management must be certain that every shared Article has been translated correctly in language, culture, and meaning and that nothing in the content is offensive to readers in the new market. Publication layout and design must appeal to readers in the new country, and the publisher must be sensitive to the fact that colors, symbols, and photographs mean different things in different countries.

Finally, literacy rates are often lower in emerging countries than in industrialized nations, and for a publishing company to succeed, there has to be a critical mass of individuals able and willing to read.

NEW MARKET OPENS

Recognizing the limitations of their own home market, the top executives of EMI decided to expand into foreign markets, particularly into countries with emerging economies and not-yet-mature media markets. Corporate management soon identified a country--Newland--in which it was interested. Newland had the strongest and most consumer-oriented economy in its region, although by Western European standards the living conditions of the population were bleak. Nevertheless, a recent decision by Newland's government to liberalize the economy and open the country to Western investment had drawn a flood of North American and European companies into the market and set off a mini economic boom. As part of its decision to liberalize its economy, the Newland government announced that it would allow limited foreign ownership of the print media, as long as at least 50 per cent of each publishing company continued to be held by a Newland company or individual.

That announcement set off a publishing land rush and Western media companies dashed across the Newland border to grab a piece of the market. Among Newland's advantages as a publishing market were its emerging economy and the resulting strong demand for news and information that would be useful to both business managers and consumers as they came to grips with their new environment. There also was an almost insatiable interest among the Newlander public in Western products, fashions, and ways of doing things, which boded well for Western publications. Also an advantage was the fact that the country enjoyed comparatively high literacy rates for a nation in its economic situation.

Finally, Newland had a reasonably sophisticated transportation infrastructure in its major cities, making it possible for Western publishers to consider the possibility of printing publications in their home countries and shipping the finished product into Newland. On the downside, Newland's primary language was unique to the country, which has a relatively small population. Thus, there would be little ability to capture economies of scale in production for Newland, and there would be virtually no opportunities to export editions produced for Newland beyond that country's borders as was possible for EMI's German and English language publications. Newland also was different culturally and politically from Germany and other Western nations, and despite the Newland public's interest in things Western, there remained a strong undercurrent of resentment in the population against the incoming Western investors, their ways of doing things and their apparent affluence in comparison to Newland citizens. The cultural differences between Newland and the West extended to the business culture.

Within Newland companies, everything from accounting methods to relationships between employers and employees operated very differently from what would be normal in a Western European or North American company. In Newland, when people took a job, they expected it to be for a lifetime. Pay was low, but employees rarely quit and they generally did not need to worry about being fired or laid off.

On the job, productivity expectations were minimal and workers felt little pressure to be efficient. With the sudden influx of Western investors, the expectations of both managers and employees in Newland changed in some ways but not others. Employees expected that their unwritten lifetime employment contracts would continue, as would their managers' previous standards of productivity. But at the same time, the employees wanted their pay to increase dramatically and their working conditions to improve. Newland business managers, on the other hand, wanted the chance to become part owners in Western-funded business ventures, and they wanted those ventures to make them rich quickly. But with capital in Newland scarce, local managers had little money of their own to invest in new business opportunities.

In the publishing industry, it was no different. Newland publishers' were not familiar with Western business methods. Nor did they have experience doing business in a competitive publishing market because before the government opened the economy, there had been few magazines available in Newland and most received government subsidies. Although EMI's management was fully aware of these challenges, company leaders decided that Newland still was an attractive market. Therefore, the company announced that it would begin publishing in the Newland market.

ESTABLISHING THE NEW VENTURE

As required by Newland law, EMI's initial entrance into the Newland market was structured as a joint venture with a local Newland company. EMI met its partner through a third party, who contacted EMI on behalf of the Newland partner before the Newland government had announced its decision to liberalize its economy. That partner, a Newlander publishing entrepreneur, anticipated his government's decision and decided to find a Western partner with deep pockets. In return, he offered EMI his knowledge of Newland and its readers, his contacts in Newlander government and industry, and the two small electronics magazines he had recently launched that complemented EMI's stable of publications. Under the agreement worked out, each partner held 50 per cent of the new joint venture. The partnership agreed that it would begin by publishing three different monthly consumer electronics magazines and two annual publications. The monthly magazines included EMI's flagship publication, Electronic Gadgets Today and the two small Newland magazines that the local partner published. The annuals included EMI's special yearly electronics industry soft-cover book and its annual catalog.

The fledgling joint venture was named EMI Overseas Ltd. or EOL for short. EMI's first priority was to establish the monthly magazines in the Newland market and stave off competition from similar publications that might be launched by other Western European publishers. The expectation was that once EOL's monthly magazines established a loyal Newland readership, there would be strong demand for the company's special--and more expensive--annual publications.

But that expectation was only a hunch. Indeed, almost all of EMI's decisions about the Newland market were based on guesses. Because of the suddenness with which Newland's market had been opened by its government and because of the rapid influx of other publishers into the market--each one trying to establish its dominance in a particular market niche--there was no time to do the kind of careful research that would have been done before launching a new publication in a Western European market. Instead, EMI and other Western European publishers simply leapt into Newland without looking. They had only the most rudimentary information about Newland market conditions, readers' habits and desires, and cultural norms. On this occasion, speed of action took precedence over caution and information. It was a high risk strategy. Moreover, there was a lot more to setting up a new transnational operation than just deciding what to publish. There was a whole series of critical decisions to be made about how the new Newland magazines should be published, with each decision being important to the ultimate success or failure of the new venture.

Content Issues

A major issue to be resolved by management involved the source and orientation of the content for the Newland publications. A number of options were available. One possibility was to have the magazines produced locally with Articles focusing on Newland. A number of Western publishers entered the Newland market using this model of content production. A second option--again, one widely used by Western publishers breaking into the Newland market--was to use the copy and art that were being produced for a publication's current home market edition and have it professionally translated into the Newland language. A third choice was a cross between the other two approaches: depend on the local staff to produce some or most of the content for the Newland edition, but also offer them all of the content and art from the company's home market publication so that they could use any material they believed appropriate for Newland readers.

A publishing company using this model also gave the local magazine staff the right to rewrite and refocus the Articles borrowed from the parent publication so that the angle of the story would be more appropriate for local subscribers. For example, the German edition of an EMI magazine might focus on the upgrades for a new product promised by the manufacturer in coming months, whereas the Newland version of the story might focus on approaches to maintaining and repairing that same product.

After much consideration, EMI and its joint venture partner decided to use the third content model. It was expected that some content--such as product test results--would be translated directly from the German editions of EMI's publications because the Newland EOL partnership would not have independent product testing facilities. Most of the copy--roughly two thirds of each Newland edition's content--would be produced locally and would be unique to EOL's publications. The other one third would be either test results translated directly or Articles published in EMI's German magazines but reworked for the Newland market.

Who Runs the Show? The next crucial questions were how would EOL's Newland publications be produced, where would they be produced, and by whom would they be produced? Again, there was a number of possible options. Some Western investors published their Newland editions in their home countries and simply shipped the finished product to Newland for distribution to readers. In such cases, the Newland staff or translators usually worked in the company's international headquarters turning out the publication for their distant readership.

Other Western publishing companies set up operations in Newland but staffed them largely with their own personnel. The Newland partners functioned only as advisors and sometimes only as window dressing. Using an almost entirely Western staff ensured that the new publications operated the same way as all of the parent company's other publications, maximizing production and management efficiency and minimizing cross-cultural misunderstandings on staff. A third organizational structure adopted by some Western investors transplanted Western managers to run the local operation, but hired local workers for nonmanagement positions. This increased the publication's sensitivity to cultural conditions as well as to readers, while ensuring that the business end operated according to Western standards and processes.

Finally, a fourth approach was to completely staff the local venture with Newlanders. This maximized a magazine's relevance to Newland readers and created goodwill among readers and the government by demonstrating that the Western owner was willing to create jobs and share power and prosperity.

After much consideration, EMI agreed to adopt the last structure for its nascent Newland venture. EMI management and its local Newland partners hired Newlanders for both the management and staff positions in EOL. However, EMI insisted that the person hired to head the EOL subsidiary be brought to Germany for extensive training at company headquarters in Western business, accounting methods, and publication production processes. EMI's management also reserved the right to maintain control of major decisions, such as launching a new magazine or any other issue that would have major financial impact on the company. Those decisions would be made in Germany.

Other Decisions

There were other key issues facing EMI's management in the prelaunch days of its Newland subsidiary. Western publications used higher quality paper, higher resolution photographs and printing processes, and much more colour than most Newland magazines before the government opened the market. For this reason, many Western investors arranged to have their publications shipped to Western Europe to be printed, with the finished product being shipped back to Newland for distribution. EMI was fortunate, however. Newland boasted two printing facilities capable of producing high quality four-colour glossy publications, and EOL was able to secure a printing contact with one of them.

Another question concerned advertising. Should the EOL subsidiary focus its efforts on securing advertising primarily from in-country sources or from Western advertisers? If the company went after Western advertisers, should the company screen the advertisements submitted for local culture-appropriate content and for product availability?

Although from a financial standpoint, the desirable strategy obviously would be to sell as much advertising as possible and publish it regardless of content, Western publishers had found in the past that such a strategy can backfire in a less developed country. In some instances, local readers had resented the role Western-owned publications played in helping foreign businesses move into the market and compete with local companies through advertising. In other cases, readers had objected that they could not afford the products that were advertised and accused the Western-owned magazines of using the ads to flaunt Western wealth to them.

In such cases, the result of an open advertising strategy had been to create reader resentment and a loss of subscribers. The final significant management issue facing EMI and its EOL subsidiary was how the publication would be distributed. In the first months after the government opened the market to foreign publishers in Newland, publishers had little choice about distribution. Although the government had opened its publishing market, it had not yet deregulated its magazine distribution system. The government required that all magazines be distributed through the Newland Post--even those that went to newsstands for sale off the rack. Readers and kiosk operators who wanted a publication did not contact the magazine. They contacted the Post. Magazine publishers never knew who their subscribers were or how many copies were sold through subscription and how many were sold on newsstands. As the distribution system was set up, the Post told publishers how many copies of their publications it wanted.

The publisher was paid 90 per cent of the magazine's cover price up front, with the Post keeping the remaining 10 per cent as a sales commission. The Post took responsibility for distributing and selling the magazines and, if some did not sell, the Post absorbed the loss. The distribution system had worked very well for Newland before the government opened the publishing market to outsiders. In the old days, there had been shortages of paper in the country and, as a result, publishers could not produce enough magazines and newspapers to meet demand.

Thus, almost every edition of every publication sold out. That had meant the Post had faced little financial risk in paying publishers for the magazines immediately. At the same time, having the contract for all magazine distribution gave the Post a critical and consistent source of revenue that helped the government provide its citizens with affordable mail service. Loss of revenue from magazine sales would have been a major financial blow to the nation's postal system.

A Good Beginning

The first year of EMI's new venture in Newland went far better than expected. The influx of Western businesses had set off an economic boom in the country and--perhaps even more importantly--the conviction in Newlanders that unlimited economic prosperity was here to stay. Consequently, the conditions for reader interest in nonessential consumer electronics products were ideal.

Moreover, the country's long isolation from the West had created interest in information and contact with Western ways of doing things, and so there was strong demand for Western-based publications that carried Western advertising and discussed Western products. Finally, because EMI and its Newland partner had been discussing a partnership before the Newland government had even opened the market to Westerners, they had been able to set up operations very quickly. Consequently, they were publishing their Western-quality magazines months before most other Western publishers had been able to break into the market.

Not surprisingly, then, the circulation for the three monthly consumer electronics products magazines zoomed during the first year. Circulation for the Newland edition of EMI's flagship magazine, Electronic Gadgets Today, topped 75,000 at one point during the first year, an impressive level for a start-up publication in a less-developed country with a population of only 10 million. EOL's success with advertisers was equally great. Western electronics manufacturers and retailers were no less eager to grab a piece of the Newland market than were publishers, and magazines and newspapers were the most cost-effective way for those companies to advertise their wares to potential Newland buyers. With little competition from other electronics magazines, much of the advertising found its way into EOL publications.

Through the first year, about 30 per cent of the revenue for Electronic Gadgets Today came from advertising, whereas the other two monthly magazines were booking about 20 per cent of their revenue from advertising. By comparison, most U.S. consumer magazines depend on advertising for around 54 per cent of revenue, whereas subscription and newsstand sales provide the other 46 per cent. At the end of the first year, EOL also produced Newland editions of EMI's two annual publications. Those were particularly slick publications, carried lots of advertising and were sold at a premium cover price. They were marketed to Newlanders as Christmas gifts and as status symbols. They were, for example, marketed to Newland companies and executives as something to leave on their waiting room tables for clients to see and read. The newly affluent among Newland citizens also bought copies to display in their homes.

Newland circulation for the Electronics Industry annual book was 50,000 during the first year, and for the catalog, 90,000. Both were immediately profitable. Although EMI executives were ecstatic about their Newland venture's first year results, that did not mean the company was producing large profits. In fact, only under the most generous calculations could it be claimed that the operations were even breaking even.

With a circulation of 75,000 and 30 per cent advertising revenue, Electronic Gadgets Today was bringing in enough cash to cover its direct production costs, including editorial, advertising and printing. The other two magazines were not quite as successful but were still managing to cover most of the direct production expenses for each edition. However, none of the three publications was covering administrative costs, particularly not the higher expenses incurred by EMI's German operations as a result of travel, training of Newland personnel, and other expenses associated with running a transnational subsidiary.

One of those additional expenses included hiring someone fluent in the Newlander language to work in EMI's German headquarters. EMI had realized after its EOL subsidiary published its first magazine that there was no one at corporate headquarters who could read the publications and double check them for quality, accuracy, and possible legal problems. Some publishers with transnational operations did not worry about having in-house readers for their overseas publications, trusting their foreign employees to produce quality magazines without headquarter's oversight. But EMI felt strongly that the company's reputation had been built on the quality and expertise of its publications. Consequently, EMI executives wanted to make sure the editors and reporters in their Newland subsidiary knew what they were doing when it came to publishing a magazine and knew what they were talking about when it came to writing about consumer electronics products. EMI hired a Newlander who had been living in Germany for some time and had electronics expertise to monitor the new publications.

Their concern was not unwarranted. During the early months of the EOL venture, the local Newland staff proved unable to get their publications out the door on deadline. Instead, they produced the magazines in stages as they were accustomed to doing. This meant that it took 2 to 3 months to get each edition to the printer. Given the fast change in the consumer electronics market, that meant most of the magazines were outdated long before they reached readers.

An honest assessment of the EOL subsidiary's financial standing at the end of its first year would also have had to acknowledge that the operation was not anywhere close to being able to repay its German parent company for its start-up investments or any of the interest being incurred on those loans. Under Western accounting methods, all of those expenses also would need to be covered by revenue from the publications before the overseas subsidiary would be considered profitable.

Still, EMI's executives had few complaints about their Newland venture. They understood that it normally takes several years--and sometimes much longer--before a start-up publication achieves true profitability. They also knew going in that because of the higher administrative costs of managing a transnational subsidiary, it would take even longer for their Newland venture to become profitable than it would have if the company had been domestic. Finally, EMI's management team was fully aware that advertising and circulation figures for new publications are usually highly unstable for the first few years after start-up as reader and advertiser interest ebbs and flows. Stability and consistent growth comes only when a publication succeeds in building a solid base of loyal subscribers who attract loyal advertisers. For most publications, that happens slowly. So, the fact that the EOL publications were generating enough revenue to cover most of their direct production costs was more than EMI executives had expected.

The Venture Hits Hard Times

If EMI's executives were happy with the results of the first year, their Newlander partner was not. Far from it, in fact. The Newlander entrepreneur had expected the magazine company to produce a handsome return on his investment in I year. Instead, his German colleagues were telling him that the magazines were losing money when all expenses were calculated. The total costs of producing the publications--including interest, overhead, and administrative expenses--were more than what the publications were bringing in from advertising and circulation. The EMI executives also pointed out that, as an owner of the company, the Newlander partner was expected to continue to provide some of the cash that would have to be pumped into the EOL subsidiary on an ongoing basis until the company became truly profitable--2 or 3 years down the road.

And even if his German partners considered his Newland-market expertise as part of his contribution to their joint venture's efforts, as a 50 per cent owner, he should expect to contribute something close to 50 per cent of the money needed to cover continuing financial short falls. For the Newlander partner, that was simply an impossibility. He did not have the capital and, in capital-starved Newland, neither did anyone else. In the meantime, there were other stresses on the partnership. Because Western and Newland business practices were so different, there were frequent misunderstandings between the partners. A common business term meant one thing to the Germans and something else entirely to a Newlander.

Because of the Newland law requiring all companies incorporated in the country to have at least 50 per cent Newland ownership, EMI was left with two choices: fold its Newland operations and go home or cover 100 per cent of the venture's losses although its additional investment would not result in a greater share of ownership. There was never much doubt what the company would do. EMI executives had a long-term view of the opportunities in Newland. The company would stay. EMI's Newland partner had a short-term outlook, however, and for him, as the company moved into its second year, the situation became decidedly worse.

The first thing that happened was that Newland's economic boom--which had been fueled more by optimism than cash--collapsed. Suddenly, Newlanders realized that the overnight prosperity they had anticipated had not materialized, which meant that many of them had been spending money they did not have and were not likely to recover anytime soon.

At the same time, competition in the Newland publishing market was stiffening. Although EOL's publications had been the first in their niche on Newland newsstands, by the beginning of the second year there were plenty of imitators. Some were copycat magazines that had been started by local entrepreneurs. Most were Western joint ventures run by publishers like EMI that had similar magazines back home and had deep pockets to fund their move into the Newland market.

The combination of increased competition and economic downturn hit the EOL venture hard. Suddenly fewer people had the money to be interested in consumer electronic products, and those people--and the advertisers that wanted to reach them--had a lot more publications from which to choose. Circulation for EOL's publications plummeted. For Electronic Gadgets Today, the venture's mainstay, circulation crashed from a high of 75,000 to 22,000.

EOL's other two monthly publications and both annuals suffered similar circulation losses. At the same time, advertising revenues plunged from 30 per cent of revenues for Electronic Gadgets Today to 20 per cent, and averaged across all three publications, advertising was generating only 15 per cent of the venture's revenue. EOL's group of publications was no longer bringing in enough money to cover its immediate production expenses.

To make matters worse, in the midst of these setbacks, the Newland Post announced that it was changing the way it distributed magazines. The Post's policy of paying for publications up front and absorbing the risk of selling them was only feasible if it could be sure of selling almost every copy it had. During the days before Western investment, there had been only a few publications available in the country, so selling all copies of all publications had been a sure thing. But with the flood of new publications on the market from around the world, selling every copy was now an impossibility. The Post had no choice but to change the way it did business with publishers. Under the new system, publishers were still required to distribute through the Post. The Post also determined how many copies of each publication it would distribute. Now, however, it did not pay for the publications when it received them.

Instead, the Post waited four weeks and then paid the publisher 50 per cent of the net revenue from sales up to that point--having already taken out its sales commission--and waited another 3 or 4 months to pay for the rest. In other words, the Post would order 50,000 copies of a magazine and sell 30,000 during the first month. After 4 weeks, it would pay the publisher for 15,000 copies--or half of the total it had sold. The remainder of the revenue for the other 15,000 that had been sold was paid a month or more later when the Post felt it had a final accounting of sales for that edition.

In the meantime, the publisher already would have had to pay all the bills for producing 50,000 magazines, although it had received only a fraction of the revenue from their sales. Moreover, eventually the 20,000 unsold magazines would be returned to the publisher. Those magazines, of course, generated no revenue.

This created serious cash flow problems for all publishers in the Newland market. Moreover, the system shifted all of the financial risk onto the publishers, with only limited means for controlling those risks. Magazine publishers had to rely on the ability of the Post to forecast how many copies of each edition would be sold and, therefore, how many should be printed. If the Post overestimated, the publisher had to absorb the loss. Worse yet, the Post's new system meant that there was a significant lag time between when an edition was printed and when the Post calculated how many copies of that edition had been sold. In the meantime, the publisher would have printed several more editions without any chance to adjust print runs--and therefore production costs--to account for declines in circulation or, for that matter, to take advantage of increased reader interest. As the problems created by the Post's distribution system increased, several Western publishing companies met to discuss ways to maneuver around the Newland law that magazines had to be distributed through the Post. The group contacted a magazine distribution company in a country near Newland. The distributor agreed to try to get copies of the Newland Post's subscription and distribution list for each of the publications in the publishers' group. The idea was that the cross-border distributor would use the list to start sending the publishers' magazines directly to Newland readers and newsstands from outside of the country. That would reduce the risk and cash flow problems of the Western publishers involved in the plan, as well as give them control over their own lists of subscribers.

The plan, if the Western publishers were successful, would circumvent their host country's regulations, but the publishers in the group felt it was unlikely that the Newland government would be able to enforce any real penalties against them. Nevertheless, when the group of Western publishers approached EMI's executives about joining them in the plan, EMI declined to participate.

Restructuring, Relaunching, Renewal

By the end of EMI's second year in the Newland market, things were looking grim for the EOL partnership. EMI's Newland partner was shocked by the failure of the venture to produce profits, irritated by the ongoing cultural and professional misunderstandings with EMI, and disheartened by the sharp downturn in the joint venture's fortunes as the country entered a recession. As the second year wound to a close, EMI's Newland partner announced that he was"resigning from the hardships of the market."

EMI was without a partner. EMI was not alone in facing this crisis. Western investors around the country were experiencing similar problems as their capital-short Newland partners faced the recession with empty pockets. Under pressure from the business community, the Newland government repealed the law that required 50 per cent ownership by a Newlander citizen in order for a publisher to do business in the country. EMI was now free to go into the future using the corporate structure of its choice for its Newland operations.

The choices, of course, were several. EMI could restructure EOL as a wholly owned subsidiary. It could look for a different partner--another Newland investor or a Western partner--or it could decide to cut its risks by shutting down EOL and licensing its publications to another publisher. In the face of the recent hardships of the Newland market, Western publishers were doing all three things. Some of them were leaving the market altogether. With the first wild"gold rush"into Newland over, the fallout among publishers was beginning. Only the best, hardiest, and most determined were going to be able to stay. Even as EMI's management team were considering these options, the phone rang. On the other end was the chairperson and CEO of another German publishing company that had entered the Newland market the previous year with a magazine that focused on crafts and hobbies. This new publisher, Hobby Magazines Inc., had also encountered problems with its Newland partner. The chairperson of Hobby Magazines suggested that his company and EMI form a new joint venture for their Newland operations.

EMI's management team was intrigued by the possibility. For one thing, although crafts and hobbies had little to do with consumer electronics, at least Hobby Magazines was producing the same type of publication EMI was, that is, a special interest magazine that provided readers with news they could use. As far as EMI was concerned, that made Hobby Magazines a better fit for a partnership than a movie star or fashion magazine publisher. Nevertheless, examination of Hobby Magazines' record in Newland was a bit discouraging. The company had been a late entrant into the market and had already reorganized its Newland subsidiary twice. Circulation of its hobby magazine had never been strong in Newland and had declined with the recession, just as EMI's publications had. The pool of potential advertisers for the hobby publication was smaller than for EMI's consumer electronics magazines and the companies producing hobby supplies had much smaller advertising budgets.

Still, the hobby magazine was a proven performer in Germany and in other Western European countries where Hobby Magazines Inc. had operations. If EMI managers took a long-term view, they had reason to believe that it might be equally successful in Newland 5 or 10 years down the road when the economy stabilized and the citizenry started having more disposable income and leisure time. Moreover, Hobby Magazines Inc., although a German incorporated and managed company, was actually owned by a major Canadian magazine publishing company. Thus, if EMI partnered with Hobby Magazines, EMI's executives would have the advantage of working with a management team that shared their language, culture, and business outlook, while being backed by the very deep pockets of a truly multinational publishing corporation.

After several months of negotiations, the two companies agreed to go forward together in a joint venture. The newly created partnership was not 50-50, however. With EMI bringing in five publications and Hobby Magazines bringing in only one, the joint venture was structured with EMI holding 94 per cent of the company and Hobby Magazines only 6 per cent. One of the first orders of business for the new partnership was to relaunch one of EOL's consumer electronics magazines. The magazine, one of those originally started by the Newland partner, had never overcome its production problems. The publication's focus had wandered from issue to issue and content was usually outdated by the time it reached readers. During the recession, both readers and advertisers had abandoned it, and circulation had fallen below 10,000 with advertising producing less than 10 per cent of revenues. After careful consideration, EMI decided not to kill the publication but, instead, to relaunch it. They pulled the publication off the market for several months and hired a market research company to survey remaining readers about why they read it. The survey results identified a central area of the magazine's coverage that had attracted readers. That became the new focus of the publication.

Once plans for the new focus were completed and the publication was redesigned to have a new look, EMI hired a public relations firm to advertise the relaunch of the made-over magazine. Initial response to the relaunch was quite positive, with circulation climbing above 15,000 for the first 2 months of the new publication and advertising producing about 17 per cent of the magazine's revenue.

With the market beginning to shake out and the number of magazines published in Newland falling, EMI's management team recognized that it was time for their Newland subsidiary to change the way it did business. Up until then, the venture had been operating as a start-up company, a phase in the life cycle of organizations during which quick decisions and risk taking are important. But as the other would-be publishers in the Newland market departed, EMI's management realized that they needed to focus on a long-term strategy for slow, stable growth. EMI temporarily shelved plans to buy, launch, and absorb additional publications in Newland. Instead, it started an ongoing programme of market research to help its existing magazines be more successful. The company also began bringing on new employees, doubling its staff in just 1 year. Finally, a marketing firm was hired to develop a consistent advertising and marketing plan for each of the publications.

EMI also came up with a plan to minimize the problems caused by the Newland Post's distribution system. The company placed an advertisement in each edition of each of its publications offering readers a small gift for sending in their names, addresses, and comments to the editors. This not only provided EMI with reader feedback, it also allowed the company to start developing a list of its readers and subscribers.

With a basic subscriber list in hand, EMI was able to start developing programs to improve reader retention--a key issue in publishing. Almost immediately, these changes began paying dividends. By the end of the third year of operation, circulation for the subsidiary's flagship Electronic Gadgets Today had climbed more than 45 per cent from its low at the crash, topping 32,000. Circulation for the other two consumer electronics products monthly magazines was more than 25,000 and one of the annuals sold more than 60,000 copies during the third year of operations. Advertising revenue also was climbing. By the end of the third year, Electronic Gadgets Today had averaged a 33 per cent advertising-to-editorial-pages ratio for the 12 months and had, in one memorable issue, broken the 50-50 mark. For the company as a whole, about 20 per cent of the Newland subsidiary's revenues were coming from advertising and the percentage was slowly climbing. Although the company was still slightly in the red for all of its operations for the year, it had finished the year showing strong and steady growth on all fronts.

EMI's executives projected that, all things remaining equal, they could expect the Newland subsidiary to be booking 40 per cent of all its revenues from advertising by the end of the next year--their fourth in the market. They expected to achieve profitability--true profitability--the year after.Five years to profitability had been about what they had expected going into the Newland market and, despite a few surprises along the way, the company was pretty much on track. For EMI's management team, that meant only one thing: It was time to begin looking for a new market in another country with an emerging economy. It was time to expand their transnational operations again.

7

Managerial Decision Making

Managers usually make decisions the way most people breathe, without thinking about the process. However, decision making is at the heart of the managerial process, just as breathing is central to life. Simon, probably the most noted scholar in the area of decision making, equated the process of decision making to the process of managing. Making decisions without considering the process works reasonably well on a day-to-day basis. However, decision making is a skill. To improve that skill, managers must think about the process they use to solve problems.

DEFINING DECISION MAKING

Definitions of decision making abound. For example, Simon wrote,"Decision making comprises three principle phases; finding occasions for making decisions; finding possible courses of action; and choosing among the courses of action". Harrison defined a decision as,"a moment, in an ongoing process of evaluating alternatives for meeting an objective, at which expectations about a particular course of action impel the decision maker to select the course of action most likely to result in obtaining the objective".

Many of the traditional definitions of decision making concentrate on the process as a rational one that involves a person or a group with common goals. However, Taylor emphasized the role of social and political context of organizations and their environments. This approach suggests that decisions are not as deliberate as often assumed, but occur from interaction among people and groups with sometimes conflicting goals.

The range of definitions for decision making suggests that defining this process is somewhat arbitrary. However, some concepts are common to most definitions. Decisions almost always involve resources; they usually address goals or objectives; they always involve people; and the environment in which these people work almost always affects decisions. With these common concepts in mind, we define decision making as the allocation of scarce resources by individuals or groups to achieve goals under conditions of uncertainty and risk. This definition has six important terms. First, allocation means that objects have been distributed among alternatives. Just as a family allocates its income for food, clothing, housing, transportation, and entertainment, media managers must decide how to distribute their resources. Scarce resources reflect the fact a manager never has all of the resources he or she would like.

Available resources are people's time and money. To a degree, these two resources are interchangeable. If you have money, but need time, you can hire others. If you have time, but need money, you can sell that time. Certainly, other forms of resources are available, but all are related to time and money. For example, technology is a way of increasing the effectiveness and efficiency of time and is acquired with money.

Other forms of resources are derivative of time and money, or are ways of improving the allocation of time and money. The word scarce is equally important. If resources were not scarce, decision making would not be central to management. With a limitless supply of money and time, people could try every alternative until they found the one that worked best Scarce resources limit the time and money spent on a decision. The third term includes individuals and groups. Decisions can be made by one person or by two or more people functioning as a unit. All other things equal, it takes less time for one person to make a decision than it does a group. However, ease of decision is not the same as effectiveness of decision. Groups make some decisions better than individuals do.

Goal is the fourth term. In our definition, goal means a decision has a purpose. The nature of business goals is complex and has been the subject of much debate and research. The cases may or may not state specific goals, but no decision can be made adequately without considering the goals of that decision and the overall goals of the organization. In pursuing goals, managers act either in a strictly rational way or with bounded rationality. Managers act in a strictly rational way when their goal is to maximize some aspect of business. Simon (1957) defined a rational decision as occurring when a decision maker confronted with alternatives selects the one that has the highest return. This definition of rationality is the basis of classical economic theory and has resulted in the idea that business should maximize some goals, whether it be profits, revenues, or sales.

Acceptance of the assumption of rationality began to crumble after World War II, as scholars began to recognize the limits of the"rational man"approach. Cyert and March (1963) said the profit maximization assumption for businesses was not realistic because people within organizations do not have single-minded purposes. People pursue a variety of goals. Cyert and March also added that firms do not have the perfect knowledge necessary to maximize profits. Maximizing profits occurs when the cost of an additional unit of a product equals the price a consumer pays. This maximizing point is a theoretical idea, because such detailed price and cost data are impossible to collect In place of this rational assumption for decision making, Simon suggested the principle of bounded rationality. This principle recognizes that humans cannot be rational in the strict, traditional sense, but Simon was not willing to say people act randomly. Rather, he proposed that humans pursue goals in a purposeful manner but this pursuit is limited by nature of people and by the social environment in which they live. As a result, people will seek goals and make decisions that work to satisfy instead of maximize their benefits from the decisions.

This satisficing approach means people adopt goals and decision outcomes that are acceptable within the constraints faced by the organizations. Uncertainty is the fifth term of the definition that needs discussion. We define uncertainty as meaning all decisions are probabilistic. No decision outcome is 100 per cent certain. Reducing uncertainty starts with a subjective estimate of the probability that an outcome will occur. A graduating public relations major, for instance, might estimate that he or she has a 50 per cent chance of finding a job within I month. Part of the estimate is figuring out the factors that affect outcomes. Once a person has made such an estimate, the reasons behind the estimate can be used to reduce uncertainty.

These estimates of probability may be as crude as a statement that an outcome is more likely than not, or they may be as sophisticated as a derived mathematical statement of probability. For instance, a person might"bet"another person that Michigan State University will beat the University of Illinois in a football game. This is a statement with subjective probability, as is the statement that there is a 60 per cent chance of rain tomorrow.

However, all such subjective estimates share two characteristics:

- They are based on analysis of information;
- They also are based on assumptions about measurement and time that limit their objective nature. The accuracy of the information and the quality of analysis determines how well the subjective statement of probability predicts rain or the football game winner.

Uncertainty then rests on a continuum from 0 per cent to 100 per cent uncertainty about a decision outcome. Because perfect knowledge is impossible, 0 per cent uncertain decisions do not exist, and a 100 per cent uncertain decision would be a random solution. As Bass (1983) pointed out, in the absence of other information, people fill in questionable space with their experience or that of their acquaintances. As uncertainty increases, the difficulty of making an effective decision increases.

The word risk the final term in the definition, is used differently here than in traditional decision-making literature. Risk refers to the amount of resources committed to accomplishing a goal and, therefore, the amount of resources that might be lost. Risk also exists on a continuum. The risk runs from small to great Small means few resources are allocated, whereas great means a large number of resources is involved. As with uncertainty, rarely will organizations operate at the ends of the risk continuum.

Few organizations will allocate a large percentage of their resources to a given project, much less a single decision. Risk is a relative term. Allocating $1 million would be a huge proportion of resources at most weekly newspapers, but a relatively small proportion of resources at a large media corporation, such as CBS or Microsoft. The greater the risk for a company, the more important the decision.

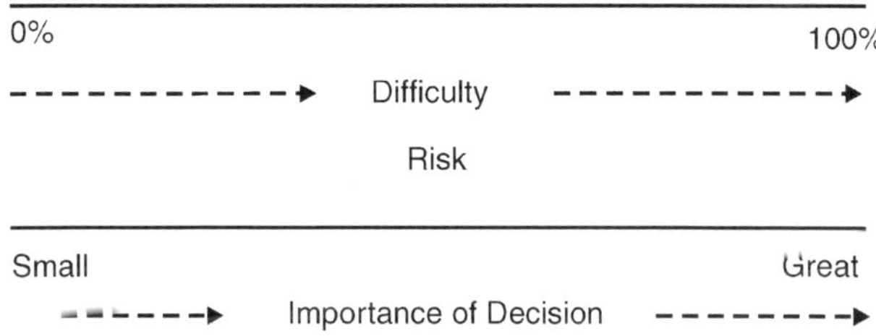

Fig. The Relationship Between Uncertainty and Risk.

A decision that concerns a relatively great risk and a high level of uncertainty is important and difficult. In fact, such a venture might not be undertaken. A decision that has little risk and uncertainty would be relatively unimportant and easy to make.

TYPES OF DECISIONS

Decisions fall into two types: programmed and non programmed. A programmed decision sets up a rule that states an action will take place once a certain condition has been reached. A non programmed decision is one that cannot be made by referring to a rule. Programmed decisions tend to be highly structured, with established goals and channels of information. Non programmed decisions have poor structure, vague goals, and ambiguous information. Determining an employee's pay every month is an example of a programmed decision. Publishers at a newspaper do not have to decide how much money to pay their employees at the end of each month. The amount and form have been set up in advance, usually on an annual basis, and larger organizations have computers that will issue the checks.

Non programmed decisions require information and analysis that is specific to a particular decision. Selecting a new news anchor at a local television station is a non programmed decision. The taste viewers have for a news anchor change, and making decisions about new anchors with old data about the audience is likely to lead to lower ratings. Non progmmmed decisions, such as selecting anchors or hiring journalists, happen too infrequently to develop an effective, programmed policy. Each time, new information and analysis are essential for an effective decision. The distinction between programmed and non programmed decisions is an important one. If a decision can be programmed effectively, it is wise to do so. The greater the number of programmed decisions, the more time a manager will have to spend on difficult non programmed decisions. Whether or not a decision can be programmed depends on the uncertainty and the risk involved. The lower the uncertainty and risk, the more likely a programmed decision will work. The two types of decisions often occur in the same process. News selection, for instance, involves both programmed and non programmed decisions. News values are a form of programmed decisions.

If an automobile accident kills several people in a city, it will be on the evening television news in that city. It has the news values of proximity (it is local) and impact (extreme consequences). There is little debate because applying the news values to such events has become programmed. The difficulty comes in deciding if an event truly represents certain news values.

Proactive and Reactive Decisions

Another way of categorizing decisions has to do with the impact of external events and trends on an organization. Managers tend to react to changes in the business environment with either proactive or reactive decisions. Proactive decisions are made in anticipation of external changes, and reactive decisions are made as a result of external changes. Examples of these two types of decisions can be found in the reaction of a newspaper company to web sites that provide information about the newspaper's community.

If the newspaper went online in 1995 with a web site about it's community, it is likely that managers made a proactive decision to establish a source of information before other companies did. If the newspaper managers waited until 1998 when competitors had already established a community web site, then they made a reactive decision.

Proactive decisions can work well when they promote solutions to problems before they become particularly burdensome. Reactive decisions often occur after a company's competitor has gained a foothold in the market, which can put the reacting company at a disadvantage. On the other hand, a company can be proactive to an imagined problem and end up wasting money solving a problem that does not exist. Successful proactive decisions require accurate predictions of future external trends and events. Successful reactive decisions require that an organization not wait in responding to changes in the business environment. Timing is crucial.

THE DECISION PROCESS

Despite variation in the names given to the steps in the decision process, most models of decision making are similar. For example, Drucker gave six steps: classify the problem, define the problem, specify what the decision must do, seek the right decision, build in the action to carry out the decision, and use feedback to test the effectiveness of the decision. Griffin and Moorhead offered a model that incorporates the difference between programmed and nonprogrammed decisions and that acknowledges the role of information at each step. The model is called a decision wheel because it represents the cyclical nature of the decision process. It differs from the Griffin and Moorhead model in two ways. First, it does not include the idea of programmed versus nonprogrammed decisions. Programmed decisions, although important, are not the basis of the case study approach. Although creating a policy may be the solution to a case, this solution results from a nonprogrammed decision process.

A second difference between the decision wheel and other models is the central placement of the collection and analysis of information. Just as a decision making is the heart of management, the collection and appropriate analysis of information are the hub of decision making. All steps of the decision-making process must involve the collection of information and its appropriate evaluation. Analysis, which breaks down the information and then examines and classifies it so it can be used, is a key to effective decisions. Correct analysis with little information often is more useful than poor analysis with abundant information.

Defining the Problem

The first step is defining the problem to be solved. It involves the collection of information about some form of behaviour, either inside or outside the organization, that is a problem for the media firm. This information must be analyzed in a way that allows the managers to frame the problem appropriately. For example, a television news department that is losing audience has a problem. To define the problem behind this decline in ratings, management must develop a list of possible causes and collect information about them. Then the information about the potential causes must be analyzed to decide what the cause may be.

Perhaps the audience does not like the hard-news focus of the news shows, or they may not like anchors. Each problem holds several possible causes, and in many cases, problems may have more than one cause. The ability to reverse the sliding ratings, however, will depend on management's ability to define the problem in a way that the causes can be identified correctly.

Specifying Goals

After the problem is defined, the next step is specifying the goals of the decision. The goals need to be concrete. Vague statements about reversing a trend will not allow for effective decision making. The goals should be as specific as the problem and available data will allow. Usually the decision process will address multiple goals. All goals should have a time frame for accomplishing them.

In the television news example, the station president and news director may decide that the station should increase its early evening news ratings by 3 points and its late evening news ratings by 2 points within the next 6 months.

(A ratings point equals 1 per cent of the TV households in a station's market.) These very specific goals allow for better monitoring and force a manager to use detailed analysis of data. Managers may set up several goals across time. So, the station management may want a 1-point increase in ratings within 3 months and an additional 2-point increase during the following 3 months. The crucial element of goal setting is degree of specificity. To do this, one must collect as a much information as a possible and analyse it effectively.

Developing Solutions

The third step in the decision wheel is developing alternative solutions. This step should yield as a many alternatives as a possible. Inadequate solutions can be rejected, but a solution that has not been considered never can be selected.

A weeding-out process follows the listing of the solutions. Here, the obviously unsuitable solution can be dropped, leaving those that have some possibilities for accomplishing the goals.Just as a with all steps, the narrowing process requires the acquisition of information and its analysis. Two questions for developing this list are:

- Will the solutions actually accomplish the goals?
- Will the costs of the solution outweigh the gains to the organization? If the answer to the first question is no, then the solution should be dropped. If the answer to the second question is yes, then the solution should be dropped.Using the problem of declining ratings, we can list possible solutions to this situation:
- Hire new anchors.
- Increase the time devoted to weather.
- Increase the time devoted to sports.
- Introduce new segments to the newscast, such as a a health information segment.
- Use more live coverage.
- Change the nature of the news by presenting more feature material and fewer hard-news stories.
- Hire a new sports announcer.
- Hire a new weather announcer.
- Create a web site to promote the news.

These are just some of the possible solutions. Only a few of these will get serious consideration, but examining all possible alternatives will help managers identify plausible ones.

The two-question test can be applied to eliminate some of the alternative listed. First, based on a recent viewer survey, the news director might reject solutions 1, 7, and 8 because all of the on-camera talent received good evaluations from the viewers (no answers to question a). Solution 5 can be dropped because the station does not have the money needed to buy technology that would allow more live coverage (yes answer to question b).

Selecting a Solution

With a short list of solutions, a manager moves to the next step, which involves the selection of one solution to the problem. The solution may be a combination of more than one alternative solution, but the next step requires a decision to pursue a specific solution. The collection and analysis of information are crucial at this point. When one solution is selected, the alternate solutions should not be forgotten. Often the original solution does not work as well as management would like. As a result, managers have to return to the problem and either generate new solutions or choose one of the solutions dropped previously. It is a good idea to prioritize the solutions not used based on information and analysis. This may save time if the chosen solution fails.

Selecting solutions is always a matter of costs and benefits. Often, more than one solution will work, so the correct option involves one that balances costs with benefits. One solution may generate more viewers than another, but the costs would be so high as to consume the entire increase in revenues from getting more viewers. At the same time, a solution may be inexpensive, but the results will not reach the specified goals. Returning to the television news department, we find the managers considering the five solutions that remain after discarding ineffectual solutions. They reject changing the nature of the news because a recent survey of viewers indicated they generally were pleased with the mix of news being carried. They also reject the web site option because the survey indicated only 18 per cent of the households access the web. The three remaining solutions all involve the allotment of time. The comparison then becomes one of costs versus expected audience increase. Adding time to weather and sports would not require additional reporters because these two segments already have more material than they use. The potential for increasing audience exists, based on the recent viewer survey, but the survey also revealed a significant segment of the viewers who did not care much for sports.

Considering the potential negative impact of more sports, the managers narrow the solution to either more time for weather or a new daily segment about health. Either solution will require the expense of promotion and advertisements. The costs of the health spot include loss of time for other news and the expense of training a reporter to cover health issues. The potential for an audience increase appears greater for the health spot for three reasons. First, no other station in the market has such a spot, which means it could be promoted and advertised effectively.

Second, this type of spot has attracted viewers in other markets. Third, research has indicated a growing awareness of health issues by the general population in the United States. The increase in weather coverage cannot be promoted as well because another station in the market already broadcasts more weather information and cable has a 24-hour weather service. The managers decide that a daily segment devoted to health issues would be the best way to increase their ratings. As a back-up approach, they decide an increase of about a minute each for sports and weather would be best. However, they delay the decision about the exact content to be included in the new health spot. They want more information about what types of health news other stations have included in their spots.

Implementing the Solution

Once the solution has been selected it must be implemented. This is the fifth step in the decision wheel. The solution means nothing unless it is applied correctly. This requires a detailed plan of action with a timetable for specific actions, a budget, and a breakdown of who has responsibility for carrying out the changes. The details should be as specific as possible. Again, the collection and analysis of information are important at this stage. Much of the information at this point deals with internal organization issues. The budget, timetable, and delegation of responsibility reflect the resources within the media company. It is important to note that the people with the responsibility for carrying out aspects of the solution must be given the power and budget to do so. Responsibility and power should be connected always.

Our television managers, for example, have selected one of their reporters to be in charge of the daily health spot. This reporter was a science major in college and has an interest in this area. The reporter will work directly with a particular producer. The spot will be introduced in 3 months, following an extensive promotional effort, and will occupy about 2½ minutes every weekday on the early and late evening newscasts. The spots on the two newscasts may or may not cover the same topic, but they should have different angles. The time will be taken mostly from the news hole, but 30 seconds will come from the sports segment. Approximately $5,000 has been set aside to fund workshop attendance by the reporter, and $10,000 has been allocated for researching viewers' responses.

Monitoring the Solution

The final step is monitoring the implementation in the fight of the goals. This monitoring should provide feedback on a regular basis to judge progress toward the goals and be part of the implementation plan. For example, the television news managers have decided to evaluate the effectiveness of the spot on a monthly basis, as well as through informal weekly discussions with the producer and reporter. Every month, the managers will have a meeting with those involved to discuss the content and any problems. After 3 months, the managers will have meetings with several small groups of viewers to get their comments on the new segment. Also, after each ratings period, the data will be analyzed to determine if the new spot is having an impact on the ratings. Crucial to the monitoring system is a timetable. A solution that is not working should be given an adequate test period, but a media organization should not remain committed to a solution once it becomes obvious that it will not work. Times should be established during the implementation process at which the managers must decide to continue or end the plan.

This monitoring process makes the entire decision process cyclical. If the solution is not working, this becomes a problem that starts a new cycle of decision making. The same steps are taken in a new cycle but some may take less time and effort because the previous decision process already provides relevant information. However, managers must be careful not to assume they have all the information they need. An effective manager continues to acquire information until the cost of additional information outweighs the probable benefit from having that information.

CONSTRAINTS ON THE DECISION PROCESS

The decision wheel is an ideal. It is a blueprint that rarely is followed exactly because of practical constraints that fall into two types: who makes the decision and time available for the decision.

Decision Makers

Table: Advantages and Diables Advantages of Group Decision Making

Advantages		*Disadvantages*
	Timing	
Slower decision process		Slower decision process
Division of labor for complex task		Disagreement over goals may result in no decisions
	Uncertainty	
Larger amounts of information		Political behavior of group and knowledge generated members reduces acceptance of information from others
Fewer errors in analyzing		Groupthink--tendency of information group members to think the group is infallible
More alternatives generated		
	Goals	
Groups can clarify goal understanding		Groups sometimes act in ways inconsistent with goals
Participation increases acceptance of group goals		Group think

Individuals and groups make decisions. Whether a group or individual makes the decision influences the efficiency and effectiveness of the decision. In some cases, individuals may decide best. In other cases, group decisions work better. Huber (1980) listed three advantages and four disadvantages of group decisions, whereas Harrison (1987) gave nine strengths and four weaknesses.

Griffin and Moorhead (1986) presented six advantages of group decision making and three advantages of individual decision making. Table summarizes the advantages and disadvantages of group decision making and categorizes them under the headings of timing, uncertainty, and goals. Interestingly, weaknesses of group decision making can be strengths. For example, one of the advantages and disadvantages of group decision making is its slow process. Group decision making usually increases the time needed for a decision because of problems in organizing meetings and the long process of forming consensus among people with conflicting positions. An individual decision maker does not have these timing problems. Whether the time element is an advantage or a disadvantage depends on the decision. If timing is crucial, individuals make quicker decisions. If timing is not crucial and risk and uncertainty are high, a slower process has advantages.

Deadlines exemplify the timing importance in news departments. News stories do not get used if they are not ready by the printing or broadcast deadlines. So, individuals make most decisions about what stories will run. However, exceptions to this rule involve important stories. The inherent lack of speed in group decisions is not the only advantage or disadvantage of groups. When complex tasks are involved, groups have the advantage of division of labour. Dividing tasks among group members can speed up the process because one person does not have to learn the wide range of information required for complex decisions.

Buying a new computer system for a newspaper is an example. Because such systems often serve multiple departments, it would make sense to include someone from each department in the decision-making process. It is easier to have people from each department who know the department's computer needs than it is to have one or two people learn about the computer needs of all the departments. Advantages and disadvantages of group decisions also fall under the heading of uncertainty.

Group decision making can reduce uncertainty in three ways. First, having more than one person will increase the amount of information and knowledge brought to the process. Second, it can decrease the number of errors. The cliché"two heads are better than one"applies here. Having more people also can reduce information errors because people can evaluate each other's information and analysis. Third, groups generate more alternative solutions. The ability to compare alternatives with each other can result in better solutions.

Although uncertainty will decline with some groups, it can increase with others. The probabilities that develop from the satisficing approach are subjective. This subjectivity is influenced by the attitudes and perceptions of other group members. Political behaviour among group members can create doubt as to appropriate goals and the desirability of solutions. For instance, when a city editor and a sports editor try to persuade other group members that their departments are key to improving quality overall, the very process of persuasion can cast doubt on either department being effective at attracting readers. The result is uncertainty of actions.

Just as dangerous as political behaviour, which can divide, is the phenomenon of groupthink. Groupthink occurs when group members are so set on sustaining unanimity among themselves that they fail to properly appraise the alternative solutions. Although the group feels they have reduced uncertainty because they agree on the best alternative, they actually have decreased the probability that any one solution will work. The solution does not get an adequate evaluation. Because of the number of people involved, groups often will develop a better understanding of the organization's and decision group's goals. Reading a statement of goals adopted by an organization does not mean that the employees understand those goals. Hearing others discuss the goals can help clarify them.

Another advantage is that participation in group decision making will increase acceptance of the goals and solutions that are adopted. Increased acceptance can translate into increased effort in accomplishing the goals. People tend to accept more readily those decisions in which they participated. A disadvantage of group decisions with respect to goals is the tendency of some groups to develop their own goals that may be inconsistent with the organization's goals.

For example, a group set up within a media organization to develop ways to cut costs may decide that cost cutting is not a proper goal. The result will be a conflict of goals between management and decision group. Resulting decisions are less likely to accomplish the aims of management. The advantages and disadvantages of group decisions create problems for deciding when groups or individuals should make decisions. Vroom and Yetton (1973) said that individual managers are likely to make decisions when the problem is well structured, information is plentiful, a previously successful solution to a similar problem is available, and time constraints require a quick decision.

Individual Decision-Making Styles

As with all human skills, managers vary in the style of decision making they use. A decision-making style has to do with common patterns of reaching decisions. Most managers will exhibit more than one style, but often a particular style emerges under pressure. The way managers use information and how they focus on solutions. Use of information involved either satisficing or maximizing. As mentioned earlier, satisficing requires collecting information to reach a"satisfactory"conclusion that may not result in as good a result as possible. Maximizing involves collecting information until a decision maker has enough to reach the"best"decision.

The difference is related to how long the decision makers win collect information before acting. Solution focus concerns the use of data to identify possible solutions. Unifocus people collect information and identify one solution they think is best, whereas multifocus people collect information and provide a variety of solutions to a problem.These two dimensions were combined to produce the following five decision styles people use:

Decisive Style

This style involves people who are satisficers and are unifocused with respect to solutions. A limited amount of information is collected and acted on quickly. Once solutions are identified, the decision makers are unwavering in their support of the solution.

Flexible Style

Flexible decision makers are satisfiers who are multifocused on solutions. Limited information is acted on, but more flexibility is shown in using solutions. If one solution fails to work, another is chosen.

Hierarchical Style

This style involves maximizing and unifocus. Large amounts of information are collected in order to select the one best solution, which is pursued using a very detailed plan. People who use this style act slowly, due to the time they spend on getting information.

Integrative Style

People using this style are maximizers with multifocus solutions. Collecting and evaluating information takes time, but unlike the hierarchical style, more than one solution to the problem is considered.

Systemic Style

This style incorporates both the integrative and the hierarchical styles in a two-step process. The first step involves evaluating large amounts of information and dealing with multiple solutions. The second step is more hierarchical because solutions are prioritized with one or more criteria being considered the "best." This style is more contemplative than the hierarchical style but involves more organized and active solutions than the integrative style. These types of decision-maker classifications can be useful in understanding decision making, but care must be taken. Often managers will exhibit a combination of these styles with individual decisions and in decisions over time. The usefulness of the classification is its emphasis on types of goals (satisficing and maximizing) and on nature of focus (unifocus or multifocus).

Types for Group Decisions

Just as individual decision makers exhibit different styles, so do groups. McEwan (1997) listed 10 ways that groups can reach decisions, which vary by the degree the entire group participates and by the quality (how effectively the decisions result in reaching goals) of the resulting decisions. The group styles are:

Decision by Authority Without Group Discussion

This is not really a group decision, although it may be presented as such because one person makes the decision for the group. It yields a fast decision, but the group does not become involved.

Decision by Default

A group failing to make a decision can be a form of decision. Group inactivity results in either someone else making the decision or the problem going away.

Self-Authorized Decisions

One or more members assume they have the authority to make a decision when they do not. Such decisions have little support from members left out of the process.

Decision by Clique

A few individuals form a subgroup to make decisions and then impose that decision. This breaks the decision-making group into competing factions, which reduces quality of decisions.

Decision by Expert

A person within the group makes the decision, but how the"expert"is selected can create internal disagreements.

Decision by Averaging Individual's Opinions[ssh]

Members' opinions are asked separately and the results are averaged. Group members have no actual part of the decision because group interaction is missing.

Decision by Authority After Group Discussions

Group members advise the person who has authority to make decision. This can result in competition for authority's attention or telling authority what the group members believe will please him or her.

Decision by Minority

A subgroup is given the authority to make decisions. This makes other members wonder why they were put in the group.

Decision by Majority Vote[ssh]

The group does as the majority wants. The effectiveness depends on everyone's commitment to this method, whether they are in the majority or the minority.

Decision by Consensus

The group reaches a decision that everyone can support, but it can be very time consuming. This may be the best method if time allows because it results in high quality conclusions. All of these types of divisions have advantages and disadvantages depending on the goal of the decision. It is helpful for groups to understand how they are making decisions because it will allow them to analyse the weaknesses of these decisions. Suppose a magazine company appoints a committee to plan a long-term strategy for incorporating the World Wide Web (WWW) in its market strategy. Members should represent the various departments in the company, as well as a variety of web experience and technological knowledge.

The group might be tempted to let the person with the most technological knowledge (decision by expert) make the decisions, but that person might not know how advertisers and viewers want to interact with the Web. The company's chief executive officer (CEO) might make the decision after hearing all sides (decision by authority after group discussion), but the techies and nontechies might form subgroups and compete for the CEO's support. The best type of group decision making depends on a variety of factors about the problem and the people involved. One of the most important factors is timing of decisions.

Time and Decision Making

In addition to classifying decisions by type of decision-making style, decisions can be broken down on the basis of time available. Three general timing patterns seem appropriate. Nonprogrammed decisions can be classified as immediate, short-term, or long-term. Immediate decisions must be made quickly.

The time that is available between step I and step 5 in the decision wheel is measured in hours or even minutes. Story decisions on deadline are the prime examples in media. As a result of deadlines, it is common to find individuals making content decisions at newspapers, magazines, and television news departments. However, the deadline pressure hides the danger that individuals will begin making all decisions quickly and alone out of habit. No decision should be made before time requires it. If a decision need not be made immediately, participation of others should be sought. Short-term decisions are ones that need not be made immediately, but they must be made within a reasonable period of time. At a newspaper, the plans for a breakdown of news and advertising space for the coming week would be short-term.

Small groups usually make these decisions, even if one person has that responsibility. For example, the publisher, who has final authority for space in a newspaper, may meet with the advertising manager and editor to determine news holes for a week. Often the publisher has determined a breakdown for the year between news and advertising space. The meetings are monitoring sessions by which the three managers discuss news-editorial needs in light of the year's goal, previous use of space, and the newsroom's space needs for the week.

Long term decisions are those that affect the organization over a period of years and, therefore, warrant a longer decision-making process. This type of decision includes the television news ratings problem discussed earlier and format changes at a magazine or newspaper. Because of their complexity, these decisions require participation by a large number of people in groups and as individuals. In effect, a long-term decision, such as what next year's budget should be, requires hundreds or thousands of smaller decisions.

Overall, time acts as a constraint on the process shown in the decision wheel by limiting the time available for each of the six steps. These limits determine how much information can be collected, how much analysis can be conducted, and how many people can participate in the decision. Immediate decisions allow very little time for each step and for information collection and analysis. Long-term decisions should include adequate time for each step.

The timing of various types of decisions places a premium on different types of managers. When an immediate decision is needed, a satisfactory solution is more important than an optimal solution. So the person who has command of a great deal of information in an area and who can analyse quickly will perform best. This person need not be as good at working with people as a manager who deals with short- and long-term problems. Decisive and flexible decision styles work well here.

A manager faced with short-term decisions needs both people skills and the ability to reach decisions within a reasonable time. On the other hand, managers who must make long-term decisions are better served by skills that allow them to work with people and that allow them to examine a problem from several angles. This person should be good at analysis, but it is analysis with a different time frame. This manager must be good at developing many alternatives and evaluating them against each other. The variation of needed skills explains why some people make better upper level managers, such as editor, than lower level managers, such as assistant city editor. Long-term decisions that involve high risk and uncertainty work best with integrative or systemic styles for decision makers. The key to effective decision making is to put people in positions where their abilities will serve them best and then to train them in the areas where they are weakest. The ability to understand and handle time constraints is essential if a person is to be promoted within the media organization.

TOOLS OF MANAGEMENT

Just as decision makers and time constrain decision making, so does the quality of information and analysis, which relate directly to the skills of the decision maker. As with all skills, collecting and analyzing information can be improved through learning. The next section addresses briefly the sources of information and some of the tools of analysis.

Sources of Information

Because information plays an important role in all six steps, it is useful to examine where one gets information. Basically, information comes either from one's own efforts or from the efforts of others.

The efforts can take various forms, however, and those forms can affect the quality of information. The two main types of efforts are experience and research. Experience involves participating in events or processes, and research is the application of generally accepted systemic methods of examining events or processes. Someone who works at a news magazine has experience in magazine journalism.

Someone who conducts a survey of news magazine reporters is conducting research about magazine journalism. Experience differs from research in that it does not have accepted standards for analyzing data. Experience is inseparable from the person having the experience. But a researcher, if conducting research properly, should have a minimal impact on the events or processes being studied.

Research should be more objective and systematic than experience. Should be are more important words because quality of research depends on the researcher's skills, just as quality of experience depends on the wisdom of the person experiencing the event. Experience can be analyzed systematically and somewhat objectively by a manager, just as a researcher inadvertently can alter the result of research through poor use of methods. Managers have roughly four sources of information: their own experiences, the experiences of others, their research and the research of others.

The tendency among media managers is to depend on their experiences and the experiences of trusted colleagues. Experience has the characteristics of being detailed and specific to a particular situation. This can be an advantage when a decision must be made about a situation similar to previous events. However, using one's experience becomes a liability when that experience is applied to a problem that differs from the original experience.

The result in such cases is often a poor decision. Managers should know the value of all forms of information and seek diverse sources of information, especially in the monitoring step.

A successful manager analyzes past decisions so the next decision can be more effective. The results of every decision should become information for future decisions, but the usefulness of this information depends on the ability to use tools of analysis.

Cost-Benefit Analysis

A manager with few analytical skills or with little knowledge and experience will end up depending on others to judge the reliability and validity of information.

This can be a problem. Managers who understand analysis are in a better position to select information appropriate for decisions. Analysis involves ways of processing information. Several different types of analysis, which vary in complexity, are available. Perhaps the most recognized analytical tool is cost-benefit analysis, which is an attempt to estimate the costs and the benefits that result from alternative actions.

McKean listed five steps:

- Identifying benefits to be achieved,
- Identifying the alternatives that will reach the goal,
- Identifying the costs for the alternative methods,
- Developing a model or set of relationships that explain the impact of alternatives on the costs and benefits, and
- Selecting the preferred alternative with a criterion involving both costs and benefits.

These steps sound familiar because they correspond to steps of the decision wheel. The traditional approach to cost-benefit analysis is to place a monetary value on all costs and benefits and compare the resulting differences. Because this is difficult to do with many types of costs, cost-benefit analysis may include the"dollar-equivalency technique" which is the development of money equivalents for costs that are difficult to measure in dollars. Obviously, this becomes problematical when costs and benefits involve human behaviour.

Two concepts are useful in dealing with the nonmonetary aspects of cost-benefit analysis: opportunity costs and intangibles. Opportunity costs are the expenses that accrue from giving up alternative actions. It is equivalent to the old saying:"There is no free lunch."For every alternative selected, a person loses what she would have gained from another alternative. For example, a manager is hiring a reporter and must pick from two candidates. The first is stronger at writing and the second at reporting. If the first is hired, an opportunity cost is the reporting ability that will be lost from not hiring the second. If the second is hired, an opportunity cost is the writing skill that will be lost from not hiring the first. Intangibles are the things that cannot be measured well. This may be leadership in a manager or the ability of some people to raise morale in an organization. Whatever the attribute, a dollar amount cannot be assigned adequately. These intangibles often are ignored in formal tools of analysis because they cannot be measured well.

Opportunity costs and intangibles are the Achilles heel of cost-benefit analysis and most other types of formal analysis. These two concepts relate to all decisions, although sometimes they are more important than at other times. Despite these two problems, cost-benefit analysis can be useful even if it simply allows a manager to think more clearly. The following example demonstrates the potential use of cost-benefit analysis in a situation where quantification is difficult.

The Times-Leader recently conducted a readership survey in which 48 per cent of the readers said they would like to have more in-depth local coverage. Managing Editor Jane Smith has been assigned to come up with a plan for doing this. Her first observation is that it can be done either by hiring a new reporter or by using existing staff. She comes up with the benefits and costs presented in Table.

The monetary benefits f or either alternative are equal in Table and amount to $54,000 per year. These benefits are based on retaining 250 readers a year and attracting 250 readers annually as a result of increased in-depth coverage. Two main areas of monetary benefits are saving $4,000 from not having to replace the 250 readers and making $50,000 in advertising revenue that would be lost if the 500 readers were not buying the newspaper.

Both approaches also have intangible benefits in the form of staff morale and promotional advantage of having in-depth coverage that will generate recognition of the newspaper's journalistic efforts. The use of existing staff has added advantage in that it will increase morale of the staff because they will be allowed to spend time on more lengthy projects.

Monetary costs of hiring an additional reporter are about $20,000 more a year because the new reporter would earn $30,000 a year, whereas overtime needed to use existing staff would only amount to $10,000. Both alternatives have opportunity costs. Each alternative would require about the same amount of additional editing, which would have to come from the time spent on editing of day-to-day stories.

Two opportunity costs and two intangible costs stand out as important factors. First, having a new reporter could create dissatisfaction among the existing staff members who would like to pursue in-depth reporting. In-depth work usually is looked on by reporters as reward because it is more satisfying and interesting than most day-to-day coverage. On the other hand, taking time from day-to-day coverage has the opportunity cost of reducing the amount of space and effort spent on everyday reporting. This could negatively affect circulation.

Table: Cost-Benefit Analysis of Increasing In-Depth Reporting at the Times-Leader

	Alternatives	
Costs	**Hiring a reporter**	**Using existing Staff**
Monetary	$30,000 a year salary	$10,000 a year additional overtime
	$5,000 a year expense for travel & research	$5,000 a year expenses for travel & research
	$13,000 for 26 additional pages at a cost of $500 per page	$13,000 for 26 additional pages at cost of $500 per page
Opportunity	Dissatisfaction among existing staff because	Use of staff for In-depth reporting
	they will not be allowed to do in-depth work	will reduce time for day-to-day reporting
	Editing time lost on day-to-day coverage	Editing time lost on day-to-day
	due to increased editing needs of day-to-day coverage	coverage due to increased editing needs of day-to-day coverage
Intangible	Possible negative impact of new reporter in the newsroom	Added effort needed to balance indepth coverage
Benefits		
Monetary	Save $4,000 needed to gain 250 lost readers	Save $4,000 needed to gain 250 lost readers
	Save $50,000 in advertising revenue	Save $50,000 in advertising revenue
	that could be lost with decline of 500 readers	that could be lost with decline of 500 readers
Intangible	Increased morale among staff from in creased quality of the newspaper	Increased morale among staff from increased quality of the newspaper
	Promotional value of expected recogni tion from in-depth coverage	Promotional value of expected
		recognition from in-depth coverage
		Increased staff morale for those who do in-depth reporting

The intangible costs also involve the staff's reaction to a new plan. If a new reporter is hired, he or she may alter the chemistry among people in the newsroom. This impact, combined with the possible resentment, may have negative consequences. On the other hand, a new reporter might add to the newsroom chemistry. Whether this becomes a cost or not would depend on who is hired as the new reporter. The use of existing staff means an added cost for the editors because they must ensure that the in-depth assignments are distributed fairly. Otherwise, staff resentment could develop.

By examining Table, a manager could see that the question of which approach to take comes down to whether the additional $20,000 cost of a new reporter and the potential newsroom disruption exceeds the impact of reducing the day-to-day coverage in the newspaper. This, in turn, is related to the adequacy of the current staff. If the newsroom is understaffed already, expanding the work required could be disastrous. More readers might drop the paper because of poor day-to-day coverage than would buy the paper because of increased in-depth reporting. In order to make an appropriate selection, a manager needs to have an understanding of the nature of the reporters currently working and an awareness of the informal organizational setting in the newsroom.

An important point of this illustration is that many of the costs and benefits are not quantifiable. But this should not lead to these costs and benefits being ignored. A second point is that the analysis is only as good as the information that goes into it. The monetary costs and benefits should be accurate, but the knowledge of the people in the newsroom needs to be just as reliable and valid.

SOCIAL SCIENCE THEORY

Successful use of cost-benefit analysis depends greatly on the quality of the information used. Poor information will result in poor decisions. However, another analytical tool is available that can improve the quality of information, whether it be from experience or research. This tool is called theory. Social science theory is a system of abstract statements that describes a set of behaviors.

Theories can provide one or more of the following:

- A method of classifying behaviour, called a typology,
- Predictions of future events and behaviour,
- Explanations of past events or behaviors,
- A sense of understanding about what causes events,
- The potential to control events or behaviour.

The usefulness of a theory depends on how many of and how well these functions are fulfilled by the theory. All of the five possible functions of theory would be useful to a manager in making decisions because they help reduce uncertainty. Useful theories can be found in sociology, psychology, and economics, and many of these are discussed in this volume. One example of applying theory would be the use of equity theory. Equity theory states that people evaluate how fairly they are being treated by an organization in four steps. First, a person evaluates how he or she is being treated. Second, the person evaluates how a"comparison-other"is being treated. This other is someone the individual considers to be equivalent to himself or herself in some way from the organization's perspective. Third, the individual compares the treatment of himself or herself and the other. Fourth, the individual feels he or she is being treated either equitably or inequitably.

As a result of the comparison, a person who feels equity is motivated to continue the current situation, whereas the person who feels inequity may take several different steps to reduce the inequity feeling. An important implication of this theory is that absolute amount of a pay raise given a person is not as important in many cases as the evaluation of the raise with respect to others in the organization.

Equity theory is one of many behavioral theories that can be used to analyse behaviour. If an employee displays lack of motivation or poor performance following a pay raise, for instance, it may be a result of inequity feelings. A manager who explores this possibility may be able to work with the employee by examining the employee's approach to equity. It may be that the person's comparison-other is inappropriate, that the comparison-other got a large raise because of something unusual, or that the inequity feeling was justified. Whatever the case, theory can be useful in classifying and understanding the behaviour of people in an organization.

Using theory in decision making involves five steps. First, a person must be familiar enough with theories to identify which are useful in a given situation. Usually, behaviour may fit more than one theory. Second, a manager applies several theories and selects the one that might be useful in understanding the given behaviour. Third, more information is collected to better fit the behaviour to the theories. Fourth, the behaviour is examined in light of the appropriate theories. Finally, the resulting information is fed back into the decision wheel process.

Across time, managers will find some theories more useful than others in explaining behaviour. However, they should be careful not to apply a theory just because it worked in other cases, and they should make an effort to keep up with theories that develop.

Looking at Past Decisions

People very often make important decisions without preparing properly or examining fully the decision process. The purpose of this assignment is to have you think about your decision-making process by concentrating on a specific decision. Select some important decision (choosing a college or college major, moving in with someone, etc.) that you made during the past few years that has disappointed you. Think about how you made that decision and why you were disappointed. Now, using the decision wheel try to remember the actions you took that would have fit into the various steps in the wheel.

Using Individual and Group Decision Styles

Dan Smith, publisher of the Lincoln Daily Chronicle, sat at his desk thinking about the e-mail he had just received from one of his reporters, Susan Kelley, and from the director of advertising Jane Seymore. Both messages concerned the web site for WZZY, the local CBS-affiliated television station. The web site was not new, but, unlike the other local TV station sites, WZZY had just added a section of classified advertising.

Kelley had e-mailed Smith because she found the site while buying a set of used golf clubs. Seymore had seen an advertisement that WZZY wanted to run in the Daily Chronicle. Smith has to make two decisions. First, he has to decide whether the newspaper will run the advertisements for the classified advertising on WZZY's web site. After all, WZZY is now a competitor with the Daily Chronicle for classified advertising. Second, he has to decide what to do in response to this new competition for classified advertising. Currently, about 35 per cent of the Daily Chronicle's total revenues came from classified advertising. Before the Web, the cost of delivering classified ads to consumers had kept down competition for this lucrative market.

Looking to the Future

Technology has created a rapidly changing business environment for the media companies. In such an environment, a company needs to make proactive decisions to keep up with media consumers' demands and with the competition. These decisions are non programmed.

8

Leadership and the Work Force

Media managers in the next decade will be focused on profit margin, competition, and employee needs, but the internal and external contexts will be driven by two powerful forces: demographics and technology. That is, managers will be dealing with shifting demographics that affect the needs and uses for media products and services in the marketplace. Demographic dynamics also affect the internal operations of media companies adjusting to the changing characteristics of media employees who mirror the larger work force.

Emerging technology will affect not only the delivery and production of services and products to consumers but communication options between and among staff members. Managers will have available several tools for hiring, training, and assessing employees. Managerial excellence will be tied to effective and efficient use of the technology available to managers. Something that will not change, however, is the need for managers to be leaders. Although all leaders are good managers, all managers are not good leaders.

GENERAL PROFILE OF MEDIA COMPANIES

In December of 1997, the U.S. Department of Labour (DOL) released a 10-year projection for the U.S. work force. The DOL predicts that by 2006 the overall supply of workers will increase by 15 million with the largest increases for workers in the 45 to 64 age group. On the positive side, this grayer work force will offer a great deal of job experience and stability. These workers understand professional work standards, have faced crises and know how to improvise.

They will, however, present some management challenges. For instance many will require training. In addition, they may consider themselves semiretired at age 55 and not want to work full time. Salary may not be the key issue for them, but rather benefits (like health insurance) may be most important in recruiting and retaining this group. Traditionally, businesses have considered middle-age employees less adaptable, flexible, dynamic, and responsive to new ideas and technological changes than younger workers. However, because there will be fewer young workers and competition for jobs will be intense, media companies will need to move beyond stereotypes. Training sessions and adult education programs will be required for both middle-age workers and younger employees. Middle-aged employees will need training in technological developments and general skill upgrading. In addition, younger workers may need basic educational tools because school reform has not kept pace with the needs of business, and the gap between the education schools provide and the education workers need is widening. According to one researcher, U.S. businesses lose $20 billion each year due to illiteracy in the work force.

The newest generation of the work force also are of interest to managers. Because they realize that companies can no longer guarantee lifetime secure employment they often are described as the generation on a compressed fast-forward professional cycle. Apprenticeship used to be part of the traditional way new employees"learned the job." However, today's work environment includes Generation X workers who may be with a company only a couple of years (or in some instances a few months). In some cases a 23-year-old might even be hired to oversee a staff unfamiliar with a new or developing media product (like a web page).

The compelling criteria for hiring this generation is not"who you know"but"what you know."The emphasis on skills and expertise is good news, however this can come packaged in an employee with inflated expectations that put the product and customer last. Management and communication skills as well as judgment and experience may be limited or nonexistent. Vigilant overseeing, explicit instructions, and careful explanation of company values and expectations will be required to help this younger worker fit into the company productively--especially if the employment is short term. Although Sheppard concluded that males and females experience organizational life differently, it is difficult to analyse management data on a gender basis because so little of the research has included significant numbers of female managers. Although mid-level media management jobs are held by women, only 4-6 per cent of women hold top-level positions in companies they have not started themselves. Some theorists claim women have a more circular, consensual, and relationship-based style of leadership than men who tend to use linear models. They predict that as female managers increase they will create a new working climate because of their tendency to spend more time with subordinates, listen more carefully, and develop more participative management environments where negotiation and relationships are important tools of decision making.

Asian and Hispanic workers will increase faster in the general work force than any other groups, with predictions calling for Asians to account for 5 per cent of the total work force and Hispanics to hold 12 per cent of all jobs. Black employees also will account for 12 per cent of the work force. However, it is hard to predict growth rates (in the media) for these workers from educational statistics alone. Becker and Kosicki reported race/ethnicity enrollment records for journalism students have not been carefully or consistently recorded. For instance, although 1996 figures show that White student enrollment decreased from 1995 levels and Black student enrollment increased, data also indicate that overall there is a"persistent gap"between the percentage of students of colour enrolled in journalism programs and those who actually graduate. This suggests retention and completion problems. It is impossible to know why students abandon journalism or media studies in college, but graduation rates compiled by Becker and Kosicki confirm a very small pool of non-White students hold degrees in the field.

They say 9 per cent of all joumalism degrees in 1996 were obtained by Black students, 4 per cent were earned by Hispanic students, 3 per cent were earned by Hispanic students, 3 per cent were obtained by Asian students and.9 per cent were earned by Native Americans. The competition for non-White media professionals with journalism degrees will be intense unless both college enrollments and retention rates increase. The research concerning non-White managers is largely underdeveloped and anecdotal. However, the few media executives who have crossed the colour barrier are instructive in their observations. One Hispanic media manager said his supervisors had difficulty when he adopted a style of management that was comfortable for him and his Chicano staffmembers. He said it was"natural"and effective to develop a working climate built on affiliation rather than authority.

He used a model that was closer to a family than a hierarchy. Although the leadership style he used worked well for his staff and took into consideration the ethnic culture from which they emerged, his traditional White male supervisors were uncomfortable and questioned his sense of closeness with the staff because he did not distance himself from his employees. He added that even at a corporate training session on leadership there seemed no understanding of the wisdom of adapting corporate climates to employee needs. He said the management training session was set up to indoctrinate executives into a preconceived management model. There was little room or time for discussion or acceptance of styles that were diverse or that deviated from the White male traditions.

Although growth will not be dynamic for White non-Hispanic workers, they will still hold the largest numbers of jobs with 73 per cent of all workers falling into this category. They also will continue to have the highest levels of educational preparation for media work. Leadership is a dynamic activity, and the next decade will hold even more examples of challenge to the traditional corporate model as diversity within the ranks increases. More women, people of colour, and older workers will merge with current employees to create a need for a more complex and encompassing leadership model. In the next decade families and work also will be combined by both women and men. National research suggests leisure time--not money--may become the status symbol. Managers will be expected to recognize and capitalize on the characteristics of a diverse work force. Cultural and demographic differences will impact training, motivation, production and turnover issues for managers, who will find their jobs challenging.]Managers in the next decade may deal with tension, resentment, and conflict among workers who do not share common backgrounds or cultural orientations. Diversity (unlike affirmative action) is not meant to correct past inequity but to ignite dynamic think ing tuned to market demands and service opportunities for the media.

Efforts during the 1970s and 1980s to diversify the work force commonly met with hostility, misunderstanding and even backlash. However, development of global markets has contributed to an understanding that a multicultural work force is not just"politically correct"but a smart and necessary business move. However most managers recognize that teams and groups of workers do not bond without help. It is the job of the manager to initiate and support the process. Managers can lead the effort by first assessing what strengths belong to the group.

For instance, if a manager notices that the work force of baby boomers is generally suspicious of authority and perpetually engaged in preserving youthful images then the manager might construct an autonomous rather than authoritarian work climate. He or she might build into technology training the message that technology provides access to and integration with youthful ideas and audiences. For some employees trust may be the most important determinant of a satisfying work environment. These workers will not invest themselves or become motivated unless they have a working relationship with management that they consider trustworthy. They may define trust as consistency between written/verbal communication and managerial behaviour. Or trust may be defined as the ability of management to"let go"of some of its power when employees have expertise, experience, and/or ability to perform without close supervision.

However, managers cannot and should not guess at what is important to a particular set of employees. Each employee and work place have their own peculiar characteristics. Educational, professional, experiential, and personal backgrounds will vary, and managers should regularly talk with employees to note changes in expectations and employee needs. Managers also should note abrupt changes in employee behaviors (e.g. a usually prompt employee abruptly becomes tardy on a regular basis). Managers who are alert to cues sent by employees can avert and extinguish many problems before they become general morale or production nightmares.

Most work force experts predict that educational backgrounds may be the most challenging demographic variable to manage in the future. Some staff members will lack basic educational background and require technical training, whereas others will be highly educated professionals who are specialists in their fields. In fact, DOL predicts that jobs for people requiring at least a bachelor's degree will grow by 25 per cent. Studies within the field of journalism support these overall findings with Becker and Kosicki reporting that an estimated fall 1996 enrollment of 149,256 students in U.S. journalism and mass communication programs was the highest total figure since 1991. They say analyses of the trends over the past several years suggests continued growth for journalism and mass communication college majors.

Employment projections for the next 10 years support continued growth in media-related jobs with public relations and management fields ranking third among the top 10 industries. Technical support employees including database administrators, computer support specialists, and other computer scientists will increase by 118 per cent and computer and data processing services will increase by 108 per cent according to DOL projections by Franklin (1997) and by Silvesti (1997). Media managers will be expected to analyse the strengths of each employee and merge talents in a way that benefits company goals.

LEADERSHIP THEORY

A manager who is also a leader may be defined as someone who oversees tasks, is accountable for meeting goals, pays attention to profit objectives, and has a"vision"of where the company is going and why. Decisions reflect an understanding of larger long-term goals. Early research in the field includes the Michigan Leadership Studies, which involved interviews with managers and subordinates to determine effective leadership behaviors. The studies isolated and identified at least two major supervisor orientations. They were job-centered or task-oriented behaviour and employee-centered or relations-based managerial behaviour. Researchers assumed the two types of managerial orientations were exclusive and represented two ends of a continuum with managers being one or the other but not both.

About the same time, researchers at Ohio State University were conducting similar leadership studies. The research, which included data from military and industrial institutions, focused on relations-based decision making. The studies identified at least two typologies that were called consideration behaviour and initiating-structure behaviour. In the former, the manager considers the needs and ideas of subordinates before making decisions. In the latter, the manager clearly defines the duties of subordinates and communicates their functions to them. These were similar to the Michigan typologies, however the Ohio State researchers suggested that managers were not necessarily one kind of leader. Rather, they concluded that a manager could possess more than one orientation and successful managers could and did alternate styles as circumstances changed. The research described previously was helpful in identifying and confirming certain leadership behaviors. However, it was not complex enough to account for different organizational settings or individual deviations, nor did it explain how employees interpreted apparent inconsistencies when they witnessed managers adopting alternate styles of management as circumstances changed. Fiedler's contingency theory suggested that leadership effectiveness is related to a leader's personality and the situation. His research proposed that leaders have basic personality preferences that make them task versus relationship motivated, and that these preferences are constant and measurable for leaders. The research suggested that when a manager's dominant need was matched favorably with those of a company culture then job fit and satisfaction were generally favorable.

All media managers must fit their personalities to an existing culture when they join a company. The cultural context, therefore, bears important consideration in all discussions of leadership behaviour. As media companies expand into international arenas, it makes sense to understand the various dimensions for cultural analysis. That is, symbols, language, task definitions, and acceptable behaviors vary between workers, countries and even media. A good manager will balance personal style or preference with complex situational variables. Culture is a construct that underlies behaviour and beliefs within a company and the society in which it operates. It guides, explains, and predicts processes and products of a media company. Organizational culture can be"observed"through categorizing and noting patterns of behaviour, styles of dress, backgrounds of those hired and promoted, and so forth. Culture also can be defined in terms of shared values or assumptions workers hold about the world and human nature. Such common belief systems result in predictable behaviors and confirming rituals. Hofstede noted that North American and West European countries stress individualism rather than collectivism.

This impacts how workers and managers regard their own relationships as well as those between the company and the individual. If organizational culture is seen as opposed to individualization or as something that impedes or diverts the individual, then supervisor-subordinate conflict is sure to occur in companies where Western values are prevalent. Such conflict affects morale and, in turn, employee production. Early research by Lewin, Lippitt, and White, who studied boys' clubs, found that autocratic leadership produced the largest number of completed tasks, at least while the leader watched, but morale was best under democratic leadership. Interestingly enough, mixed and different results were found when the study was replicated outside the United States within different cultural contexts.

The democratic style was effective if the task was easy, but the autocratic style was preferred if the task was difficult. Meade found in India that the autocratic style was best on all criteria. Other studies have found similar differences between cultures and between types of businesses. For instance, Heller and Wilpert found that managers in Sweden and France were consistently more participative in their management decision making than were managers in Britain, the United States, West Germany, and Israel, and that participative management styles are more characteristic of the oil and electronics industries than in banking and public transportation fields. Such studies serve to remind us that leadership styles must be considered within the context of worker values and expectations that may be tied to national, professional, and personal cultural orientations. Quite simply, effective leaders are not necessarily interchangeable across international borders, industries or even departments.

Regarding media news cultures, a shared U.S. value is high regard for competition. The cultural context for this competition includes the notion that being first with the news is being best, and being best translates into more market share and higher profits. Competition can entice managers into considering almost anything short of lying appropriate behaviour. Media companies informally monitor one another and through professional groups sometimes even design codes and agreements for themselves that temper the cultural support for such values as competition. There are also unwritten rules that occasionally have resulted in excommunication of members who violate them. Within large media companies there are several subcultures that reside in departments.

They may support or be in conflict with each other as they struggle to maintain a dominant culture that ensures their survival and supports their collective belief systems (e.g. the business department may include norms that are consistent for accountants in general as well as for accountants who work primarily for media companies). However, subcultures will be allowed to exist only if they do not conflict with dominant company philosophy, which may be articulated in a mission statement or through daily work habits.

The Times Mirror Company Mission Statement in the late 1980s included nine separate objectives with,"attract, motivate and retain a high quality work force that reflects the diversity of our society, and provide a positive work environment that allows employees' talents to be developed to the fullest,"listed as the seventh objective. The Indianapolis Newspapers, Inc., mission statement also includes diversity among its six objectives and says the company will,"encourage the professional growth of our employees, reward them for their contributions and strive to maintain a staff that reflects the diversity of our community."Both media companies promise commitment to diversity, but the promises vary in specificity and intention. Managers working for the companies would be expected to make daily decisions that are consistent with the mission statement of their company.

All official communication such as employee handbooks (which outline hiring, firing, performance review, and promotion procedures) as well as informal communication concerning daily assignments or even meetings also would be expected to reflect the spirit and purpose of the mission statements.

SOURCES OF POWER

Power is defined in several ways, however within the context of this discussion, it means the ability to accomplish an act or event or to influence an outcome. Media managers are expected to have the authority, ability, and influence to provide expected or desirable outcomes. The bases of leadership influence were identified by Weber as:

- Rational or resting on legal or normative rules;
- Traditional, resting on the legitimate status of those exercising authority; or
- Charismatic, which could involve leadership arising out of devotion or heroism.
- Expert power, which allows leaders to control via expertise or information they hold that others need.

That is, although leadership types are recognized most easily because they possess titles, fulfill functions on an organizational chart, and have hierarchical recognition, the third type may operate informally and without institutional identification.

This type of leader can develop out of positive needs for entrepreneurial development within an organization or out of negative or oppressive situations where workers feel disconnected, unappreciated, and devalued.

The fourth leadership power arising out of expertise is dependent on a leader being able to convey, in a subtle, nonthreatening way, his orher possession of information. In addition, sometimes unauthorized leaders emerge out of situational factors that provide platforms for recognition. These types of leaders might be considered "renegades," especially if they threaten traditional, hierarchical corporate authority. Much of the early leadership work focused on studying"current"leaders, and then identifying the steps on their rise to power. These studies found that people accept or are chosen for legal and traditional leadership positions because they possess certain cultural backgrounds that are acceptable to the current organization. It is still not clear how important personality is in the leadership formula, but it is clearly a variable related to the organizational situation as well as the level of expert competency required for the position. It also is clear that"leaders"who are named through static bureaucratic or institutional edict and are successful within that context may be very different from leaders who"emerge"because of dynamic situational factors growing out of crises or special need.

MEDIA PROFESSIONALS

Communication theorists and historians agree there are significant professional differences between media workers and suggest such differences can be traced to the early origins of each medium. For instance, advertising theory and practice grew out of understanding and adherence to principles tied to profit margins, and the radio and television industry developed from entertainment interests. Research by Powers and Lacy outlined a model to illustrate how:

- Factors within journalists,
- Leadership characteristics,
- Organizational settings, and
- Market factors affect a local television newsroom. All four factors affect the perception of goal accomplishment or effectiveness, which in turn affects job satisfaction.

Powers and Lacy found that employees are more satisfied with democratic-oriented leadership than with leadership that is autocratic in nature. They suggested that;"this does not mean news directors cannot make their own decisions, but rather that many, if not most, decisions should also include participation by the journalists". If leadership is seen as a dynamic activity, then managers will need to explore intellectually and pragmatically what is effective for the moment as well as for the long-term corporate climate.

Newspapers are the products of historical institutional clashes. Typically newspapers have crusaded against political and government entities, business organizations, religious groups, military structures, and others. Indeed, in the United States the First Amendment is written specifically to protect what U.S.'s founding fathers felt was a crucial voice of future dissent. Therefore, the conflict between the news department and all other departments of a medium is to be expected and supported, some scholars say. Bagdikian suggested such tension between the news department and all other departments is a necessary ingredient in media companies.

And, according to Bagdikian, the health of the industry depends on corporate support of the uniqueness of the news department in both broadcast and newspaper companies. The tendency for news editorial employees to be skeptical, untrusting, and suspicious of colleagues within their own news organization, may be seen as anhistorical "condition" sanctioned by professional expectations of those within the field. It is, however, also an obvious and peculiar managerial challenge to provide leadership for employees who routinely are rewarded for their instincts to question and resist authority. Indeed, one editor readily and proudly agrees that the editorial office of a newspaper is a"subculture"within the larger newspaper culture. He believes a newspaper ultimately must be a reflection of personalities who are willing to become identified with and take a stand for what their product is. This notion of personalizing the media company has ample historical reference with Pulitzer, Hearst, Luce, and even more recently Neuharth and Turner providing identity for famous successful media conglomerates.

Personalized Management

Weber distinguished his concept of charismatic leadership by defining it in terms of a psychological need of followers to become committed to a leader who might guide them out of a difficult situation. It is beyond hero worship, Weber said, and has a base in the idea that the charismatic leader should recognize this quality and act on it. He went on to say that this devotion by followers can arise out of enthusiasm, despair, or hope.

It appears then, that charismatic leadership would not occur in a traditional corporate setting unless employees are ripe for deliverance via personality-based leadership. Also, the bond between charismatic leader and follower requires a unidirectional model in that followers are seen to be acted on by a leader. That is, followers tend to see themselves as subordinate to the professional abilities and strategic thinking capabilities of the leader. Charismatic leadership is recognized as a legitimate category that is distinct from more routine definitions of managers or administrators. Charisma is often discussed in terms of transactional and transforming leadership. The former is as an exchange between leaders and followers that could be built

on economic, political, or psychological bonds that continues only as long as leaders and followers find it mutually beneficial. Transforming leadership involves the initiation of a relationship with followers that has each encouraging the other through motivation and morality. Interactive relationships suggest that leaders do not act on followers but that followers somehow agree to the relationship because it is a satisfying one. Yet, it is still clearly the leader who is the definer of what is important. That is, goals are set by the charismatic leader--not by the leader and followers working together. Efforts to quantitatively measure the effectiveness of charismatic leadership have been mixed and generally disappointing.

However, charisma retains powerful anecdotal meaning within the context of media and other businesses, so it is included here as one of several legitimate recognizable leadership styles. Several media executives have been known as charismatic leaders. In summary, the research on leadership has been built upon several theoretical assumptions:

- Criteria for measuring leadership vary. They can include but are not limited to: task completion or production quotas, goals set by supervisors and organizations, or they can be subordinate morale.
- Certain leadership characteristics are thought to be identifiable and measurable and thus capable of being studied and taught.
- Leadership criteria cannot be assumed to be culturally adaptive, and differences in findings among different cultures are present.
- Personality factors contribute to leadership.
- Situational as well as legal, traditional, task, and charismatic leadership are recognized.

EFFECTIVE COMMUNICATION

Everyone agrees that communication is key to the efficient and effective management of a work force. Managers who are adept at communicating can unite, commit, and motivate employees to cooperate successfully for a common goal. Managers who are poor communicators can alienate, distract, and destroy employee momentum and energy. Managers communicate informally and formally with staff and intend for messages to be heard and understood. However, they should be aware that misunderstandings are to be expected, and feedback with quick correction should be built into any corporate communication system.

Traditional theory was built on the assumption that leaders are rule givers who tell employees what to do and when to do it, act as disciplinarians and punish those who do not obey company procedures. Although media managers do share some of these responsibilities, they most often supervise employees who are comfortable with autonomy and limited supervision. In addition, the media are change-oriented and technology driven so that work systems have to be constantly reconfigured to meet customer needs for new and better products, markets, and delivery systems. Clearly leadership requires a productive relationship between managers and employees, but there is not much agreement on the nature of that relationship.

Leaders, according to Schein, have the ability to communicate organizational messages in at least five different ways:

- By focusing on and measuring and controlling variables;
- By reacting to crises or other important events;
- By coaching and teaching;
- By promoting, recruiting, and excommunicating.

If leaders are consistent in actions supporting these five criteria and if they embellish these actions with stories, myths, and formal statements, the culture can be"managed"and maintained quite effectively. Cultures can be upset by contrary evidence that the criteria in place are wrong or inappropriate, by the emergence of a charismatic leader who readjusts the value system, or by the current culture's failure to meet expectations in some important way. That is, if a media company has as one of its major values community service, and employees have an abiding understanding of that value, the products the employees help develop will reflect that value.

However, if for some reason the products become unimportant to the community, or the employees decide because of leadership or self-initiative that the internal value should be social responsibility, which they see as the antithesis of community service, the company culture could change dramatically. Basically, leaders remind staff"who we are"and"what we do."Confusion, and even anarchy, can occur when management delivers unclear or dysfunctional communication. Therefore, it is important that leaders explore all the options they have to communicate.

Written Communication

Typically employee handbooks offer managers the opportunity to communicate with staff in all five ways outlined by Schein. That is, they clarify how staff will be hired, fired, and retired; outline hours of work and attendance policies; identify holidays; explain payroll deductions and set paydays; specify when and how performance will be reviewed and promotions considered; outline how salaries will be determined; list vacation time allowance; define insurance benefits; and outline behavioral and professional expectations. A handbook is generally desirable for five or more employees, essential at 10 and imperative for companies with 15 or more employees because Federal Civil Rights, Americans with Disabilities, and Pregnancy Leave Acts apply to companies with 15 or more employees.

It is important for employees to know what is expected of them and what can be expected in return. Job satisfaction is enhanced for employees when benefits and disciplinary policies are well known, and the company has a measure of assurance that managers will take basically the same course of action in similar circumstances. Because they serve as a contract, they are written in formal language meant to outline expectations (on the part of both the company and employees) and resolve or mediate future workplace conflicts. They should promise equitable and consistent treatment of all employees. Expected standards of behaviour also should be included in the handbook.

An example of this content is the Employment Opportunity Commission's (EEOC) definition of sexual harassment, which is,"unwelcome"sexual attention, whether verbal or physical, that affects an employee's job conditions or creates a hostile' working environment". The EEOC guidelines were issued in 1980 and unanimously affirmed by the Supreme Court in 1986. Many companies not only have a written statement about harassment but also require training sessions for certain managers to help understand the meaning and spirit of the law. However, some media companies either do not have employee handbooks or fail to use or refer to the ones they have. This increases their vulnerability to lawsuits or claims from government agencies. For instance, if a manager fires an employee for being late the company may face a lawsuit or a claim from a government agency if there is no carefully spelled out written policy on tardiness--particularly if other employees have suffered no consequences for tardiness (a lack of consistency in enforcing rules can be grounds for discrimination claims). Written job descriptions not only assist in hiring the best possible employees but set the standards for future performance reviews. All job descriptions should state the job title, list the purpose of the job, state the essential duties and responsibilities, outline education and experience expectations, and describe required skills.

For in stance, a news manager hiring a person to start a web page might advertise for a webmaster (job title); with a journalism or related degree (education); with at least 2 years production experience on a web page (level of experience); who knows HTML, link translations, scanning procedures, and Associated Press (AP) stylebook (skills); who will compose and produce a weekly web page; that will appear every Thursday by 12 pm with rewrites of major local, national, and international news wire stories about lifestyle, sports, and business topics and include movement, colour, graphics, and real-time media (essential duties). A detailed description provides guidance for equitable analysis and selection of job applicants, suggests relevant interview questions, provides standards for reward/discipline and assessment, and specifies standards for dismissal.

Verbal Communication

One of the most important conversations managers and employees will hold occurs during the job interview. Media managers should thoroughly discuss not only job expectations but the motivations workers hold. For instance, it is not unreasonable for managers to ask prospective employees what would cause them to resign and what their overall professional goals are. Such blunt and direct conversations about expectations rarely have occurred outside of mandated or written union understandings. However, it makes sense for managers--and employees--to initiate such conversations before employment commitments are made. One media manager said such a discussion is now a part of all her interview conversations with prospective employees."I don't want any surprises after I spend the time and money to hire someone."

Discussions should occur on a regularly scheduled formal basis with all employees. This can occur on a monthly, semiannual, or annual basis. These reviews provide managers with the opportunity to discuss problems, recognize outstanding performance, and motivate workers who may need support or encouragement. However, informal encounters are also important and should be scheduled so that managers can observe and notice behaviors and complaints that need minimal, immediate attention before they build into major problems. In the formal setting, employees have the opportunity to self-report about their work-related successes and complaints, and in the informal setting managers have the opportunity to observe how employees are working. Both events should be recorded by the manager. Although the best communication is face to face and all formal performance review sessions are conducted in this way, much can be accomplished by phone, e-mail, or meetings.

Phone and e-mail provide opportunities for discussion as well as debate. If the manager has a good relationship and high trust with the employee, then the informality of the phone and e-mail may work in a positive way. With minimum effort, e-mail as well as voice mail can provide the opportunity for sharing news at the same time with many employees. E-mail also allows employees to ask questions as well as clarify and discuss options even if everyone involved is not in the same office location or same time zone. Meetings, however, are probably the communication mechanism of choice for managers. Mosvick studied meetings from 1981-1995 and found that the average number of meetings jumped from 7 to about 10 a week for all business professionals. Unfortunately many meetings are simply a time drain rather than a productive event. A study by 3M Meeting Network, an online resource, says that managers spend between 25 per cent and 60 per cent of their time in meetings but as much as 50 per cent of that time is unproductive. Studies even show that meetings can trigger stress in employees unless they foster creativity, reach collective agreement, or gain consensus. All meetings should have an agenda, time limit (20-40 minutes is ideal), and provide follow-up information about decisions made following the meeting.

Team-Building Implications

Work teams are among the business trends that have been integrated into media companies. Emerging technologies, expanding international markets, and the necessity for interdepartmental collaboration have fueled the effort. The purpose of a team is to work efficiently and effectively to identify opportunities and problems, which may seem short-term but in reality have long-term implications. For instance, the decision to"try out"a new media product (e.g. a newspaper zone edition, a"smart"TV, or a web site) requires a team effort to research, develop, produce, distribute, and assess its viability. This kind of team would be task-oriented with a specific product as its goal. Decision teams, on the other hand, might define goals, prepare budgets, or study changing political and economic climates to determine long-term company strategies.

For teams to succeed, the commitment must be strongly supported by management--particularly top levels. This means that mission statements mention teams, and at least one top corporate officer is assigned to develop and provide resources for teams. Secondly, criteria for measuring and rewarding team efforts must be clear. Pay or salary need not be the reward for progress, but something of significant value (to team members) must be offered. Third, resources must be clearly allocated. This is usually time and money. And finally, the purpose of the teamwork should be clear with specific questions and problems identified.

If the team is working well, then the goals are strong and clear to everyone (everyone in the group can independently state objectives that match what others say and think). Everyone in the team understands their role and knows how that role contributes to the results. The work climate is positive, supportive, and trusting. People willingly communicate in open and direct ways sharing data, information, and opinions. When differences occur they are recognized and resolved through negotiation and consensus. Everyone participates in decisions without regard to title or power. Everyone agrees to follow decisions made by the team. A manager must know how to select and coach a team of employees as well as how to train them to work as a self-directed entity. Team members may have different backgrounds, levels of education, expertise, experience, and company titles. Team members also might have different professional needs for achievement, power, or affiliation. Making a diverse group of employees into a productive team is not an easy task, however it is essential. Teams should spend considerable time agreeing on a common set of goals or a shared vision of what they want to accomplish. Next, they must see diversity as a positive value. That is, they should identify skills, backgrounds, cultures, expertise, and experiences that may impact their collective result. There should be a commitment to using all the resources and strengths of the individuals to help the team.

Leadership of the team can occur several ways. The team can have an appointed leader who has direct influence and control. Or the leader can organize, train, and facilitate the team but not directly influence its work. The team can select its own leader, rotate leadership, or it can even operate without a leader (committee of the whole). The team also has flexibility in terms of how often and how long it meets.

For some teams sharing information by e-mail or by phone is satisfactory, but other types of teams might require a high level of interaction. A team working on a new book might meet once to agree on content, time frame and style rules. E-mail or phone conversations would occur as questions arose or changes were ordered by the publisher, but most of the teamwork would be accomplished independently. However, a news team putting out a special edition on a hurricane that just passed through town would work closely conferring every hour about new information, pictures or film that were available, interviews that had been completed, and overall presentation choices.

A team is only as effective as its ability to plan for and deal with predictable problems. One such difficulty is passive behaviour by team members. Sometimes artificial agreement occurs when team members are dependent, immature, and have no desire to confront controversial issues. Or team members may have learned over time that conformity is the least stressful option when dealing with a particular leader. Some team members may resist participation if they have little or no trust in the leader and feel they must protect and guard themselves. Other problems may occur between team members if they do not trust one another or they are unwilling or unable to accept differences.

However, most problems can be reduced to differences in expectations. If behaviour of one person does not meet expectations of another person then negative reactions result. If there is no resolution, the team members can become hostile and the team effort destroyed. Therefore, one of the most important tasks of any team, is to identify not only general expectations for the team, but expectations each individual holds about his or her role and the role of all other members of the team. For instance, if Team Member

A"expects"everyone will turn in their work on deadline there must be verbal and written agreement and commitment (from all members of the team) for that expectation to be met successfully.

The Case of Planning Human Resources For WXPT

WXPT is a network affiliate television station in a southern city with a population of 300,000. It is the centre of a metro area of 500,000 people and 216,000 households. You are general manager of the station, and your investment in the local television news department during your 3 years has paid off with growing ratings and shares for both the evening and late-night newscasts.You credit your success to the heavy emphasis of local coverage in your newscast. In your 3 years as station manager the news budget has grown by 50 per cent. Your newsroom now has one director, three producers, six news reporters, two anchors, one sports anchor, one sports reporter, two weather reporters, and 10 camera people.The 5-year strategic plan calls for expanding the early evening newscast to I hour from its current 30-minute format.

The local news will run from 5:30-6:30 pm with the network newscast moved to the 6:30 pm slot. In addition, the station is upgrading its equipment and studio, and production training will be required for nearly all staff. The changes are scheduled to take place in 6 months, so it is important that a human resource plan be developed. The current staff include the following: Jim, a White, 51-year-old man, has been an anchor for 12 years and a reporter for 20 years. He is managing editor and is perceived by viewers as steady and trustworthy. Although Jim is well liked, it is clear he enjoys his status and frequently reminds younger staff members of their lack of experience when he thinks they are acting arrogant. Sandy is a 25-year-old White woman who has been working as co-anchor with Jim for 2 years.

Recent research indicates both men and women in the market think she is beautiful and pleasant. She is not a strong reporter and did not attend college although she has worked as an anchor for two other stations prior to joining this one. Jim frequently corrects her pronunciation and her adlibs, which invariably include factual errors. She has worked hard to achieve her current position and is proud of herself, although she quietly resents Jim's oversight of her work. She thinks she could take over as anchor if Jim were to leave the station.

David is the 57-year-old White weatherperson. He has a college degree in meteorology and is highly respected by viewers, however he has been hinting that he might retire unless the terms of his 5-year-contract (which expires at the end of the year) are favorable. David is very task-oriented and does not appreciate wasted conversation or work time. Although not rude, he is curt and does not socialize with staff members outside the station. Janice is a 30-year-old African American who was born and raised in the area and has been at the station as a weatherperson for 4 years. She is not a certified meteorologist, but she is a quick learner and has been trained well by David who thinks she does a wonderful job. She appreciates David's training and help but wishes she had a mentor who was better at communicating. She enjoys relationships, and she would like to be better friends with more of the staff, but she is afraid David will disapprove if he observes her casually talking with coworkers.

The sports anchor is Harve, a 42-year-old White man, who joined the staff 14 months ago after he was recruited from the second-place station in the market. He has fit in well except for a few conflicts with Jim over treatment of sports news. Jim wants him to deal with social issues and sports whereas Harve wants to just give highlights and scores. Harve is well liked by the staff who enjoy his jokes and friendly ways. The staff sense tension between Jim and Harve and hope it never escalates into open warfare.

Susan is the number two sports anchor. She joined the station I year ago after she left the local newspaper claiming sexual discrimination. She is currently suing the newspaper publisher for repeated sexual harassment. The station received a large amount of positive mail from viewers when it hired her. She was hired because of her expertise in baseball and car racing, both important sports in the area. In addition to anchoring the weekend sports spot, she also reports during the week. She has received good but not glowing evaluations during her first year on the air.

Her weak points have been coordinating film with words, although her evaluations acknowledge her outstanding writing. When Susan first arrived, she was grateful to have a job, but recently she has become disenchanted with the station and wonders if she made the right decision. She does not like editing and cutting news into small pieces, but she is excited by the upcoming changes that will provide more news time. She secretly hopes the station will consider giving her a leadership role in the planning phase because she likes analyzing and coordinating ideas and details. However, she is reluctant to make her desires known because she feels she is too inexperienced and new to offer suggestions.

Leslie is the star reporter. She is a 30-year-old African American who grew up in the area. She joined the station immediately after graduating from the local university with a degree in journalism. She has been named Outstanding Broadcast Journalist for the state for her in-depth reports on problems facing cities. Many people have pointed out she could be working at a network or in a much larger market, and indeed she has turned down such offers because of family commitments in the area. Although she is achievement-oriented, her most striking professional need is affiliation, and she values the relationships she has made at the station and with her sources. The major skill that has contributed to her reporting success is her ability to put people at ease and to build trust. That is the same characteristic that draws people at the station to her. She is the best-liked and most respected member of the staff. The other reporters are all White males and relatively new to the business although they hold college degrees in journalism.

Shutting Down and Moving On

Nancy is the public relations (PR) vice president for a corporation that is facing a corporate move to another state. Her department is small, but she must figure out a way to complete the department's work with even fewer people because the corporation only will be able to move four people including herself. She has not been able to tell her staff of the move because the president has asked all vice presidents to keep the news to themselves until he makes an official announcement in 2 months. Her task is to cut her staff and to reduce department salary lines.

Her first consideration is expertise and level of production. She needs to retain people who work quickly and efficiently and fire people who are marginal in their performance. She also wants to retain people who can work together well because increased patience and cooperation will be required in the months ahead. And finally, she appreciates staff who are creative and take risks because many times her department is called on to develop campaigns and projects that are unusual, clever and memorable. The president has told her to cut $150,000 in salaries from her budget.

Although Nancy has been in charge of the department, she has not worked closely with the staff because she serves as the personal advisor to the president and delegates direct supervision of the department to 52-year-old Marge, who earns $64,000 per year. Marge is a design expert and has purchased the software and hardware necessary to create most PR packages internally saving thousands of dollars over the years. Nancy hired Marge and considers her a loyal and valuable employee. Ed is the chief technician and photographer, and his work on the recent annual reports has won national awards for the corporation. His work is creative, professional and always produced on deadline. He has, however, taken many personal leave and sick days, which Marge suspects are spent with his family and Church, because he is very religious. He earns $45.000.

Charlie is 28-years-old and has a background in news. He is a graceful writer who prepares copy for all the corporate publications including the annual report, the brochures, and promotional packages. He is very ambitious and has made friends with several corporate officers. He tends to gossip, and so Marge tells him little about the overall office chores unless he is directly involved. Although she appreciates his talent and performance, she is cautious with him because she believes he is more concerned with his career than with the corporation. He earns $38,000. Madeline is 22-years-old and started with the corporation as a college intern when she was 20. She is a graphic designer and works with Ed.

She is very creative and although she is young and relatively inexperienced she has made several suggestions that have been followed by the department. She is quiet and has not made friends easily, and Marge is not certain she is happy although her performance has been excellent. She earns $29,000.Paul is 35 and has many of the same skills and background Marge has. He is well respected by the people in the department and is very witty. Many times he has helped Marge with personnel issues because he recognizes problems and is able to diffuse them with a kind or witty word that generally soothes egos. Although he is very respectful of Marge he wonders if she is best suited to manage the unit because her communication skills are sometimes too harsh. He genuinely loves his work, but he wants a raise. He has been reluctant to ask for one because he has heard rumors the corporation is moving and will fire some people. He earns $40,000 and needs his job because his wife has just had a baby and quit her job.

9

Online Networks

ONLINE PUBLISHING WORKS

The narrowband online industry is not new. In fact, it is the oldest and richest sector of the electronic media industry. Although our attention in recent years has been grabbed by the headlines about the rapid growth of CD-ROM markets, revenues generated by all forms of packaged media still remain-despite recent growth-small compared to online. By the end of 1995, the world market was probably worth $14 billion compared to a total for CD-ROM titles of about $3.5 billion. The difference is that online has taken 30 years to reach its current level while CD-ROM was invented only 10 years ago (1985). In fact, the history of the online industry is of a slow and faltering business model which, for some years, looked as if it was running into a commercial dead end.

We will not go into the details of that history now but we can establish some basic understanding of how online works today by examining some of the key factors determining the past developments in this sector. Most important of these is how online has attempted to leverage the unique attributes of digital information delivered over a one-to-one network and what we can learn from this about current and future business models in this sector. Before we look at these unique features, it will be useful to clarify what an online network is and how the traditional business model for online publishing works.

There are three important elements to a commercial online system. At its heart is the information to be commercialised. This is hosted as a structured database on a host computer. The host is the basic repository which is drawn upon to provide customers with the information they need. Attached to the host (or sometimes a part of the same computer) is the server. This provides the computing power needed both to regulate the flow of incoming enquiries and to inject responses into the network. The host-server system is linked by an ISDN or faster line into the telephone network which acts as the link with customers. In the jargon of the industry, the computers that customers use to connect themselves to the online service are termed clients. In practice they are usually conventional desktop PCs equipped with a modem to allow an exchange of digital data over the telephone network. Each client is given an identification code and some access software by the online publisher which allow it to dial up the service and make contact with the server and host computers. The client can, in principle, be anywhere in the world where there is access to a telephone line.

In practice, operators of online services often establish a distributed network of subsidiary servers in key cities which feed the central server and host. The advantage of doing this is that it means clients need dial up only their most local server and this cuts telephone bills substantially. For example, a client in London using a particular online service may be accessing a host physically located in the United States. If the client has to make direct contact with the host, the client has to pay the cost of the telephone connection.

This would make it unlikely that such a US host would have many UK clients. But if the online publisher has built points of presence in Europe and, in particular, in London, the client needs to make only a local call to get into the online system. The telecommunications charges between London and the United States still have to be paid, of course, but in this case they are absorbed by the online publisher and reflected in the charges to the client. This shifting around of telecommunications charges is important because online service operators can negotiate special bulk rates for long-distance phone traffic because they bring to the telephone companies a large number of individual users. This means they can get access to long-distance telephony at a fraction of the cost to individual users and make the process of intercontinental online communication relatively painless.

The traditional business model for an online publishing operation of this kind is usually based on a single strand of revenue generation. Customers subscribe to a service, usually for an annual payment, and are then charged for access to the service on a pay-as-you-go basis. Specifically, charges are most commonly calculated on the length of time that a user is actually online to the service. This process of connect-time charging is increasingly giving way to other forms of access deals but still remains the backbone of the industry.

The Uniqueness of Online Networks

Now we should return to the key attributes of online information which form the basis of the commercial offerings of these services. There are five really important ones:

- Infinite storage
- Searchability
- Real-time updating
- Global access
- Communications

Infinite Storage

The database hosted by an online system can be huge. It is constrained only by the memory of the host computer and since such memory can always be extended by simply bolting on some more hard disk, the database can effectively be any size you want. Massive databases can offer a comprehensiveness in a given subject area that no other medium can match and this can be a persuasive feature in such areas as law, medicine or engineering, for example, where access to all available information can sometimes be the difference between success and professional disaster. However, size can bring its own problems.

Simply because there are no real constraints on the size of the database or databases hosted, the publisher, in pursuit of comprehensiveness, may allow the product to become too large. Indeed, because comprehensiveness can become such a strong issue, online publishers in the past have gone to extremes, including much material that is never likely to be accessed. This leads to unnecessarily large databases, requiring users to make ever more lengthy and elaborate searches in order to find what they want. It has also meant that many databases that should never be issued commercially have found their way into the online industry. As a result, for most of its 30 years, online has been a slow-growing business characterised by terrabytes of unwanted and unused data clogging up computer memories all over the world. In other words, the lack of constraint on size sometimes led to a lack of editorial discipline in designing the products and a lot of bad publishing.

SEARCHABILITY

Online information is, of course, searchable. Comprehensiveness is hardly a benefit if users cannot get exactly what they want out of the data mountain, quickly and accurately. The key to this is the search and retrieval software provided to users. This software is effectively the electronic pair of hands which sift the data and locate or correlate information to give users the answers they need. The way the software works, the kinds of searches it can perform and the interface through which the user communicates with it, largely define the power of the online product.

REAL-TIME UPDATING

Online data can be updated on a moment-by-moment basis. This means that online publishing can provide access to fast-changing, time-critical information. In the late 1980s, it was this key feature that transformed the online industry. Up to then, the kinds of databases held online were largely historic in character. In other words, the currency of the information did not change much over time. Then a major transformation reshaped equity, commodity and currency markets as financial centres all over the world became computerised. Known jocularly as 'the big bang' it had very serious implications for international traders handling transactions often valued in billions. Access to the most up-to-date financial information-the raw data of fluctuating exchange rates, commodity values, stock prices-was vital to their competitiveness. In order to make the right judgements at the right times, traders had to pay whatever it might cost to get moment-to-moment feeds of information. Suddenly, online data came into their own purely because of their instant updatability; real-time financial information services exploded as a new and burgeoning sector of the otherwise moribund and slow-growing online industry. Such services carried very high price tags but the value they delivered was commensurately high. After all, a transaction worth many millions could depend on the intelligence delivered by such a service. Its price, therefore, was almost irrelevant.

By the end of the 1980s, nearly 70 per cent of all online revenues were generated by such services. Today, the proportion has settled at around 60 per cent. Although the real-time financial information services are a vitally important sector, they represent a large but specialist niche. However, they illustrate how a single unique feature of online data can be richly commercialised if the economic need exists in the market-place. They also suggest an important message for the future of online publishing. Online is good at delivering access to fast-changing information. This has value in itself in many sectors beyond international finance.

It is worth noting now that even at a consumer level there is much time-critical information that users value-sports, weather, travel information, for example-and in designing services for these markets, even though they are radically different from such niches as finance and more general business applications, online's incomparable ability to deliver volatile information should always come high on the list of features to exploit. It is also worth remembering that access to volatile information not only delivers operational value to those who need the up-to-date-ness but also-where it is important as a sales proposition conveys a dynamic experience to its users. This can be a key feature in exciting and retaining interest among users, particularly in consumer markets.

GLOBAL ACCESS

Online services recognise no territorial boundaries. Just as we can make telephone calls all over the world thanks to the interconnection of national telephone networks, so we can access online systems from anywhere we can get a phone line. Apart from the unprecedented market reach this gives online services, it also has striking implications for the rights to exploit content. Traditionally such rights are defined by such criteria as the particular form of exploitation intended, the length of time the right to exploit subsists and in which territories-defined by geography or language or both-the exploitations may take place. Online services-particularly those hosted in environments such as the Internet where it is hard (though not impossible) to lock out particular territorial users-place real strain on conventional rights agreements and are pushing such deals towards routinely incorporating a global approach to the licences they embody. There are, of course, other more complex legal issues such as jurisdiction-particularly where a liability issue would be interpreted differently under different jurisdictions.

The obvious issue would be to decide whether illegality took place where the server is located, where the user was when infringing material was accessed or whether the passage of material across the network constituted some kind of moving, international infringement. But, aside from these issues, most online publishers are attracted by the ease with which they can reach international markets. Reach is not the same thing as results, of course, and while networks can span the globe, it is still a major challenge for nationally based services to market their online products effectively on the international stage. The issue, however, is vastly different from having to ship material products like books or CD-ROMs where a traditional distribution value chain has to be commercialised. In the world of online networks the product is in the form of bits not atoms, and distribution in the traditional sense is no longer as important an issue as signalling to the market that you exist, have something to offer and are available from any nearby phone.

COMMUNICATIONS

Finally, online systems can provide communication as readily as they can provide content. This should not be surprising since they utilise networks dedicated to offering one-to-one conversations. But traditionally, this attribute has been the least exploited. The reason is obvious when we look back on the origins and early development of online publishing. The original business objective of such systems was to make access to information available to users on a commercial basis. On the whole, therefore, they were viewed exclusively as publishing operations with little interest in leveraging networks other than as distribution channels-albeit interactive ones-for content. The online systems were therefore configured in the form of a central server with clients accessing the hosted information bolted onto or a part of the server. Electronic mail, of course, was already becoming an accepted part of corporate local area networks-as distinct from wide area commercial publishing networks. But even electronic mail was not the point. Such mail was no more than a messaging service, valuable to be sure, but a million miles away from stranding the kinds of communications experiences into online activity that one day will create true virtual communities bound together not by operational synergies-as in corporate systems-or by geographical locality-as in most real-world communities-but by common interest, aspiration or belief. Increasingly, this notion of virtual community created by the communications power of networks is becoming the key to building a thriving new wired world.

The Evolution of the Online Industry

With so much happening today, we should not dwell too much on history. But history is neither bunk nor boring. Above all, it provides invaluable context. A picture of how online publishing has evolved in recent years tells us much about the way it works today and suggests how it might develop in the future. We have already touched on some of the past trends so we can afford to be brief and provide just the headlines. First, however, we need to emphasise a key distinction between the majority of commercial online networks in the past and a particular and distinctive network environment-the Internet-that has become of overwhelming importance in the 1990s.

The distinction is that, before the emergence of the network as a global publishing and communications phenomenon, online was a world of proprietary networks. In other words, services were kept technically distinct-so that only those paying for access could use them-and were specifically designed for their customers. By contrast, the Internet was created to meet a particular non-commercial need amongst highly computer-literate users-mainly academics and researchers with an urgent desire to exchange information, research threads and ideas with colleagues in other institutions anywhere in the world.

No single commercial organisation decided to create the Internet and no such organisation, therefore, can claim to own it. The Internet's software protocols-the technical infrastructure which makes it work and is largely responsible for what it can do-are available to anyone who is interested in them. That is why there is such a massive industry today amongst individual organisations selling various flavours of Internet access software, usually packaged with Internet access. Because the Internet was designed not by ordinary folk but by people who understood computers, it is an unfriendly and complex environment, only now beginning to be tamed for a wider constituency to use. Neither is it surprising that it is proving so difficult to build structures on the Internet to allow the secure trading of services and products. The Internet was never conceived or designed for the purpose. Proprietary networks on the other hand-if they are wisely implemented-can be made simple and attractive to use and optimised from the outset for commercial exploitations.

It is ironic, however, that the early online services were actually anything but easy to use. Indeed, in the 1970s and for much of the 1980s, the available networks were hard to access, difficult to navigate and expensive. Not a cocktail designed to promote rapid growth and, sure enough, growth was slow and unsteady. The reason why the original proprietaries were so unsatisfactory by today's standards was not a reflection of commercial incompetence but a natural result of the primitive state of computing and telecommunications. Surveys in the early 1980s, for example, demonstrated that one of the reasons why customers resisted using online services was because of the difficulty of logging on. And logging on was difficult simply because telephone connections often did not work, or worked and then broke down in the middle of the online session. In Europe, during this period, as many as one-third of all online transactions were aborted because users could not make the telephone call needed to secure an online connection.

Even if users managed to make a stable connection, their problems were only just beginning. The databases offered were typically very large and the search and retrieval engines were accordingly extremely powerful. But power brings its downside-particularly in the Stone Age of the early 1980s. Because the search systems had to perform complex tasks they were difficult to use. The command languages needed to make them search quickly and accurately were unfriendly and difficult to learn. The problem was compounded by the cost of using the services. Connect-time was priced very highly and forced users to get in and out of the databases as fast as possible in order to minimise charges. This placed added pressure on being able to drive the search software efficiently.

The usual solution, still common today, was to use trained intermediaries skilled in using a range of search engines, to carry out the searches for the actual end users of the information. In other words, those needing the answers had to convey their questions to the intermediaries who would plan and devise a suitable search strategy to sift the required information from the online database. Once they were sure of the strategy they would log on and plunge into the database, grab the results of their search and log off. Needless to say, this was the framework for a low volume, high priced publishing business aimed at academic, corporate and professional users with a very strong 'need to know'.

The high cost of connect-time, coupled to the unfriendliness of the search software, had another result. Any readers who are also Woody Allen fans will remember that sublime moment in Manhattan when Allen and Diane Keaton are in the back of a taxi travelling through the neon-lit streets of New York. Allen, gazing at Keaton, murmurs: 'God...you're so beautiful, I can hardly keep my eyes on the meter.' The experience of using traditional online systems was much the same. The information may well have been the most desirable of prizes but the pressure of connecttime charging meant that users were always aware of a figurative meter ticking up the ultimate bill. In other words, there was no time for gazing, just for grabbing what was needed and getting out.

This meant that browsing in online services was unknown. The traditional charging model was not designed to encourage users to maximise their use of services but actually to minimise it. Even today, the paradox of charging for online services on a connect-time basis is that it serves to inhibit online activity rather than promote it. Given the difficulties of using these traditional forms of online service, it is not surprising that their market was confined to computer users with a strong operational reason for wanting information delivered online. There was certainly no element of pleasure or entertainment-raw need was the driver. Nonetheless, the computerisation of the world's financial markets in the late 1980s gave-as we have seen-a major boost to the industry and together with improvements in telecommunications, more intuitive search engines and more flexible charging models, online database publishing markets have continued to grow at an annual rate of between 9 and 12 per cent, with the lowest level reflecting recession in the world economy at the end of the 1980s. Today professional, corporate and academic online is a substantial and mature industry with about 5,500 databases offered by around 850 online hosts around the world.

But even while the high priced, low volume industry was making its unsteady progress during the 1980s, other operators were creating fledgling services aimed at a radically different market. Companies such as CompuServe, Prodigy and America Online had their eyes on a business based on the low priced, high volume economics of the mass market. The belief fuelling the ambitions of these players was that the routine use of computers in academic, professional and corporate sectors would soon migrate to the home and a new generation of consumers would seek interactive information, entertainment and communication over easy-to-use, low priced networks. In the 1980s when these services first launched their offerings, the vision looked a very distant prospect. But, in the early 1990s, the market they had foreseen suddenly emerged. The computerisation of the home, first and at high speed in the United States, and then at a more leisurely pace in Europe, is creating the installed base of computer users that the consumer online services had been hoping to see.

The Making of a Consumer Market

It is worth reminding ourselves that the story of the evolution of the online industry exactly parallels the growth and development of CD-ROM publishing. In both cases, their origins and commercial centre of gravity lay in the professional and corporate sector. Their business models-based on low volume, high priced products-were similar. And both have changed out of all recognition in recent years with the rapid emergence of an unprecedented market among home users. Of course, none of this is coincidence nor is it the least surprising. Both online and CD-ROM publishing markets track the use of computers.

They have to because computers give access to their offerings and they therefore must follow the patterns of computer usage to find their customers. As the demographics of computer users has widened, so the online and CD-ROM market has grown in line with the change. The reason why major consumer markets for online and CD-ROM have suddenly emerged is because the markets are now tracking the shift of computers into homes. The underlying driver, therefore, has nothing to do with online or CD-ROM in themselves. It is the computerisation of the home with powerful desktop technology that is pulling with it the purchase of CD-ROM drives and modems. The consumer online market, therefore, is a recent phenomenon even if consumer online offerings have been around since the early 1980s. The only difference between then and now is that the service operators have some customers.

Indeed, growth in the market has been phenomenal. Most of the action so far has been in the United States because computerisation of homes has taken place there much more quickly than anywhere else in the world. By the end of 1995, there were around 40 million US homes with at least one PC in them. Out of these, approximately 20 million had PCs with modems making them potential customers of online services. It is important to use the word 'potential' because, as we have already stressed-and this should be engraved on the heart of everyone in the electronic media industry-the possession of technology does not necessarily imply its use.

In 1994, for example, a survey of PC homes with modems in the United States showed that 32 per cent of the modems had never been connected to a telephone line. In other words, ownership of modems, while obviously necessary to the growth of the consumer online market, is not enough to guarantee that growth. Consumers need both the technology and the motivation to use the technology. In the case of online networks, this means not only modems but also a perception that online services are worth using. This is a key area for anyone trying to predict growth patterns to consider. We have spent years in the digital media industry struggling with various statistics purportedly indicating the rise of installed bases of hardware. The logic was obvious.

The rise in the numbers of CD-ROM drives and modems being purchased indicated the rise in the number of CD-ROM drives and modems being used. This was a fair assumption so long as the equipment was relatively costly and purchased as add-ons to computers. Today, the hardware is cheap and is increasingly sold integrated with PCs as part of a routine value package. In other words, PC buyers are getting CD-ROM drives and modems whether or not they particularly want them. Many, of course, may use them avidly, extensively and for ever.

Others may try a CD-ROM title or two or may accept an online service's promotional offer of some free connect-time but then dismiss either or both as unsatisfactory. The underlying market reality, therefore, is that while CD-ROM and online publishing track the demographics of the PC market, the link between the installed base of hardware and a revenue-generating market is weakening. We can no longer rely on the traditional assumption that another modem sold means another long-term customer for online services. The onus is on industry players to commercialise the installed base. They cannot assume that the installed base will come to them.

Consumer Online Networks

We will look first in this section at the rise of proprietary online services, leaving the Internet's remarkable growth in use and influence until later. In reality, the two strands are closely intertwined and the evolution of proprietary services has in recent months and years been largely shaped by the development of Internet services and the extraordinary growth in their use by all kinds of online customers. Indeed, the concept of a network that is, in the traditional sense, proprietary may soon vanish altogether.

To understand the impact of the Internet on the proprietary industry, we need to step back to the time a few years ago when the Internet was simply not an issue in consumer markets. In the early 1990s, the few networks designed for consumers were just beginning to feel the impact of an emerging market-place. At the end of 1993, the total number of subscribers to consumer online services was around 3 million, almost all in the United States. Two years later, the number had grown to around 10 million. The rapid growth brought both joys and anguish.

The proprietary networks suddenly had customers and their huge infrastructure, content and marketing investments could at last be clawed back. But with customers came competition and an increasingly savage battle for market share. The battle-fought almost exclusively in the United States-has resolved itself into fierce competition between the three major players: CompuServe, the only one with a long-standing presence outside the US market, America Online (AOL), the fastest growing of the three, and the IBM/Sears joint venture, Prodigy, arguably the weakest of the main contenders. The ferocity of the competition was fuelled by a single disquieting factor. As the numbers of subscribers grew, it became increasingly evident that consumers using online services were not easily persuaded to spend money on those services beyond the initial subscription. To understand the implications of this we need to examine the basic business model on which all the main services are based.

Consumer online services have a very simple and persuasive proposition for subscribers. They offer for a modest monthly payment-typically a few dollars-access to a 'warehouse' of content and service offerings. CompuServe, for example, has over 3,000 products on the shelves of its warehouse and rightly argues that amongst such a vast selection there must surely be something to attract everyone. This tells us something important about subscribers to these kinds of services. They form a potentially large but very unfocused constituency. No single thread of interest or common concern has drawn them together, merely the attraction of a low cost key to a treasure house of information, entertainment and communications. The implication of this proposition is that the networks have to attract very large numbers of subscribers to make their business model work. In other words, the approach is to build a high volume of users, each spending relatively small amounts.

But networks ardently hope to be able to increase those relatively small amounts by getting consumers to spend money beyond their basic monthly subscriptions. While the subscription buys the key to the door, users generally only get a few hours of free connect-time-currently varying between five and ten hours per month-and if they remain online longer they are billed at a modest rate per hour.

Additionally, not all the products and services in the warehouse are free. Many of them may be considered premium offerings, attracting an additional charge for use, based either on connect-time or a flat fee. Some genres of services, of course, are always free. For example, transactional services such as home shopping or travel reservations are free to users-who could imagine charging a fee allowing entry to a shop?-with networks getting a commission on the value of transactions conducted by their subscribers. Taken together, therefore, consumer networks aim to generate enough revenue from all these sources to cover their continuing investment in computing and telecommunications infrastructure, marketing and content.

The cost of content, of course, varies enormously but the key point to appreciate about network operators is that traditionally they have owned none themselves. In other words, all the content offered from their warehouses is licensed from content owners. We will look at the basis of these licences shortly but for now it is important to understand that the networks are merely packagers of content acquired from third parties. As packagers, their decisions about what to license and how to deploy services based on what they license, crucially distinguishes them from their competitors and ultimately determines whether or not they attract and retain customers.

We now need to return to the realities of the market-place. We have outlined the way that consumer networks attempt to derive revenue from their subscribers. Their objective is to build a large constituency, retain and grow it and ultimately commercialise it by generating revenue from its use of online services. The reality has been a shattering blow. It is still not entirely clear what consumers like doing online but it is apparent what they do not like doing. Sadly for the online companies, they do not like spending money. In other words, typical consumers pay their subscriptions and then use no more than the 'free' connect-time included each month.

They tend to avoid premium services and use instead the free services such as electronic mail and communications-based offerings such as forums and real-time chat areas. The position is easily confirmed. Just look at the revenues that consumer online services generate compared to the average number of subscribers they have. The arithmetic is changing fast now that access to the Internet has become a part of their offerings but, on the whole, in 1995 at least the total revenues of the companies could be roughly calculated by multiplying their average number of subscribers by the average cost of subscribing to the service. This has one very powerful message for the big players among the proprietary online services. They have a vital battle to fight to gain as much market share as possible. The only way they can build their revenues-at least, based on the traditional charging model-is to increase the raw number of their subscribers. On the basis of their experience, it does not seem to matter who their subscribers are-there is no one demographic group that appears to be prepared to spend more than another-so sheer quantity is the issue. The result has been two-fold. First, the majors have launched aggressive and sustained marketing campaigns. Vast numbers of floppy disks are being given away embodying access software for their networks combined with trial offers providing a free access for limited periods. Second, the fierce competition has driven down monthly subscription and additional connect-time charges. In an increasingly vicious spiral, this has in turn served to intensify the need to win even more subscribers.

A key weapon in this competitive free-for-all is content and, in particular, strongly branded content. We need, therefore, to consider how the network operators are managing the acquisition and deployment of content in order to attract and retain customers. Traditionally, the proposition for content companies has not been especially appealing. The arrangement was known as the '80:20' deal meaning that the network licensing the content retained 80 per cent of all revenue generated through use of the content, leaving 20 percent for the content owners. In practice, this percentage break varied around 15-30 per cent going to providers of content, depending on how badly the network wanted the particular content concerned. A strongly branded product such as a bestselling magazine or globally acclaimed news service might be so desirable that networks would pay up to 50 per cent plus a substantial advance. In cases where the content was not going to become a premium offering and would, therefore, not generate income directly from network use, a fee was negotiated, the size of the amount again depending on the desirability of the content.

But the split of the revenue or the fee paid was only one aspect of the overall deal. Traditionally, networks would drive a hard bargain on payment and then force through other conditions. Usually, they would require partial or complete exclusivity from the content owner. They would retain complete control over the design of the service created using the content and determine its pricing. Apart from any other consideration, this means that strongly branded content would find the look and feel of its branding subsumed by the network's branding. Whoever you were in the real world and however well known you were for being it, on the networks you became firmly a CompuServe, AOL or Prodigy offering with your branding only deployed to support theirs. Lastly, network operators are able to track in detail what their individual subscribers do when they access services but all these valuable consumer data would be retained by the network. Content companies would merely receive a bald statement of usage each month with no indication even of who generated the usage let alone what they did while accessing the service. In other words, the network owned the customers and the content companies hosted on the network could gain no access to them. This simplifies what has in reality been a much more complex picture. In practice, there are many other potential ingredients in a deal and much room for negotiation between the parties. But the elements outlined above demonstrate a single, unquestionable fact. The traditional deal between consumer online companies and content owners was always strongly weighted in favour of the online companies. Why then did content consent to these unattractive terms?

The answer is telling because it reminds us of a fast disappearing attitude in the world of content. The reason that content did the deals was because the online companies were the only show in town and content had no intention or possibility of exploiting its assets independently. At the time these deals were commonplace, content was entirely dedicated to its traditional channels of delivery. The only exception was some experimentation with CD-ROM publishing. But there were few content companies who saw a future in which they might seek to leverage their assets across a wide range of electronic platforms and channels of delivery. Content still saw itself in its traditional niches dedicated to its usual forms of product and delivery mechanism. The idea, for example, that a book publisher might extend its core business by developing its own online service was a sheer flight of fancy. The possibility of getting its content hosted online-however miserly the terms-was therefore an added value opportunity and any revenue generated was a bonus.

Three important factors have combined to reshape this traditional position and have served to redefine the relationship between content and proprietary networks. First, competition has forced online players to bid increasingly highly for the most valued content assets. In 1995, for example, some of Time Inc.'s flagship magazines were prised away from AOL by CompuServe with an upfront payment well into seven figures. Second, content is now increasingly aware that markets are emerging rapidly for digital media and that content interpreted appropriately for such media will determine commercial success. Content companies, therefore, are growing acutely aware that as information, entertainment and education markets increasingly go digital, their conventional media assets are acquiring an additional and growing potential value. Third, content now has somewhere else to go and, for the first time, can seriously contemplate setting up its own online initiatives cheaply, quickly and globally. In other words, the rise of the non-proprietary Internet has provided content owners with an unprecedented opportunity to find autonomy in online publishing without the need for investing huge sums in infrastructure and software. All these factors have forced great change upon the business practices of the proprietary majors. In terms of their relationships with content companies, the old '80:20' arrangement has been widely revised to become a '20:80' deal, advantage now having swung to favour content. And exclusivity is rarely requested, except when extremely high fees or royalties are paid. The only exception among the major players to this shift in emphasis is AOL, which retains its tough 80:20 policy. Tellingly, the reason for this is that AOL is the least dependent of all the proprietaries on content, favouring instead communications-based services such as forums, conferences and chat areas-the kinds of online experiences which consumers seem to relish most. Something of a wild card also driving change in the relationships between content and online service operators has been the emergence of two new online platforms. The first, known as Interchange, was created by the online division of Ziff Davis and was subsequently acquired by AT & T as part of the break-up of the Ziff Davis publishing empire at the end of 1994.

The second was the new proprietary network created by the Microsoft Corporation and today known widely as MSN (standing for the Microsoft Network). AT & Ts Interchange is a publishing platform, a software structure that can, in principle, be utilised by different proprietary players. In practice, AT & T expect to commercialise it themselves in the United States, probably delivering a business-oriented service. In Europe, it was widely expected that a company called Europe Online would deploy Interchange as the basis of a new consumer service. It has since changed its strategy and Interchange is beginning to look like an answer in search of a question.

The MSN by contrast is a full consumer online venture and is never likely to be utilised by anyone other than its creators. Indeed, not only is it highly proprietary but also it has been promoted in an intensely proprietary manner. Launched at the same time as Microsoft's important new operating system, Windows 95, in August 1995, access to MSN was embedded in the Windows software. This meant that every new user of Windows 95 would need only to click an icon on their Windows worktop to enter and try out the online service. Since the number of Windows 95 users could grow to tens of millions within a few years, Microsoft's marketing ploy was and is a powerful one-so powerful that it has attracted the eye of the anti-competition regulators in the United States together with the anger of other competitors in the online market. Pressure may now ease, however, since-as we will see when we consider the impact of the Internet more generally on proprietary services-Microsoft, only months after launching the network, is now completely rethinking it, abandoning the original proprietary model and using MSN instead as an influential access point for the subset of the Internet known as the World Wide Web.

Despite their dissimilarities in design and commercial prospects, the reason why we should bracket together the Interchange and MSN as originally conceived is because they present a radically different proposition for both content companies seeking to be hosted online and for consumers seeking to find an online service that both holds their attention and offers an attractive charging model. Unlike the online services which preceded them Interchange and MSN both offer a high degree of autonomy for content companies. To examine this, we will concentrate on Microsoft's original plan for MSN since Interchange is anyway looking increasingly like a lame duck, unlikely to have much future impact on the market.

MSN's original proposition for content companies is interesting because it not only offers a financial deal along the lines of the 20:80 arrangements increasingly becoming current but also allows content companies to build and operate their own sites on the MSN. Using Microsoft's own development tools, contributors to MSN can design the appearance and interactivities of their offerings-so ensuring that their visual brandings are preserved-and control the pricing of their services. This means that MSN is positioning itself not as the ruler of the network, only as the reliable owner of a huge virtual mall. Using this analogy, MSN is the landlord who makes sure the mall is heated, lighted, well signposted and clean (no bugs!) and who does his best to attract and direct visitors to the various stores located in the mall.

The content companies pay their rent to MSN and can then design and set up their own shop fronts, determine what goods they will put on their shelves and how they wish to price them. MSN also deals with all billing and customer management so the payments by users for services purchased are always assured through MSN's secure, centralised procedures. Perhaps most crucially of all, MSN is ready to share information about the demographics of users of the mall and will allow shop owners to access the names of visitors to their stores and to track their activities while inside. This is not perfect since MSN still retains a strong proprietary interest in the data and will not reveal the details of the gross, mall-wide data. However, it is a vast improvement over the usual practice of online operators keeping the data entirely for themselves.

The proposition for MSN subscribers looks less appealing. The underlying concept is to offer a pay-as-you-go experience. Monthly subscriptions to MSN are very modest-just enough to pay for the upkeep of the mall-and charging thereafter depends on the sites within MSN that are visited and the charging policy determined by each site owner. This a la carte approach to an online service appears to make good sense. After all, subscribers can decide for themselves what they buy and the network as a whole does not have to pass on the cost of maintaining a huge body of licensed content via high monthly subscriptions.

The flaw in the logic is obvious. First, a la carte is fine until the bill comes in. Subscribers may find it all too easy to meander around sites buying piecemeal here and there without realising how much money they are spending when it is finally aggregated into a single bill. Second, the low cost of entry to MSN no longer looks especially attractive. Competitive pressure has already driven down the entry cost of accessing the traditional proprietaries. Moreover, those established players show up the weakness of the a la carte model. As efficient packagers of content, their proposition cannot be bettered. Low cost entry into an established body of products or services which are-on the whole-freely available to subscribers. The key point here is not merely a matter of competitive analysis-the issue of whether MSN will succeed against established players-but the continuing powerful role of information intermediaries in online publishing. The traditional online companies are aggregators of both content and consumers. In this sense they act as powerful go-betweens, mediating the relationship of content and its market.

They offer content companies access (at a price) to their powerful, multimillion-strong constituencies and they offer their constituencies low cost access to a distinctive bouquet of content. When we come to examine the role of content on the Internet, we will return to the importance of intermediaries because their strategic influence lies at the heart of successfully commercialising online markets.

CONSUMER ONLINE SERVICES IN EUROPE

Although the underlying principles apply anywhere, many of the commercial activities and market developments we have discussed have been taking place in the United States. And, although we have emphasised that networks do not recognise national boundaries, they are sensitive to market demand. Europe, therefore, has been an arena distinct from the US consumer online market and needs to be examined separately. We will not attempt detailed analysis of European developments-such coverage would be beyond the scope of this book-but it is important at least to examine some of the main themes that are emerging and touch on the principal initiatives that are emerging.

Although the penetration of PCs into European homes has leaped in recent years, the growth of the installed base of modems has been modest. This is not surprising since there has been little infrastructure of consumer online services-outside the business and professional sectors-to attract and drive usage. The only such service with a broadly based offering has been CompuServe which, though based in the United States, has systematically built an infrastructure of points of presence and subsidiary companies in many parts of the world. In Europe-where it began marketing its service in 1989-it has today about 45 points of presence. Its only two success stories so far, however, have been the UK and Germany and even here penetrations have been modest. At the end of 1994, for example, CompuServe's European subscribers numbered around 200,000 compared to its US customer base of around 2 million. In 1995, it has greatly increased the number of its European subscribers but still has fewer than 500,000 compared to about 3 million in the United States. These figures are approximate but give a strong sense of the real centres of gravity of the market-place.

But as the computerisation of the home proceeds and as interest builds in the United States in online markets, a range of European initiatives are emerging, targeting the consumer market in the belief, no doubt, that 'if we build it, they will come'. At the time of writing, for example, Olivetti-Telemedia-the new media arm of the Italian-based computer hardware and communications company Olivetti-has been the main investor in two online ventures: Italia Online in Italy and UK Online (UKOL) in Britain. Both services are strictly national initiatives with no panEuropean ambitions. Elsewhere, pan-European objectives are firmly a part of the recent alliance between America Online and European media giant Bertelsmann. The first fruits of this alliance, announced early in 1995 and now branded AOL Europe, has been the launch of a new German online service with French, British and other national roll-outs planned for 1996 and 1997.

Similarly, Europe Online-a Luxembourg-based start-up with backing from Burda in Germany and Pearson in the UK-has a strong pan-European agenda although, at the time of writing, it is rapidly shifting its strategy towards the Internet and is seemingly struggling to gain the kind of content base that will distinguish its offering to the market. Meantime, despite its dramatic change of strategy at the end of 1995, Microsoft's MSN-conceived ultimately as a global service with points of presence all over the world-is also being strongly promoted in Europe and will become increasingly significant as the preferred portal to the Internet as Windows 95-with which MSN access is bundled-becomes more popular with European PC users.

Although, as we have noted, there have been few broadly based online services in Europe in the past, these relatively new developments are being delivered alongside some existing infrastructures. We mentioned CompuServe's existing presence in Europe as if it was the only significant service but we should not forget that videotex services, particularly in France and Germany, while not fully fledged online services, nonetheless have traditionally provided users with an extensive, broadly based 'near online' experience.

In France, for example, France Telecom has been offering its Teletel service since 1981, available largely through Minitel terminals which were given away in millions to kick start the viability of the underlying service. This radical strategy has borne fruit with over 6.5 million terminals now installed serving up to 20 million regular users of the service. Although about half of all usage is business related, France Telecom believes that over one-third of all French homes have a Minitel terminal. Turnover for France Telecom in 1994 from Minitel business was over £1.3 billion with the most common use being to check telephone numbers. Indeed, Minitel-as it is commonly known-was originally positioned as the answer to printed phone directories which were largely withdrawn when the service was first launched. Other major uses today include business-to-business services, home banking and chat services-particularly les messageries roses (literally 'pink mailboxes') which offer the chance to enjoy what are euphemistically called 'adult' communications services (when in reality that is the last thing they are!).

Despite its success, however, growth in Minitel has petered out. The installed base is not growing significantly and although the use of the service still generates huge revenues, France Telecom is urgently trying to shift its emphasis away from the fairly primitive, low-resolution experience it gives now to a more sophisticated PC-based environment. As a part of this strategy, France Telecom is also actively developing modern new online services as France-en-Ligne-intended to shift the Minitel market into a mainstream online market-and Wanadoo, a consumer entertainment service created through a joint venture with the French publishing giant, Havas.

In Germany, the national telecommunications company is also a major player in online services. Originally called Datex-J, Deutsche Telekom's videotex service has been offering page-based online information for business users and consumers since the mid-1980s. In recent years, Deutsche Telekom has been upgrading and modernising the service and successfully migrating new subscribers towards accessing it via PCs rather than videotex terminals. Subscriber growth has been rapid with over a million by the end of 1995, almost twice the number using the service in 1993.

We will not examine either of these important services in detail. The key point about them, however, is that they indicate how different the commercial climate is for the emergence of online services in Europe from the United States. Whatever we think of France Telecom's or Deutsche Telekom's current offerings, the fact that two state telecommunications companies-both with immense political clout-have a major grip over two of Europe's most important markets is a major complicating factor for independent online initiatives. Indeed, it is one of the reasons why so little has happened so far in Europe and why newly spawned initiatives-such as the AOL Europe or Europe Online initiatives-have a much greater level of competitive pressure to cope with than the otherwise somewhat blank European online scene would suggest.

Europe is also distinct from the United States for a related but much more prosaic reason. Local telephony in the States is largely free, meaning that most online connections do not incur the cost of a local phone call. In Europe, current regulatory restrictions prevent most telecommunications companies from offering a free local service and-for now, at least-going online will mean paying both online service providers and the telephone companies. This is not a killer for online growth but it will plainly inhibit growth. For this and many other reasons, Europe must be seen as a distinct arena for online (and offline) developments and while analysis of the US industry is important to indicate the processes of change which will ultimate shape market opportunities in Europe, we have to remember that the European metabolism is different. The pace and character of change may be broadly based on US indicators but those indicators need careful reinterpretation before they can be applied to Europe with any accuracy. There is one thing we have learned very clearly from the pioneering quality of the US market which applies unconditionally to European developments. The proprietary networks which have both suffered and enjoyed such huge growth in recent years have all run into the same wall. The message of their experience is that the real future of online services is dominated not by narrow proprietary interests but by the wide open spaces of the Internet.

THE INTERNET

The history of the Internet is well documented elsewhere and we will concentrate here only on establishing the main themes. To some extent, because it is impossible to discuss the background of online markets without immediately referring to the Internet, we have already begun to explore these themes above. But, at the risk of being repetitious, we will reprise some of this material in order to make the story of the growth of the Internet clearer and more accessible.

The Internet has been the subject of immense hype, particularly by the popular press. There are even some influential thinkers-such as Professor Nicholas Negroponte of the Massachusetts Institute of Technology Media Lab-who believe that the hype is actually an understatement of the likely impact of the Internet on human lives. Despite all the hype, however, and-more importantly-the concrete indications, there remains a body of critics who argue that-as a commercial environment-the Internet simply does not work. Plenty of detractors who claim it is too slow, too unfriendly, too insecure, too unregulated and too light on bandwidth ever to deliver the global trading space which many are trying to create. There are good reasons for these criticisms but they all focus on a single fact which stems from the Internet's origins. The Internet was designed for a purpose that had little to do with commerce and the problems we are experiencing trying to use the Internet for trade is simply the result of us trying-necessarily-to make it do something for which it was never designed.

When the Internet was built in the mid-1970s, it was conceived as a small but crucial project in the US Department of Defence Advanced Research Projects Agency (ARPA). The idea was to create a communications system able to link a variety of different computers which would continue working even in the event of a nuclear war. Although under the auspices of ARPA, the project originally involved several US government research agencies and a number of universities. By 1978, the so-called Kahn-Cerf protocols (named after their inventors) had been developed to control communications over a prototype network. These quickly evolved into the Internet protocols (IP or transmission control protocol TCP/IP) which are today in use in millions of host computers all over the world.

The original focused aim of the protocols was soon almost forgotten as the academic and research communities, first in the United States, and then more globally, began to develop the original protocols into a full suite which offered a range of possible applications. These included file transfer protocol (FTP), which allows the transfer of computer files across the network, Telnet, which effectively makes a remote computer behave as if it was connected to the local network of a distant host, and electronic mail, which is today still the most extensively used function of the Internet. The communities of academics and researchers who built the foundations of the Internet, therefore, were, and remain today, fluent computer users. Most had already experienced the power of networking their computers on a local area basis within their own institutions and campuses but were attracted by the possibility of exchanging computer-held ideas and information over much greater distances. In other words, these communities physically located at great distances from one another wanted to talk to one another-in the most general sense-and wanted to do so electronically. The urge to link locally operated networks was the driver for the mutual development of the software protocols which, when shared among the different locations, allowed intercommunication. These protocols, therefore, effectively define what we today call the Internet-a vast, expanding global network of interconnecting computer networks.

As we noted earlier, the important thing about the Internet's protocols was-and is today-the fact that they were open to all users. They were not owned by any single entity and being non-proprietary were therefore available to anyone who could get hold of a copy and had the computer knowledge to make them work. There was, of course, one other thing they needed: access to the physical network which carried the traffic of the Internet.

Today, of course, hundreds of companies are rapidly getting rich by all being able to offer a package consisting of the free-to-anybody protocols that make computers talk the lingo of the Internet together with access-preferably fast access-into the Internet itself. But the reason there is now such a business is based on more than the fact that the underlying software that makes the Internet run is not proprietary. It is based, more importantly, in an explosion of use and a huge shift in the demographics of those who can now get benefits from touring the byways and thoroughfares of what is rapidly becoming the world's first incarnation of the long-dreamed-of information superhighway.

The Rise and Rise of the Internet

To understand the rise of the Internet we need to start with the origins we have just outlined. The key point about those origins-as we discussed earlier-is that they lay in the hands of individuals who had a deep understanding of computers. In other words, the Internet is historically an environment designed by computer users for computer users. This means that for 'ordinary' human beings-those who understand (and want to understand) little about computers and struggle to make them do something useful-the Internet has long been a deeply unfriendly and unintelligible place, a kind of technological 'no-go' area. This, of course, did not matter much because the Internet did the job it was designed for very well and those for whom it was designed knew its language and could use it for their desired ends with little or no difficulty. Even in this polarised state, however, the Internet was growing rapidly. Starting as the enthusiasm of a small group of US engineers and scientists-supported financially by the US government-the attractions of the Internet quickly fired global interest. Beyond the US academic and research networks which were first to be connected, thousands more networks all over the world gained access to the Internet and began sharing in and adding to the expanding community of users. To get some idea of the speed of growth consider these statistics from the Internet Society. In the early 1980s, the number of host computers connected numbered in the low hundreds. By 1988, the number was 33,000. By 1992, the year immediately before the Internet was opened to a much wider community, the host count had reached just under 1 million! It was impossible to determine how many individuals were using the Internet because, while it was possible to assess the number of networks interconnected, no one could know how many individuals made use of their Internet links, particularly since most networks were based on university or institutional campus where students, staff and researchers could make largely unrecorded use of the systems whenever they chose. All that was clear was that by the early 1990s, the users were numbered in millions and were growing daily.

All of this growth was reflecting enthusiasm for what the Internet was when it was created. New applications were being found by individuals all the time-the Usenet discussion groups which created the first interestcentred virtual communities, for example-so the Internet was evolving. But its centre of gravity lay with the computer-literate community of academics, researchers and students for whom it was originally designed. In 1993, however, a dramatic change took place which has transformed the world of information and media for ever.

The starting point of the revolution is mundane. A group of physicists based at the Geneva high energy research centre, CERN, led by Tim Berners-Lee, were interested in extending the functionality of the Internet. In particular, they were seeking a way of introducing hypertext linking to documents held on Internet servers so that they could follow a trail of interest among research reports, figuratively clicking on a word and being taken directly to another part of the same document or to another relevant document on a completely different server system. The team achieved this by creating a new Internet protocol called hypertext transfer protocol (HTTP) based on inserting special codes-derived from a new mark-up language they devised called hypertext markup language (HTML)-into electronic documents which would create the hypertext links they were after. In practice, the system ascribed a unique address to documents and pages within documents, held on servers. These addresses were called universal resource locators (URLs). When a code was activated, it automatically pointed the user at the URL of the related information, wherever it was physically located. Using the system, it was possible to 'jump' from page to page, document to document, server to server, creating a kind of web of interconnectivity spanning the Internet. Berners-Lee and his colleagues struck on a name for their invention which summed it up perfectly. They called it the World Wide Web.

The underlying technology of the Web is conceptually simple. A computer acting as an Internet server is turned into a site on the Web by running some software on the server that enables it to talk the language of HTTP. Once it is talking that language, it can offer documents marked up with HTML codes and allow users to link from other servers to the documents or to use the documents as jumping off points to other sites on the Web.

The World Wide Web

The creation of the Web was not a revolution in itself, only the catalyst of revolution. Despite the fact that it was simple in concept, the Web in its early days was as unfriendly and complex to use as the Internet had always been. This is not surprising. It had-like the Internet-been created by computer professionals for other computer professionals. In other words, if you happened to be an elementary particle physicist, you could manipulate the language of HTTP and navigate the Web with ease. Ordinary information seekers would find the Unix-based command language a fearsome obstacle. Of course, navigating the Web in the days immediately following its invention was a relatively short journey. In June 1993, for example, a few months after Berners-Lee and his team had released details of HTTP and HTML, there were just 50 Web sites in existence. The spring of 1996, there are already over 100,000 sites and some believe there are many more-indeed, the number is growing so fast, it is impossible to keep track of new sites as they emerge.

What has caused this explosion? Certainly not the Web's popularity among academics and researchers-although their use of it has expanded dramatically. Instead it has been the sudden appearance of ordinary computer users in their millions with access both to the Internet in general and to the Web in particular. The Web has been tamed and democratised by a single key invention-the creation of an easy-to-use, graphical point and click window through which anyone can navigate and view the Web. The window is a specialised form of software which is run on client computers to provide an instant interface for the Web. The generic name for the software sums up its use. It is known as a Web browser. The first browser to emerge appeared in the autumn of 1993, about six months after Berners-Lee published the foundations on which the Web could be built. Called Mosaic, the software was authored by a team of brilliant young programmers led by Marc

Andreeson working at the National Centre for Supercomputing Applications (NCSA), a department of the University of Illinois headquartered in Chicago. Its impact was instantaneous-largely because Andreeson and his team made it freely available via the Internet. Initially, thousands of students and academics downloaded the software via their campus Internet connections and began to surf the fledgling Web.

As news of its ease of use spread, the Internet, for the first time, became an interesting proposition for a more general audience of computer users. As the audience grew in numbers and broadened in its demographic, increasing numbers of Web sites emerged. And they were not only focused on technical subjects such as elementary particle physics. Campus Internet servers quickly became hosts to a wide range of interest-based Web sites covering every imaginable enthusiasm. Web evangelists publicised the new sites by word of mouth and through specialist newsletters.

The word of the Web spread like wildfire and ignited a major new industry. Suddenly, through the arrival of a form of software which turned the Internet from a hostile to a friendly place, millions of people wanted to get wired. Companies offering dial-up access sprang up overnight, providing low cost subscriptions that gave both admission via fast leased connections and the software needed to enjoy the fruits of the Internet-electronic mail, access to Internet discussion groups, the ability to download software from distant hosts and, of course, a Web browser to allow users to wander the fast expanding landscape of cyberspace. This process of demo cratisation-the conversion of net users from a select elite of computer literate boffins and enthusiasts to ordinary consumers hungry for information, entertainment and communications-took place with breathtaking speed. From early 1993 to early 1996, the number of consumers with dial-up access from their homes grew from zero to about 10 million worldwide. Berners-Lee's World Wide Web was the catalyst and Mosaic was the key ingredient that triggered revolution. But Mosaic was merely a jumping off point for the creation of really effective and powerful browsing technology.

While the NCSA was giving away its fledgling-and often unstable-software, commercial software companies were increasingly interested in licensing it and improving it for widespread use. Licensing deals were concluded between the Trustees of the University of Illinois and such companies as Spyglass and Spry, who immediately began making Mosaic more robust and reliable. Elsewhere, however, commercial forces were gathering to sweep aside the link with NCSA's Mosaic and build an independent browsing technology. In fact the link with the NCSA remained but merely became less formal. In mid-1994, Jim Clark, founder and former CEO of computer hardware company Silicon Graphics, created a new organisation called Mosaic Communications. To do it he did not buy the Mosaic software from NCSA but, instead, raided the NCSA for all its key programming staff. Most importantly, Clark tempted Andreeson away and with him came most of his team. With the creators of the original Mosaic successfully employed, Clark set about building a new form of Mosaic working from the ground up. The result was today's best known and most widely used browser, Netscape Navigator. All the University of Illinois could do about the perfectly legitimate and shrewd minded hijack was to force Clark to change the name of his company from Mosaic to Netscape Communications.

Clark began giving away Netscape Navigator from his company's Web site in autumn 1994. By spring the following year, more than 6 million people had downloaded the software and Netscape was well on its way to becoming the de facto standard for browsing the Web. Clark was not giving his software away as an act of altruism. His agenda was simple. Give away the software and create a huge market of users dependent on your free product. Then start charging modestly for upgrades of the product.

But, more importantly, sell Web site operators server software (for thousands of dollars) which complements the features of the Netscape browser. Although all HTTP-compliant browsers could access all Web sites, whatever flavour of Web software they were running, it was possible to add proprietary features by expanding upon and redeveloping the underlying HTTP mark-up language. This was the golden opportunity that Clark spotted and Netscape grasped. Having established an installed base of millions of users within months, Clark's proposition for the increasing number of commercial organisations wanting to build Web sites was almost irresistible: use Netscape's server software and address a vast population of browser users with the fullest possible range of Netscape features-including the ability to make secure transmissions of data between client and server, something that was possible only when a Netscape browser links to a server running Netscape software.

Commercialising the Web

The explosion in the use of the Web was startling and spectacular. But while commentators became obsessed with the sheer speed and scale of the development, commercial forces were beginning to see the presence of the Web as a stepping stone to a major new commercial opportunity. Initially, the expanding number of sites merely reflected the individual enthusiasms of Web users, particularly those with easy access to server infrastructure in research institutions and university campuses. But by early 1994, the first commercial sites began to emerge. Within a year, commercial sites blossomed as the most active sector of Web development. The types of sites were immensely varied. Large companies created sites to wave their corporate flags. Media companies went online to promote their latest movies, record albums or computer games. Newspapers set up online counterparts. Magazine companies did the same. Retailers and merchants of different kinds began exploring the possibilities of electronic shopping. The range of activity is too wide to summarise. But the basic trend was clear. The newly democratised Web was suddenly perceived as a vast new market-place where products and services could be commercialised instantly and internationally.

Most intriguing of all, it seemed as if all you needed to grab a slice of the action was a fast PC and an Internet connection. Setting up shop in cyberspace looked like a cheap and easy thing to do. Accordingly everyone stampeded towards what looked at the outset like a golden opportunity, a licence to print money. The reality has been quite different and while commentators like Negroponte may argue that the hype does not even begin to express the true magnitude of the impact of the Web, there is a serious issue of timescale to address.

The pace of recent developments has been so rapid that it is tempting to think that the Web in particular and the Internet in general will soon become a mature environment for doing business. But the truth is that we are still in the first day of school. We not only have to master and improve the technologies underpinning the Internet to make it into a friendly, secure and pervasive environment but also need to build effective, new business models to create stable businesses that will prosper and flourish long term.

10

Web Commerce

We looked at the rise of proprietary consumer networks-a phenomenon driven by the rapid computerisation of US and European homes-and the emergence of the Internet as a mainstream online environment. The single most important subset of the Internet for commercial activity-the World Wide Web. We will examine in particular the main basis for commercialising the Web and outline the key means of generating revenue from Web sites. Through examining its commercialisation, we will also be able to make sense of its devastating impact on the traditional business model of proprietary networks.

THE WEB CONSUMER

We have already gained a sense of how quickly the Web has grown in size and significance. There are many wild estimates of how many new sites are appearing. Some claim they double every few months while others struggle with the maths and come up with at least one site every minute. The truth is, no one really knows how quickly the Web is growing. The only certainty is that it is growing fast. The likely number of sites is probably around 200,000 and may double by the time it is in the hands of its first readers. Anyone can come up with numbers but it is really a matter of educated guesswork.

More solid numbers are available for the other end of the equation. There are plenty of sites: no doubt about it. But how many consumers are actually using the Web? What is the audience for this massive treasure house of online experiences? A US survey conducted by FIND/SVP in late 1995 gives at least part of the answer. It revealed 9.5 million Internet users in the United States of which 7.5 million had access to the Web. Of those using the Web, 4 million (fully 53 per cent of the total) began using it in 1995. Of the newcomers, 48 per cent were using the Web exclusively from home. Out of all US Internet users, only 27 per cent were using it via a server in an academic institution, a figure that would have been closer to 100 per cent only two years earlier.

Servers in business locations accounted for 28 per cent, indicating the rapid moves that corporations are making to embrace the Internet. The real surprise in the figures came when the researchers analysed the proportion of Internet users gaining access from specialist Internet service providers (ISPs), companies that had originally ridden high on the Internet boom and had been the main source of Internet provision since the crucial emergence of the first Web browsers. The results showed a significant decline in the influence of smaller ISPs and a rapid rise in the number of people accessing the Internet via proprietary networks. Why is this so remarkable? The proprietary networks had really woken up to the existence of the Internet only in late 1994 and had begun to use their own infrastructure to offer their subscribers Internet access by early 1995.

This emphasises the speed with which proprietary networks have taken off as an important source of access to the Internet, driving home the message that the vast majority of newcomers to the Web were the kind of people who might subscribe to populist networks such as AOL or Prodigy and, to a lesser extent, CompuServe-in other words: mainstream consumers. The figures also tell an important story about the remarkable transformation that has taken place in the proprietary network's proposition to its customers. Without exception, proprietary consumer networks have reshaped their business models so that they are now almost exclusively defined by the influence of the Internet in general and the Web in particular.

Surfing the Web

There used to be a time when nets were used for fishing, getting wired was an activity strictly for electricians and surfing was a watersport. Today, the vocabulary has assumed a different set of meanings. The particular expression 'surfing the Web' has, in only a matter of months, become one of the worst clichés of the digital world. It was meant to imply a kind of carefree voyage of discovery which users of the Web embarked upon with every click of the mouse.

Hyperlink after hyperlink would carry them through an infinite number of pathways in cyberspace. They would pause here and there to take a closer look at one offering or another but the journey was the thing: a ceaseless roaming in search of-second worst cliché-the 'coolest site' on the Web. Regular users of the Web quickly appreciate that aimless wanderings are ultimately too boring and futile for anyone to tolerate for long. The reality of Web surfing is that surfers need to be directed, they yearn for navigational aids. In the same US Internet survey we quoted above, researchers confirmed with a single finding the fact that underpins almost every strategy for successfully commercialising the Web.

Out of all the millions using the Web with its (possibly) hundreds of thousands of sites, 60 per cent of users visit fewer than ten sites on a regular basis! In other words, Web surfing is not an arbitrary wandering, a voyage of discovery. Web users find the sites they like and stick to them. If they expand the number of sites they visit regularly they do so by being directed from a site they already know, enjoy and trust. What this means is vital for Web publishing. It means that it is possible to arbitrate how people use the Web, to influence what they do and where they go. Despite the independence that the structure of the Web confers, its vastness and complexity demands the simplifying effect of navigational beacons, pointers to what is the best, most interesting and most relevant to our needs.

The idea of arbitration-expressed in different ways-is essential to strategic power over the Web and all its commercial potential. Before we look at how this works for site owners, let us consider first some models for gatekeeping the Web which illustrate the potential for finding different forms of influence. The most obvious example of a gatekeeping play is Netscape Communication's effort to turn its Web browser, Netscape Navigator, into a universal standard and to link this with a grip on Web server supply. Although we have covered much of this ground, we will reprise the main ideas in this new context. Netscape, as we saw, is the brainchild of Jim Clark, former CEO of Silicon Graphics. Clark was one of the first to spot the potential of the NCSA's Mosaic browser for revolutionising global access to the Web.

He realised that its 'point and click' approach to navigating the Web was exactly what was needed to transform it from an environment best suited to geeks to a wonderland of information and services for ordinary human beings. He also saw that Mosaic was merely a flawed precursor of the kind of browser that would eventually dominate access to the Internet and decided that he would create a company to design the new generation of Mosaic-derived Internet tools that was needed. His way of doing this was direct and uncompromising. Instead of licensing the Mosaic system from its originators and upgrading it, he poached the people who had created Mosaic in the first place and paid them to start again and design a much better version of the original. The result was Netscape Navigator. Faster and easier to use than Mosaic, Navigator is packed with features including, most significantly, a built-in security system based on a Netscape encryption technology called the secure socket layer (SSL) protocol.

As soon as the first versions of Navigator emerged, Netscape began giving them away as fast as it could. The result has been a dramatic uptake of the software. In January 1995, a survey of 73,000 Web users found that 77 per cent were using one version or another of Netscape's Navigator and even today most agree that Netscape has maintained a share of around 70-80 per cent despite a slew of new browsers coming to market. Competitors derided the figures saying it was easy to gain market share when you were giving your product away. But they missed the point. Clark was not initially trying to make a business selling browser software. His eye was on a different ball. The importance of getting large numbers of browsers into the market was to create an effective de facto standard. The reason for doing this was to sell not browsers-although Netscape, having established a huge constituency of loyal and committed users, is nowadays starting to charge for updated editions of them-but Web servers. The servers are the computers used to host Web sites and services. The software they run makes them compatible with the Web and proprietary wrinkles allow vendors of servers to offer special Internet features. Most important for Netscape's range is its SSL security system. The important point about such security protocols is that they need two halves of a 'key' to work. One half resides in the server. The other, which enables secure transfers of information, resides in a compatible browser. The heart of Netscape's strategy, therefore, was to inject vast numbers of its browsers into the market and then use the existence of an effective, strong-though not impregnable-security standard based on them to sell its servers. For those looking for a secure basis to begin Internet trading, the servers would look irresistible if virtually everybody on the Internet was already using Netscape's browser.

Domination of server supply means, of course, a lucrative business but, longer term, it also implies a gate keeping role. The reason is simple. If your browser and server together form the universal standard for Web trading, the commercialisation of the Web stands or falls on your proprietary technology. This means you can manipulate its pricing whenever you wish to control your bottom line performance. You can vary its functionality, so shaping everyone's experience of using the Web. And you can decide who and who not to do business with, so determining who gets access to the commercial opportunities of the Web. In other words, the server-browser equation is strong enough medicine to turn anyone controlling it into the Microsoft of the Internet. And that is exactly what Netscape wants to be.

In practice, of course, it is not as simple as just focusing on security because long term-as we will see later-it will be hard to resist moves to universalise an open, non-proprietary standard. The picture painted above, for example, if it was as crudely drawn in reality, would be given short shrift by US anti-trust legislation. It is not surprising therefore that Netscape has just joined with America Online, Prodigy, CompuServe and IBM to invest in a small software security company called Terisa, which is now charged with creating a single, open security protocol for the Internet. Terisa itself has created the other major Internet security protocol known as Secure HTTP, which is based on a 'public key' cryptography scheme first devised by RSA Data Security. The idea of online and Internet majors investing in it is to merge Netscape's SSL protocol and HTTP into a single, pervasive standard for the future commercialisation of the Internet. Netscape, of course, will try to ensure the final merged product looks much more like SSL than HTTP so that it can leverage its current dominant server-browser position even when the new security standard is established.

Gate keeping does not have to be based on server-browser strategies. A powerful position can also be built purely on the basis of being a dominant Internet access provider. Although we have already seen what an effective force proprietary networks have become by acting as access providers, major telephone companies also have a powerful position to leverage. The move in 1995 by MCI Communications-the second largest long-distance telephony carrier in the USA-to launch a nationwide dial-up Internet access service called internet MCI, is a good illustration.

Although we had already seen Pacific Bell-the RBOC (Regional Bell Operating Company) serving most telephone users in California-entering the Internet access market with an initiative aimed at business users and we have subsequently seen, in February 1996, AT & T launch its WorldNet service, MCI's move was the first at the time by a US carrier with national reach. As a well-known national organisation with large numbers of existing customers, it was uniquely placed to leverage its existing relationships with subscribers and to build a critical mass of Internet users quickly tied to its proprietary access provision and connection software. At the time, the only other national access providers in the United States-Uunet, Netcom, Holonet and PSI-were relatively small players compared to the financial power and commercial influence of a $13 billion corporation such as MCI.

It is important to assess MCI's move to provide national access to the Internet in the context of another announcement it had made. In addition to its access service, MCI announced it was launching an Internet shopping initiative called marketplaceMCI. This was a secure trading environment based on Netscape server-browser technology within which MCI hoped to gather a powerful group of traders offering an attractive range of purchasable products and services. The key point of MCI's approach was that market place MCI will itself be marketed from MCI's home page-the first site customers are taken to when they log on and-more important, because home pages can be changed by users-it was also to be marketed through all MCI's existing customer links as a telephony provider to millions of businesses and consumers throughout the United States. By building on its existing relationships, MCI could hope to attract large numbers of customers to marketplace MCI and by making it a compelling environment and by building into it good links with other Web sites, it would have a good chance of making the market-place the definitive jumping off place for Web surfers.

The AT & T initiative, WorldNet, could achieve everything MCI will gain in influence over the Web but on an even bigger scale. AT & T's offering at the time of its launch was extremely attractive to those existing AT & T customers seeking dial-up Internet access. The starting deal for them was five hours of free access per month for a year with additional hours at $2.50. Unlimited access was priced at $19.95 per month. For non-AT & T customers the deal was slightly less attractive with no free access and three hours a month available at a modest $4.95. The totally free service for existing customers was a breakthrough-the first time standalone Internet access had been made available at no charge. The aggressive package was all the more powerful because AT & T could immediately leverage a vast, existing customer base of 80 million subscribers. In other words, it was building instant and powerful strategic influence over the Internet in general and the Web in particular by becoming both the portal and facilitator of access for potentially tens of millions of users in the USA and-with WorldNet rolling out worldwide in 1996-throughout AT & Ts international market. With its close individual billing links with every one of those subscribers, a powerhouse like AT & T is perfectly placed to promote particular Internet activities to its constituency and-if it chooses-build an effective Web commerce operation by leveraging its reach.

This is the heart of the new kind of gatekeeping which content-rather than technology-companies can also leverage. As we indicated above, the Web is a complicated and confusing place. It needs beacons to guide people on their journeys. These beacons will define the paths people take and, therefore, whose services they access. A definitive starting point for Web journeys, therefore, will be a powerful arbiter of Web usage. In other words, if MCI or other major access providers can use their success as the springboard for building their home page entry point into the regular first stop for millions of people setting out on the Web, they will have an asset of considerable strategic power and commercial potential.

Other organisations, for example, will pay to have links inserted into the key home pages in order to point customers to their sites. There is money to be made and influence to be wielded. According to a widely publicised statement by MCI's head of Internet initiatives, the Internet pioneer Vint G. Cerf, the combined moves by MCI indicate that it is 'not just a telecommunications company any more'. Since Internet provision is of course a telecommunications service, Cerf's comment indicates that MCI is seeing its future as increasingly linked to content as well as content distribution. In other words, instead of being focused on its role as a carrier, MCI is shaping a strategic future also based on what it carries and-through its influence-making added value out of its ability to shape the pathways that people follow on their journeys around the Web. The Netscape, MCI and AT & T models add up to the same thing.

The biggest game in town, as far as the Internet is concerned, is building influence over how people get access to the Web and what they do while they are using it. There are different ways of playing the game but those who succeed will be the power brokers of what will eventually become the biggest and most influential trading environment the world has ever seen. It is a prize worth fighting for. In fact, in the digital media world, it is probably the only prize worth fighting for. Home pages-the Web page that a browser starts at when it is launched by a client-are, as the MCI example demonstrates, an important influence on what people do on the Web simply because they can rely on gaining so many eyeballs. The Netscape browser, for example, when purchased from Netscape, opens at the Netscape home page. Although this opening page is only a default setting and can easily be changed by users, the evidence so far suggests that people do not tend to bother. Because Netscape is used by millions, it is not surprising that its home page is one of the busiest places on the Web. It has acquired an instant, ready-made constituency of a size that Web publishers would have to struggle to achieve over months and years of expensive marketing efforts. Having such an instant constituency is only part of the battle. You have to make the initial offering an attractive one or they are likely to overcome their inertia and change the default setting. Netscape has been shrewd-not just in its software strategies but in creating a home site that is dynamic, full of interest and an excellent jumping off place for Web surfers looking for initial directions to take. Netscape offers hot links to other interesting sites and a direct link to key Web directories. Not surprisingly, with a big constituency of users, Netscape is also generating substantial revenues from advertisers who want the millions of eyeballs that Netscape's home page delivers.

The power of the home page has attracted many companies to buy customised versions of standard browsers which default to their home pages so that they can give these away as promotional tools. An entire division of CompuServe is dedicated to developing this kind of business. Already hundreds of companies have taken advantage of the concept. Hotel chains have placed free discs in the rooms of regular guests, for example, while in 1996 Volkswagen of America is giving away Internet software-packaged via a deal with an access provider with some free connect-time-in the glove compartment of every new car it sells and sending similar software out to 500,000 existing customers. It is a scatter gun approach but companies such as Volkswagen are obviously calculating that it makes cost-effective sense to bring traffic-hopefully, long-term traffic-to their home page and via the home page to all the retentive delights of its Web site.

The same theme of leveraging influence over how people use the Web lies at the heart of all Web publishing strategies. Most of all, of course, the central objective is to influence people to visit sites-and keep visiting them. By implication, this asks the question: what are companies really trying to achieve by building and operating Web sites? There is no single answer because objectives vary with types of companies. In some cases, there is no answer because there is no objective. In other words, some companies build their sites without even thinking through their reasons for doing so. Content companies, however, have a clear objective: they plan to commercialise some form of content asset, either leveraged out of assets they already possess in the 'real' world or via assets newly created for the online environment. The majority are seeking, more or less directly, to extend the potential of existing content and its branding. For these companies the process of Web publishing has three key phases. First, use existing brand power to build an online franchise. Second, use the franchise to create a constituency-an audience that will be loyally tied to regular use of the site. Third, commercialise the constituency. This is not rocket science-the magazine and newspaper industries have been doing it for years. What is new now, however, is the peculiar and distinctive characteristics of online environments and, most of all, how people use them.

It is worth pausing to reexamine a word we have been using repeatedly and without qualification, as if its meaning and significance were self-evident. The word is 'content' and in the online world it needs some careful re-evaluation.

Content and Online Success

The overheated and overhyped world of the Web is putting increasing pressure on content organisations of all kinds. The issue is no longer whether to create a Web presence but to decide urgently the when, how and what of that presence. Naturally enough, many companies are snatching online strategies out of the air, deciding abruptly either to get onto the Web or do a deal with Microsoft or one of the other proprietary majors or both. Sometimes fast, tactical moves work but there is already evidence that many companies-particularly those new to network publishing-are not taking the time they need to think through the realities of the new market-place, to determine where real strategic advantage lies, what existing assets they can deploy, which new ones they will have to acquire to ensure success and, at the end of the day, what kind of business model will make serious money for them long term.

The only good online strategies begin with some simple questions. What are we trying to achieve by going online? What are our expectations? What resources and assets can we deploy? What level of commitment can we afford? Where are we weak and where are we strong? Any MBA (Master of Business Administration) graduate worth his or her salt would consider these commonplace basics but the feverish atmosphere surrounding the apparent rapid emergence of a consumer online market is in danger of sweeping away common-sense deliberations of this kind. Content companies, in particular, need to draw a deep breath before taking action. A time for cool contemplation is vital.

But the pressure is growing on them to move quickly and that largely manufactured sense of urgency is pushing them to take precipitate action. It is true of course that some urgency does exist-particularly where the Web is concerned. The recent frantic pioneering activity is based on a sound policy-staking out franchises early, even before the Web can be commercialised in order to be well positioned when it is. But rushing to establish those franchises and getting it wrong could be as disastrous as thinking that the Web in particular and online in general fails the so-what test. The worst danger for content companies is that they actually believe that-in a traditional sense-content is still really king. It is the most dangerous kind of false reassurance because it contains an element of truth. But the broader reality is that it is much more than content as we have always known it that determines online success. The real threat is that the idea of content always being the dictator of commercial advantage makes owners of content complacent and less likely to take the right action at the right time.

To illustrate this we can take a brief look at some of the major issues involved in creating an effective Web presence. There are a raft of practical and technical issues, of course, which shape the design of the site, its capabilities and-most important-the costs associated with creating and running it long term. It is clear, for example, that we must increasingly try to design our sites today with the Web technologies of tomorrow. During 1996 and 1997 the experience of using the Web will have changed beyond recognition. It will commonly offer such features as real-time audio from sites, voice communications, three-dimensional graphics and virtual reality-like experiences and-within limitations-the delivery of short, windowed video clips in more or less real time. What we can offer from these sites a year hence both in terms of an online sensation as well as basic commercial products and services will be dramatically different from the possibilities being exploited today. So we have to embrace the future in today's design and build everything we do with an easy and immediate upgrade path. In this crucial sense, the Web is and will remain a highly dynamic environment.

But to put traditional content in perspective, we need to concentrate on more general issues of site design. Here too it is vital to understand the Web as a dynamic place but in a different sense. One of the most powerful attributes of online publishing is its ability to deliver fast-changing information. In the professional and corporate market, the power of online systems to deliver volatile information, even information updated on a moment by moment basis, has been one of the key foundations of what is today a $13 billion business. Users of online systems expect and demand dynamic information. They do not want to read the same information or undergo the same experience every time they visit an online site. Going online is ultimately a communications experience and, like a conversation, what you expect to get out of it is something constantly changing. Saying or hearing the same thing over and again is simply too boring to be tolerated. In other words, Web design must embody a strategy for constantly varying, updating, upgrading the content of the site.

Communications itself is a key notion too. If using the Web is essentially a communications experience, it is largely because that is what people want it to be. While it is already evident that users of online services have a relatively few favourite things they like doing online (spending money, as we have noted, is not one of them!) the one thing that is consistently high on their priorities is sharing and exchanging information and ideas with other people.

And if that is what people most like doing online, it clearly must-interpreted sensitively-be a thread of all good Web design. So Web sites must be dynamic and communications based. But there is a third crucial ingredient. The experience of using online services is very personal. If communing with an online site is more like making a telephone call than reading a book, then users of the Web want sites to respond to them personally.

This means Web design is about marketing to one person and seeing a constituency of users as a collection of well-defined and wellunderstood individuals. Personalising Web sites is not easy but with the right software tools and server systems it is increasingly possible to achieve. At the simplest level, customisation of this kind means that visitors to a site are welcomed with a personal message and a range of suggestions of what they may like to access based on their previous visits and the interests they showed during them. At more sophisticated levels, sites will increasingly offer fully filtered and bespoke information services.

None of this has much to do with our traditional notion of static, analogue content. And the implication is that owners of content may not be able to deploy as much of their existing content assets on the Web as they might suppose. Indeed, many are already concluding that the very idea of content on the Web-or any other network publishing environment-needs to be redefined. Building an online strategy, therefore, may well start with biting a very painful bullet indeed. We may have to accept that traditional content-important as it may be-is far from king on the Web. What really counts is understanding customers and building individual relationships with them. This is what lies at the heart of online success.

COMMERCIALISING A WEB SITE

If a site is successful in staking out its franchise and creating a constituency of long-term users of the site, how can it turn its promising position into one that generates substantial revenues? One thing is sure, it will need to do this quickly because the cost of entry for those aiming to build substantial and effective Web publishing operations is no longer modest. There was once a view that the attraction of the Web was the cheapness of being there. A few thousand dollars could buy the hardware, software and connection to get a server linked to the Internet.

This is still true: it does cost only a few thousand dollars-so long as you do not plan to do anything significant with the Web presence that you have created. A powerful site capable of building a substantial constituency-and retaining it-needs major upfront investment and, just as important, substantial ongoing investment to keep the site fresh, dynamic and on the leading edge of Web technology and functionality. The best commercial sites currently operating have dollar budgets well into eight figures per annum and-like making a movie, computer game or multimedia CD-ROM title-there is effectively no limit to what can be spent. So, with the cost on entry soaring, the pressure on revenue generation is increasingly intense.The first understanding that site owners must have-whatever media culture they come from-is that to stand any chance of profitability, sites will almost certainly need multiple sources of revenue. This is a familiar idea, for example, to magazine companies but a strange and largely alien one, say, for book publishers. However, it is crucial, particularly in these early pioneering years, because no one yet fully understands where the main emphasis in revenue generation will ultimately come from. Until this becomes clearer, everyone trying to make money from costly Web presences must look for revenue from every possible source.

That is why today's operators of Web shopping malls are likely to fail-because they have committed their business model to attracting visitors to their sites and then commercialising those visits via a single form of revenue generation. Of course, business models are never blunt instruments and there will, in practice, be many variations but multiplicity is a vital key in searching for ways of making the Web viable. There are at least four major paradigms for revenue generation-others, no doubt, will emerge:

- Selling content
- Selling advertising
- Conducting transactions
- Selling links

SELLING CONTENT

First, sites can create revenue from attempting to sell content or, more likely, access to content. The distinction is a fine and important one. There is a deep-rooted fear among traditional content companies that once they post their copyright assets on the Web, they will quickly be plundered. Like much of the concern surrounding security on the Web, this particular fear is based more on a perception than a reality. It also represents a danger for such traditional players who have always created businesses out of a balance between both protecting and simultaneously exploiting copyrights. At any time it is a difficult balancing act.

But in the Web environment, there is a strong sense that protection is almost impossible and exploitation, at best, problematic. This analysis would, catastrophically, counsel content companies to steer clear of the Web altogether. Fortunately, it is becoming clear, even to newcomers to the field, that protection is possible-at least to levels comparable to the real world-and that the best possible protection is not to make copyright materials accessible online in the first place. Instead, they can be showcased on the Web and sold via conventional channels. Showcasing itself can be a sophisticated process, including a sampling of the content products. Much here depends on the type of content involved. For television, video and film companies, showcasing and promotion is really the only option. Supplying product is still far beyond the capabilities of the Web. New forms of compression technologies, however, are beginning to make 'good enough' real-time video on a small window of the PC screen-probably adequate for sampling products-a near-term possibility.

For record companies, showcasing and sampling is already a possibility using existing, widely available software, although quality is still relatively poor, certainly inferior to normal CD quality sound. In other words, like the video companies, music companies (and the bands and artists themselves) are unlikely-with exceptions such as operations like the Internet Underground Music Archive in the United States and Cerberus in the UK-to attempt to deliver their products over the networks. Print publishers, of course, are the media players with most to lose and gain right now from posting their content directly on the Web because the environment is most immediately suited to text leavened with a few illustrations.

There are, of course, resolution and convenience issues-resolution determined both by the way the content is stored in the server and by the limitations of the output printer and convenience by the fact that large volumes even of mere text can take time to download over ordinary dial-up connections. For publishers, therefore, the issue is most immediate but, even for them, the obvious solution is to consider promoting rather than selling their crown jewels. That way they can be stolen only in the real world, not in cyberspace. In any event, as we saw in the previous section, the notion of content of the Web needs careful definition. While the Web may become a place where some traditional content is traded, it is more a place where trade will be based on very different notions of content than previously understood by the media industry. In fact, the old forms do not sit well in the new world. The type of content that flourishes on the Web is much more an experience than a fixed body of intellectual property in the traditional sense. This makes it much harder for Web content to be stolen. After all, how do you steal an experience? Only with great difficulty.

Even more difficult, right now, is actually generating revenue by selling access to content-whether defined in traditional or new era terms. Content, of course, drives the success of a site-by definition since there is no site without content-but to get customers to part with money for access to it is a real challenge. Those who have attempted to charge have seen the size of their constituencies plunge. On the face of it, this seems a strange difficulty. After all, most of the media industry is-on the surface, at least-based on the idea of selling access to content to those who want or need it. The direct exploitation of the content is the principal source of revenue generation. On the Web, by contrast, content is the honey that attracts interest and helps build a constituency. Revenue generation seems to come later. In fact, closer analysis shows us that even in real world media sectors, revenue generation is often more complex. Successful films produce substantial box office revenues but can often make more from video and merchandising exploitations. Magazines and newspapers rely on their content to sustain communities of regular readers which, in turn, are attractive to advertisers. Even book publishers-most obviously associated with single revenue stream businesses-actually make substantial sums from selling to third parties what they term 'subsidiary rights': the rights to serialise, adapt, anthologise original printed works or to turn books into different copyright forms such as films, plays, television programmes or even interactive products. So, in reality, the media world is less attached to just selling its content directly and is more multistream than one might suppose.

Strategies for generating revenue from access to content resolve themselves into four options. Selling access to an entire site by charging a subscription for entry is the most obvious approach. It also appears doomed to failure at present except for sites offering professional and corporate information with a strong 'need to know' character. The majority of consumer sites would find it very difficult to persuade customers to pay in such a blunt fashion. Only slightly less blunt is the idea of charging for access to content on a 'pay as you go' basis. Instead of a fixed entry fee, customers buy such content as they choose a la carte. More subtle and therefore more plausible is the widely favoured approach of providing site access free and creating a high value, premium area within the site. Those wanting to get into the premium area have to buy a password which gives them access for a subscription period. Examples of early experiments with this approach include Penthouse, Hachette Fillipachi's 'Car and driver' site and the hugely successful Sportszone, run by US sports TV giant, ESPN. More subtle still-but possibly less plausible-is the move to blur the distinction between charging for content and charging for Internet access. A number of service providers-particularly news publishers-are now offering a subscription which includes an Internet access deal.

The package is created by the content company sub-contracting the access provision to a third party company whose main business is providing such access. The content company hopes to negotiate preferential rates for its subscribers so the overall deal looks attractive. But the reality, of course, is that the charge for content and access combined always adds up to more than access alone and customers only have to do some simple mental arithmetic to appreciate the level of charging being made for the content to which they gain access. So the technique has some psychological value in fudging content charges but is not likely to fool many of the people for much of the time. That said, the deal could still look attractive if access was being provided at a heavily discounted rate. But to get a really good deal on access, the content company would have to guarantee some fairly high volume of trade. The difficulty of selling content online is striking. In the real world there appears to be little difficulty so long as the content offering is compelling and the price is right. There is probably a slew of complex reasons but one is clear. In our current media culture, people value atoms more readily than they value bits. In other words, if a digital product is enshrined in a physical medium, immediately palpable to the senses, it is more easily regarded as an object of inherent value.

By contrast, if a product is delivered online as a stream of bits, those accessing it seem less willing to appreciate its lasting value and are accordingly less inclined to pay for it. This phenomenon-which may decline as the generations roll by-is not helped by current Internet culture where information is widely seen-almost in terms of an ideology-as something that should be freely available. Even with the old altruistic culture fast being swept away by today's hardnosed commercial initiatives, the instinct that information delivered via the bitstream should be free lingers on and makes those initiatives that much harder to consummate.

SELLING ADVERTISING

Perhaps as obvious as the idea of selling content is the prospect of selling advertising. Currently the most widely emphasised approach to revenue generation, the sale of advertising on a Web site is based fundamentally on that site's guaranteed ability to deliver eyeballs to the merchants taking the advertising space. In other words, a site's ability to attract advertisers and maintain a highly priced rate card is directly proportional to the size and focus of the constituency of users. Both factors-size and focus-are crucial. A large but demographically unfocused constituency may be desirable but a smaller but more focused one might be more so. In other words, size is not everything. If a site becomes the definitive stopping-off place for the world's fly fishermen, for example, the raw size of the constituency is less important than the fact that potential advertisers have a clear idea of main interests of the individuals making it up. Plainly such a site represents a golden opportunity for certain kinds of advertisers while others can avoid wasting their money.

Clearly, this argument holds good for both Web sites and proprietary online services. Most proprietary majors, however, have large unfocused constituencies with the important proviso that large means very large indeed. At the time of writing, for example, CompuServe has about 3.5 million subscribers worldwide while AOL counts over 4 million. These are big constituencies even if they represent a very mixed bag of individuals. On sheer size alone, they are potentially attractive to advertisers. However, proprietaries by their nature offer a wide variety of offerings to their subscribers and advertisers can therefore get the opportunity to lodge adverts in areas of the service which attract demographically focused subsets of the overall constituency and so meet their need to spend their money addressing not just eyeballs but the right eyeballs. Estimates vary wildly about how much advertising is currently taking place online. The US analysts Forrester Research believe that only about $10 million was spent in 1995 but that the scale of advertising will rapidly escalate over the next few years reaching a total spend of $2.2 billion by the year 2000. The reality of 1995 was probably closer to a spend of $60 million but whatever the exact figure, most analysts agree that the number is small. The steep escalation in revenue is based on three major factors coming into play over the years leading to the millennium. First, the emergence of effective ways to audit the effect of advertising on the Web. Software solutions are already emerging to address this issue. Second, a growing confidence and understanding by advertisers of how to utilise the interactive medium and leverage, in particular, its potential one-to-oneness. And third, the rise of standardised and trusted mechanisms to allow secure payments to be made over Internet connections. Whatever the future may hold, it seems clear that substantial advertising revenues are being generated by only a relatively few high profile sites. In the course of 1995, for example, the HotWired site announced it was cash positive on the basis of its steadily growing income from advertising. Other sites such as Web directories and search engines-Yahoo, Lycos and others-key home pages, such as Netscape's, and highly popular content offerings, such as Sportszone, are all generating serious income. Elsewhere, advertising and advertising rate cards are more patchy. One thing is clear, however.

All site owners with a consumer emphasis are chasing advertising as the key revenue source for their Web operations. As we noted above, advertisers are undoubtedly at a disadvantage right now and the position will change only slowly. The key gap in the Web offering, as far as they are concerned, is auditing mechanisms for Web sites. Not only are advertisers seeking the right constituencies to address, they want to know which individuals in those constituencies have accessed their adverts and with what effect. In other words, advertisers seek some plausible way of measuring Web activity to tell them whether they are spending their (or their client's) advertising dollars effectively. Proprietary networks can deliver this because users accessing their services are individually identifiable and their actions online can be tracked step by step of the way.

By contrast, the position for Web sites is more difficult. The technology of the Web makes it hard for site proprietors or advertisers to identify visitors unless they are required to register themselves beforehand. This is accordingly a widely used technique. Registration processes and passwords, even when no charge is being made for site access, however, are time consuming and tedious and are hardly an encouragement to new users or old ones who have (inevitably) forgotten their password. Even if sites can identify visitors, tracking what they do while connected to the site is a complex process and software-such as I/Pro or NetCount-is only now emerging capable of delivering useful data beyond the usual counting of so-called 'hits' which is no more than adding up the number of hypertext links on pages accessed by users while visiting a site. Other software designed to analyse increasingly more sophisticated usage data is also becoming available and packages such as Interse's Market Focus and Open Market's WebReporter are becoming popular to save the laborious efforts of manual analysis.

There is still much progress to be made in this area of site exploitation and imminent developments will make a vast difference to the viability of sites, particularly because of the appeal that fully analysed tracking data have for advertisers. However, while server side usage and auditing software has a crucial role to play, client software is also going to contribute enormously to the personalising of site responses to incoming browsers. Netscape's browser for example now embodies a software system known as 'persistent client state HTTP cookies'. The cookies exist in the browser in order to allow site owners to tie together the various requests that a browser makes during a visit to the site.

So, instead of seeing client activity as a flow of seemingly unrelated hits, site owners can see a client visit as a contiguous session and thereby analyse usage data far more powerfully. Cookies in Netscape browsers are identifiers which maintain and store information about a visitor's use of the site during the course of a single visit. The same cookies can contain information about the kind of browser, where it has been before it visited the site and, potentially, demographic data about the browser's user. In other words, if the cookie concept is more fully developed, it could effectively add to browsers a personalised identity card enabling sites to respond in a much more targeted way to visitors than they can at present.

An example of how this principle is already being used comes from the San Francisco based online specialist, C/Net. Using its own bespoke software, C/Net offers the opportunity to advertisers to tune their propositions differently for different site visitors. By using a mix of analysis of the incoming browser header information-which indicates the domain name and software identity of incoming browsers-and of registration data stored at the server based on personal information volunteered by visitors, C/Net can automatically provide basic demographic data to advertisers who can then deliver messages with emphases appropriate to the individuals accessing their advertising.

For example, a computer supplier can ensure that the advert a Mac user sees does not try to sell PC products. Another advertiser might emphasise a corporate role in school resources for incoming browsers with 'edu' domain names and vary the offering to stress strengths in working with public sector organisations if the domain is 'gov'. Registration data could help a car manufacturer target older visitors with messages stressing safety and reliability while younger visitors receive a variant which focuses on a car's performance and design qualities. This approach to individualising site response is still in its infancy but is a crucially important future direction. Leveraging its potential, intense one-to-oneness lies at the heart of the successful commercialisation of the Web and the future of the entire online industry hangs upon it.

While the path of future direction is clear, the present reality is that for most Web sites, counting hits is the best that can be offered. Understandably, therefore, advertisers are currently cautious or undecided about the pace of their move online. The potential benefits seem clear-access to global audiences or demographically defined cuts thereof and the possibility of forging powerful, one-to-one relationships with individuals-but the price being asked plays badly against the current lack of measurable feedback. Advertisers simply do not have the reassurance they need yet that each dollar they spend online is best spent online. But advertisers face an even more challenging issue which many are only slowly beginning to appreciate. The nature of advertising online is fundamentally different from the processes of advertising in the traditional media world. The techniques that work on television or in print do not necessarily transfer to online environments and advertisers-together with all the content players of the old media industry-have to be prepared to re-engineer their skills and commercial understandings in order to make their businesses work. Most importantly, interactive advertising is a one-to-one experience so far as the audience is concerned. Accessing an advert is a deliberate act by an individual and if the person has been persuaded to access it, the advert needs data about the browser's user. In other words, if the cookie concept is more fully developed, it could effectively add to browsers a personalised identity card enabling sites to respond in a much more targeted way to visitors than they can at present.

An example of how this principle is already being used comes from the San Francisco based online specialist, C/Net. Using its own bespoke software, C/Net offers the opportunity to advertisers to tune their propositions differently for different site visitors. By using a mix of analysis of the incoming browser header information-which indicates the domain name and software identity of incoming browsers-and of registration data stored at the server based on personal information volunteered by visitors, C/Net can automatically provide basic demographic data to advertisers who can then deliver messages with emphases appropriate to the individuals accessing their advertising. For example, a computer supplier can ensure that the advert a Mac user sees does not try to sell PC products. Another advertiser might emphasise a corporate role in school resources for incoming browsers with 'edu' domain names and vary the offering to stress strengths in working with public sector organisations if the domain is 'gov'. Registration data could help a car manufacturer target older visitors with messages stressing safety and reliability while younger visitors receive a variant which focuses on a car's performance and design qualities. This approach to individualising site response is still in its infancy but is a crucially important future direction. Leveraging its potential, intense one-to-oneness lies at the heart of the successful commercialisation of the Web and the future of the entire online industry hangs upon it.

While the path of future direction is clear, the present reality is that for most Web sites, counting hits is the best that can be offered. Understandably, therefore, advertisers are currently cautious or undecided about the pace of their move online. The potential benefits seem clear-access to global audiences or demographically defined cuts thereof and the possibility of forging powerful, one-to-one relationships with individuals-but the price being asked plays badly against the current lack of measurable feedback. Advertisers simply do not have the reassurance they need yet that each dollar they spend online is best spent online. But advertisers face an even more challenging issue which many are only slowly beginning to appreciate. The nature of advertising online is fundamentally different from the processes of advertising in the traditional media world.

The techniques that work on television or in print do not necessarily transfer to online environments and advertisers-together with all the content players of the old media industry-have to be prepared to re-engineer their skills and commercial understandings in order to make their businesses work. Most importantly, interactive advertising is a one-to-one experience so far as the audience is concerned. Accessing an advert is a deliberate act by an individual and if the person has been persuaded to access it, the advert needs to deliver some real benefit. Punchy appeals for attention, or loud singleidea strap lines to sell a brand message, do not work online. To be effective, advertising has to adapt to the new medium and that means close targeting of the audience, the use of communications to create two-way relationships with the audience and an increasing and deliberate blurring of the distinction between advertising and content. Such a blurring causes immediate concerns among regulators who are rightly dedicated to ensuring people know what is an advert and what is objective content without an advertising axe to grind. But it is possible to see the process as a benign means of supporting central content offerings with advertising content-information that is contextualised with the content to which it is related and which adds value to it.

Additionally, the advertising must be genuinely interactive. It is not good enough to re-purpose advertising from the real world. Online must have what online needs and what online needs is the same for content sites as it is for advertising. So, whether a content site hosts an advertiser's offering or points from a button on the site to the advertiser's own site, it is vital that the content owner does more than sell space and walk away from the transaction. It is essential for site owners to develop a close, creative understanding with its advertisers so that the two communities can work together to create advertising that supports content and content that supports advertising. A meeting of minds is needed and every effort should be expended to achieve it. Interactive advertising in general and online advertising in particular will never work without it.

CONDUCTING TRANSACTIONS

A third key revenue stream is based on offering Web constituencies the opportunity to conduct transactions online. This has been the great hope of the consumer online networks for over a decade. It is no accident that Prodigy, for example, is partly owned by US retailing giant Sears. The original concept was that having won a large base of subscribers, Prodigy could turn into a huge, home shopping environment in which billions of dollars of business would be transacted by merchants, each of whom would pay Prodigy a small slice of the action. In fact, by 1993, electronic shopping barely accounted for 2 per cent of Prodigy's revenues. The other proprietaries have had similar success.

The mood is changing, however, and the belief is growing that as serious volumes of users emerge, home shopping will come into its inheritance as one of the major revenue generators of the online industry. With the Web expanding rapidly, opportunities for this kind of trade appear to be exploding. Analysts and forecasters are falling over themselves to predict the sheer size of the emerging market-place. Depending on who you listen to, the market could be worth anything from $6 billion to $300 billion by the turn of the century-a sure indication that no one really knows. The sense so far among home shopping specialists is that if the virtual shops and malls are built, the customers will come. Even if they do come, of course, it is worth remembering for the sake of perspective that even the most optimistic estimates of the market look tiny compared to real world shopping. The retail grocery market in the United States alone is currently worth half a trillion dollars per annum.

The reality of home shopping on proprietary services has been that the opportunities to shop have been limited to relatively few suppliers who have offered a largely unappealing shopping experience. Indeed, it is questionable whether any true shopping experience can be delivered online-replete with its essential elements of entertainment, serendipity and socialising. Probably the best that can be offered is a reliable buying experience majoring on the fact that online shops can offer limitless shelf space with a comprehensive range of products. They are also best at selling commodities rather than products with varied values and benefits. Because of this, online is a good place to offer access to large catalogues of media and software products which can be ordered online and fulfilled by conventional channels. It is not surprising, therefore, that in surveys of those online shoppers that could be found in the United States in 1995, 48 per cent tended to buy computer software and 34 per cent purchased entertainment products, especially music CDs and, to a much lesser extent, books and videos. Most (about 74 per cent) cited convenience as the main reason for shopping online. Strikingly, only a minority favoured specially created shopping mall sites to make purchases with nearly 70 per cent tending to conduct transactions at single sites which provided a transactional facility as a strand of their offering.

This suggests a powerful idea about shopping online. The fact that services on single sites are most popular may suggest that online shopping works best when the transaction facility is placed close to the point of interest that drives the impulse to buy. To understand this idea better, consider a simple example. One of the earliest pioneers of Web sites among the record companies was US label Geffen. Today at the Geffen site you can surf through a range of attractive pages that tell you more than most would want to know about Geffen artists and recordings, all colourfully illustrated and complete with sound samples. Strategically placed among the pages are buttons with the words 'I want this CD now' written on them. Not surprisingly, the buttons occur next to some of the most persuasive descriptions of latest album releases. By clicking the button, the user is instantly hyperlinked to another site run by a direct mail CD specialist called CD Now which has created a massive CD shopping presence on the Web. The link does not simply take the user to the front door of CD Now's shop, it takes them directly to that location within CD Now where users can place an order for the album they have just been reading about.

In other words, the impulse to buy has been commercialised by Geffen (and, incidentally, by CD Now) at the very moment the impulse is generated. This is a powerful model for the future of online shopping because it places shopping, like advertising, in close proximity to content. Indeed, just as we argued for advertising, online shopping may be best expressed as a strand within content, contextualised and supporting the content experience. Currently, online shopping remains in its infancy and faces particular problems on the Web. Most obvious is the issue of security on the Web and the lack of effective electronic payment mechanisms that will allow customers both to place an order and pay for the goods in a single, safe and reliable transaction. Proprietary networks have never had this problem because all data moving through their networks pass exclusively through their own infrastructures and, thanks to established subscriber management systems, consolidating online purchases within normal billing mechanisms is a simple process. On the Web, by contrast, concern about secure payment is probably the single most important factor inhibiting the growth of Web commerce.

We will consider security and payment mechanisms briefly later but for now we need only note that-despite the depth of concern that is evident among Web users-trustworthy technical solutions are rapidly emerging which will provide a small number of dominant standards by sometime in 1997 which will spark rapid and sustained growth in Web commerce during 1998 and beyond. As a revenue-generating option, however, transactions look like a strong possibility for the medium-term future. The potential, as with advertising, is based upon the creation by distinctive and successful sites of established constituencies. Just as advertisers will pay for access to such constituencies, so will merchants with offerings appropriate to the demographic of the constituency.

Selling Links

Once a site has established its franchise and built a constituency it is able to influence that constituency in important ways. Most important for proprietors of related but non-competing sites, is the possibility of gaining traffic from the 'hot' site by persuading the site owner to point its constituency at them. So far, this kind of hotlinking is usually agreed on a largely reciprocal basis but once sites have established themselves as successful and well used, they can drive much harder bargains. To some extent, the desire to generate revenue from hotlinking must be balanced with the need to add value to one site by providing links to others of related interest. Such linking is a key feature in determining a site's attractiveness and it would be ill judged to sacrifice good linking possibilities simply because a site is unable to generate revenue from the link destinations.

More interesting than one successful site merely generating hard cash by trading its constituency by selling links is the possibility of agreeing deals with paid-for sites to get preferential access terms for constituents. Proprietors of premium sites or premium areas within sites will be inclined to give substantial discounts in return for a guaranteed flow of traffic. Meantime, site owners can offer an even more attractive package for access to their own sites by, perhaps, making a subscription charge that includes free access to a number of otherwise paid-for sites. In other words, this kind of deal allows major Web sites to become packagers of other sites, offering a low-cost point of entry to a range of content and service experiences which, paid for individually, would amount to a substantial monthly cost. The key building block, however, is the ownership of a constituency which, either through raw size or valuable demographic focus, can be readily traded with others.

THE IMPACT ON PROPRIETARY NETWORKS

The idea of Web sites turning themselves into packagers of other sites may sound familiar. In fact, this emerging model for Web trade is a direct analogue of the traditional offering to subscribers of proprietary online networks. The essential proposition of such services was to offer a low cost key which would confer access to a warehouse of other people's content, licensed in by the proprietary services. Even though in practice little revenue has been generated for the third party content owners, the proposition for them was clear and apparently attractive. While network customers would have access to their content, they would have access to the customers. And networks boasting millions of subscribers had a very compelling carrot to offer to content companies with little other option for gaining access to online exploitation. Ironically, the original proposition for both customers and content providers was viable only so long as there was no consumer online market. As soon as the market emerged, the basic model began to crack under the strain of competitive pressure. The major proprietary services were desperate for market share-particularly since increasing the number of their subscribers was the only way they could boost their revenues. Online subscribers are reluctant to spend money online and the revenues generated from subscriber bases was therefore largely governed by the price of the subscription and how many subscriptions a network operator could sell.

The battle for subscribers sent subscriptions and connect-time charges tumbling and as they tumbled-and subscriber numbers rose-the potential returns for content providers, who were usually paid on a percentage of connect-time charges or a slice of subscription revenues for new customers they brought to the network, began to tumble with them. At the same time, a new and urgent element in the battle among proprietaries to win market share was the need to distinguish their offerings, particularly by including in their warehouses some highly branded crown jewel content which none of their competitors could offer.

For a few content owners, therefore, Christmas had come early because, while the majority of content companies were getting next to nothing, a few were being wooed by proprietaries offering high guaranteed payments just to get hold of exclusive access to a leading brand. In an important sense, therefore, the boot was very much on the other foot. Proprietaries had originally driven a hard deal with content owners, taking everything in terms of brand value and consumer usage data and offering them little in return. This, in a curious way, was sustainable so long as there was only a small market for online services. Once the market emerged-at a gallop-content was a key factor in the battle to win customers away from competitors and content was, therefore, in a far stronger negotiating position. This is the reason why in the two years before 1994 and 1996 the original 80:20 deal in favour of the networks flipped into a 20:80 deal favouring content.

A further nail in the coffin of the traditional proprietary business model was the emergence of the Web. One very powerful reason why proprietaries were always strongly placed in negotiating with content was that content had nowhere else to go in order to gain online exploitation. The proprietaries had invested hundreds of millions of dollars building a communications and computing infrastructure that would enable them to reach the market. The huge cost of entry, therefore, meant that content owners simply had to do business with the established network because the prospect of them building their own networks was unthinkable. The emergence of the Web changed all that and it did so quickly and decisively. For the first time, content had an alternative to doing business with the proprietaries. It could invest just a few tens of thousands of dollars and instantly gain independent online access to a global market-place numbered in millions. On the face of it, the ease, autonomy and reach of the Web looks almost irresistible. For the proprietaries, this new development made an increasingly difficult situation desperate. Not only did they now have to compete with one another for content, but also they had to compete with the lure of the Web. Their response has turned out to be a powerful one, although it implies a complete revision of their original business models.

The first step in the response was to recognise that millions of consumers were seeking safe, reliable and cheap access to the Internet. Most were getting such access via independent Internet service providers (ISPs) who were buying bandwidth from telephone companies in order to gain a pipe into the backbones of the Internet. Many were small start-up, serving relatively small areas, while a few were better funded, larger entities with national and international ambitions. For the proprietary networks, the idea of also offering Internet access was a natural and inevitable step. Whether they saw the Internet as their potential nemesis or not, they had to recognise that many of their existing subscribers were interested in the Internet and that potential subscribers would be even more attracted to a proprietary if Internet access was just another part of its overall offerings. The proprietaries would probably have preferred to de-invent the Internet. But since that was hardly an option, they reckoned that people would get Internet access if they wanted it and that they might as well get it from them. Whatever their reservations about the Internet, therefore, the proprietaries determined to make Internet access another of their offerings.

This first step-forced upon them by the realities of the market-place-has quickly led to a much fuller acceptance of the Internet. Within months of beginning to offer access during the early part of 1994, the proprietaries realised that they could deploy a much deeper business strategy. It became clear that offering Internet access was quickly turning into a major attraction for both existing and new subscribers with literally hundreds of thousands of customers signing up for it within months of the access deal becoming available.

Prodigy-otherwise the laggard of the three proprietary majors-beat its competitors to the starting post, largely because it had already decided in 1993 to completely revise its very poor user interface and to create a new one based on HTML code, the underlying language of the Web. In January 1995, Prodigy launched its first Web browser, making it available to its existing customers by downloading, and also began offering Internet access through its network. By March, 450,000 people had downloaded the software, of whom half were new customers who signed up after the Web access was announced. In under two months, Prodigy had become a bigger Web access provider than

Netcom, formerly the largest ISP in the United States. CompuServe launched its Web service next and AOL followed about mid-year. All found their offerings highly popular and saw growth in subscriber numbers-already strong-accelerate dramatically. Proprietaries quickly saw that being the point of access for such huge numbers of Internet users gave them-like MCI, AT & T and other big national and international players-a powerful influence over what people did when they used the Internet.

In particular, they could influence the use of the Web and the sites their customers were most likely to visit. Prodigy's early experience confirmed what is now confirmed by subsequent more general research on Web usage: the majority of Web users pay regular visits to only a handful of sites. This immediately suggested to the proprietaries that they could add immediate value to their access provision by including, within their own proprietary infrastructure, copies of the most popular sites. The advantages of doing this are substantial. For example, many popular Web sites can accommodate only a few hundred-or at best a very few thousand-simultaneous visitors before the server locks out any others trying to gain access. A typical site cached within a proprietary network and leveraging the powerful proprietary infrastructure can handle tens of thousands of visitors at one time. Beyond the ability to handle large numbers of visitors, caching also makes accessing sites faster and more consistent. In other words, even users with slow modems will get an acceptable experience of accessing cached sites and the speed of access will not vary with the changing overall traffic on the Internet, a frustrating phenomenon which makes general Web access fast one moment and painfully slow the next. The resulting proposition to customers was a strong one for the proprietaries and an important extension of their original positioning. In spring 1995, Ted Leonis, president of America Online services, used a striking and unusual metaphor to encapsulate the new offering. He likened the new proprietary model based on the cruise line business with the cruises being voyages of discovery on the Web.

'I see us becoming the Carnival Cruise Lines of this business,' he said. Carnival [gives you] predictable pricing. Your fare, your activities on the boat, all your meals are included. No surprises. Your berth is going to be clean, and it's going to be safe.... When you pull into a port, Carnival plans your day for you. They say:'...for those of you who like scuba diving, here are the best places to go and here are the authorized guides. For those of you who want to go shopping, we'll take you into town. If you're looking for jewelry, we feel comfortable with these two or three chains. In fact, if you present them your berth card, you'll get a ten per cent discount/ The last point is a telling one and it relates directly to our remarks about generating strategic advantage from pointing constituencies at paid-for sites. With massive constituencies, the proprietaries can now offer chosen Web sites the prospect of huge volumes of traffic. This can be done by pointing (and otherwise promoting) from within the proprietary infrastructure to sites outside it or by mirroring external sites and making them effectively a part of the infrastructure. Either way, the proprietaries can negotiate good deals for their customers, either getting discounts or free access (with the site's reduced charge carried by the proprietary).

As this new business emerged-with proprietaries for the first time embracing content that was not proprietary to them-other signs of the shift towards a Web-centric future emerged. While retaining the idea of a proprietary environment as a part (rather than the entirety) of their offerings, proprietaries also decided to hitch their wagons to the increasing number of major content companies setting up their independent online presence on the Web. They did this by mingling two strands. One was offering services that actually helped content find its way onto the Web. These services included consultancy and the opportunity to use the proprietaries' powerful access infrastructure to speed access to sites. The other strand was to joint venture the development of such sites with content partners and so, for the first time, take a direct equity stake in content assets. In both cases, the thrust of the development was to build new and closer links with content because the proprietaries perceived deep relationships with content to be the means by which they could simultaneously leverage the power of content to generate traffic and revenue on the Web and their ability to powerfully promote selected content offerings.

At a technical level, proprietaries began to shift their user interfaces Webwards too with browsers emerging as de facto standards. Indeed, newcomers to the proprietary business-especially in European outfits like UK Online and Europe Online-were effectively creating themselves as large, complex sites on the Web with content on their sites and a multitude of links to chosen external sites. Users could come and go from the strictly proprietary area-the large Web site forming the hub of their offering-and explore the further reaches of the Web or, at their choice, stick to the online environment defined by the proprietary's strategic links. The Microsoft proprietary initiative has been reinvented by Microsoft to reflect this concept with MSN effectively becoming an influential point of access to the web and its proprietary offerings being, effectively, heavily promoted Web sites with preferential access available to its own MSN constituency.

This hints at the long-term future of the proprietary business, no longer as distinct from the Web but as super-sites on the Web. In other words, the Internet and the Web become the defining factor with which all online service providers align themselves. This is the heart of the revolution which the Internet has begun.

Security and Web Payments

The commercialising of the Web depends fundamentally on being able to send messages to and from servers and clients in complete security. Much else may depend on this but being able to complete financial transactions is totally governed by it. Beyond security lies the issue of how such transactions are consummated in terms of mechanisms to handle the payments themselves, particularly when those payments may come from hundreds of thousands, even millions, of geographically dispersed individuals and the size of each of the transactions can, ideally, vary from a few cents to very large sums. The emerging systems aimed at providing such secure payment mechanisms are highly technical and commercially complex. In this section, therefore, we will not attempt to be exhaustive in our treatment but will aim to establish basic concepts and to paint the main strategic headlines. For those seeking more detail, there is plenty of material freely available on the Web itself.

Why is Internet security such a concern? The reason has to do with the way in which the Internet is organised to convey information between users. If you are a CompuServe user and you send a message via Compu-Serve to another user, the bits representing your message flow only through CompuServe's own computer infrastructure. If an Internet user sends a message, it may pass through hundreds of other people's computers on its way to its destination as it is switched from backbone to backbone across the globe. The fear that haunts the Internet community is that cyber fraudsters are lurking out on the networks hanging around switching points with sniffer programs that can invade other people's data and either copy or alter them. In particular, there are programs which can spot packets of data containing the configuration of digits that suggest the data are carrying a credit card number. The reality behind this fear is far less alarming. Apart from a few well-publicised cases of such fraud, there is no serious evidence that posting your credit card number on the Internet is any more perilous than giving your card to a waiter in a restaurant. The intensity of the concern therefore is based on a perception among users that the mysterious and abstract network with all its metaphorically open doors is a dangerous place for sensitive information. Security systems, therefore, work not only in the territory of technology but also in the realm of human psychology. In other words, they must work but, even more important, they must be trusted to work.

There are three key elements to Internet security. First, the need to keep messages private. Second, the need to prevent messages being corrupted or changed in transit-a requirement known as data integrity. Third, server and client authentication so that both ends of a transaction know they are talking to who they think they are talking to.

This is a fast-moving area and anything written now-particularly at a time of particularly intense development-is bound to be quickly outdated. So, to provide some lasting value, we will examine the current security offerings as exemplars rather than a statement of any stable and lasting position. We can at least gain a sense of the issues involved in designing such systems and get insight into the strategic direction that is being followed by the main players. In early 1996, as these words are being written, there is a raft of competing security systems becoming available, all implicitly or explicitly linked to facilitating secure payments so enabling Internet commerce to get off the ground. It is important to see that security in itself while crucial to payment mechanisms is essentially a thread that needs to run through them in order to facilitate a system that can be trusted by all its users. Trust is a key issue because technological reassurance is not enough-either for vendors or customers. This suggests that the eventual systems to dominate electronic commerce will be associated with well-established brands in the field of payments. It is no surprise and a great encouragement, therefore, to see such organisations as Visa, Mastercard, Mondex and many of the major clearing banks aligning themselves with the technology gurus of IBM, Microsoft, Netscape and other technology majors.

To gain a sense of these developments, however, we will start with the key issue of security itself and look, in particular, how one powerful and immediately available system works. We have already noted how Netscape has leveraged its secure socket layer (SSL) security technology to generate influence over the market for secure servers but the mechanism by which it offers good security is instructive and worth considering as a model of some of the more general issues important in this field. The SSL system is, of course, not the only player in the market. IBM has Internet keyed payments (iKP), Microsoft champions secure transaction technology (STT), browser giant Spyglass has its MD5 system and the US electronic trade specialists CommerceNet utilise Secure HTTP. There is considerable consolidation taking place among these proprietary offerings-Netscape and CommerceNet and other majors are, for example, collaborating through a joint venture called Terisa to create a single, common and open software standard to offer effective security on any server running the new software. However, Netscape's SSL is striking first because it is instantly available on hundreds, possibly thousands, of servers right now and also because it cunningly trades off inherent strength of security against other factors such as speed and cost.

The actual technology of SSL-like all security and payment systems-is arcane and complex, and we will gloss over the mathematic basis of what goes on for obvious reasons. With this in mind, the best way to understand how SSL operates is to imagine a real incident where a Web user with a Netscape browser visits a site offering transactional activities via a server running Netscape's secure server software.

When the server goes into secure mode, a message is flashed on the client's screen warning that the session now beginning between the browser and server will be protected by Netscape's SSL. This implies that all subsequent exchanges will be secure in the sense that the messages cannot be changed or examined by any agencies between the client and the server. There is a key symbol on all Netscape browser screens which denotes when exchanges are secure. Most of the time, it is a 'broken' key but when the browser is communicating with a secure server, the symbol is complete and unbroken. What is happening behind the scenes is technologically complex but conceptually very simple. When a secure transfer is needed, Netscape Navigator running on the client computer randomly generates a one-time token-usually a very large prime number-and this is subsequently used as the underlying mathematical basis for the encryption that will then be used to protect data during the secure session.

It is important to understand that this token is used only once for the particular session in hand and has no other longer-term significance. In order for the server to use the token for encryption, it has to be communicated by the browser in a secure way. To do this, the client makes automatic contact with a trusted third party server known as a Certification Authority which holds details of what are called 'public keys' owned by all Netscape secure servers. In practice, this trusted position is currently held by the major US security firm RSA Data, the original creators of public key encryption systems. The client gains the public key of the server and uses this to encrypt the token before sending it to the server that it is communicating with. The server uses its secret, private key (a counterpart of the public one) to decrypt the token. The server and client then both use the token for SSL encryption and decryption during the session. At the end of the session, the token is discarded. The whole sequence of exchanges involving the keys and the encrypted token takes seconds and is transparent to the users.

The system goes one step further and allows the client to verify that the server with which it is communicating is the server it says it is and that it is not an impostor. This verification is accomplished by the client asking the server to encrypt a short private test message using its private key. The client then asks the Certification Authority to decrypt the message using the server's public key. If it works, the server is what it says it is. If it does not, then the server is an impostor. Again, the entire process is automatic and takes seconds. The interesting element in this picture is the way SSL trades the strength of its encryption against other important factors such as speed and cost. Partly, however, Netscape is forced to use relatively weak encryption because strong encryption algorithms are classified by the US authorities as munitions and may not be exported outside the United States.

The weakness of SSL is, however, only relative and it is quite good enough to survive all but the most determined attacks. However, its sacrifice of encryption strength makes it much cheaper for users and, equally important, faster than any of its main competitors. The danger to its underlying security is cleverly minimised by ensuring that every encrypted session is based on a unique, once-only token. Even if the token is compromised by a breach in security all that is jeopardised is the single session and Netscape ensures that what is learned from decrypting the token is completely useless for decrypting any other tokens. The fraudsters would have to start all over again trying to figure out how to break the code. In other words, a single failure will contribute nothing to compromising any other secure sessions conducted by that browser-server or any other browser-server combination. It is worth noting that SSL verifies the server's identity but does not check the client. This gap in the loop is now being closed by a digital signature technology developed by VeriSign, a spin-off company from RSA Data.

The digital signature consists of two parts: a method of signing electronically that cannot be forged and a method of verifying that the signature was generated by the person it represents. The digital signature, of course, not only is vital to confirming identity in a secure transaction of the kind just described but also leads directly to the possibility of creating effective digital contracts and, in terms of payment systems, fully digital cheques or debit and credit advices. VeriSign's technology is soon to be incorporated in both Netscape's and Microsoft's browsers but is unlikely to remain unique. The underlying concept of the digital signature will soon be widely available and its impact on Web commerce will be huge as a component within trusted mechanisms.

Full payment mechanisms go further than security. As we saw in the imaginary transaction using SSL above, the security procedures merely protect information passing between client and server. For a secure payment process this is only the starting point. Transactions can, of course, be managed with nothing else. The server can request a credit card number, the client can send it and the server's proprietor can then manage the link with the credit card company in the same way as they might in a conventional, non-electronic transaction. The problem is that merchants hope to have hundreds of thousands of such transactions flowing through their servers every day and, in some cases, the transaction value may be quite small. The costs of managing this flow of vast numbers of, potentially, low value transactions are substantial and the prospect of an end-to-end system which takes transactions from servers through to their consummation with the relevant payment agencies such as credit card companies or banks is essential to establishing Web commerce on an effective and global basis.

There is also a security concern-more perceived than real but no less important because of it. When a credit card number is sent securely to a server, the server decodes it and makes it available to those managing the server. In other words, the merchant possesses the decrypted credit card information as indeed it must in order to process the transaction. In the real world, this situation is commonplace and universally accepted. However, in the electronic world, levels of insecurity are much higher among users. Even allowing merchants access to credit card numbers and protecting them fully on their way to merchants is not considered good enough. As a result of this need to manage a perceived threat to customers, further security technologies have emerged to keep the client credit card numbers secret right up until the point they reach the credit card company. Netscape, for example, have developed software called Secure Courier which effectively seals the credit card information with a layer of encryption carried inside of SSL. When the encrypted information reaches the server, the SSL layer is stripped off leaving only the more deeply encrypted data. The merchant does not (cannot) decrypt this but instead adds to the encryption with further data about the sum of money involved in the transaction and the merchant's own identity. This encrypted information is then sent by the merchant the last mile to the credit card agency dealing with these transactions. The agency strips off the decrypted layers to get at both the merchant's and customer's data.

Even though the examples we are giving are specific proprietary offerings, we are now beginning to see the general key elements in an end-to-end payment system. But there is a further matter of deep concern. Everything we have outlined assumes that credit cards will be used as the basis of electronic commerce. To some extent, this is a natural and desirable way of seeing future payment systems. Credit cards are widely used, trusted and are supported by a well-developed and international infrastructure facilitating payments, customer billing and subscriber management. It would be foolish not to try to fuse electronic payment mechanisms with the world of credit cards. However, many people do not possess such cards and either prefer or are constrained by their credit ratings to deal in cash.

In the record industry, for example, about 50 per cent of all products sold are sold for cash. A survey in the UK in 1995 showed that nearly 60 per cent of Britons preferred cash to cards. One way of addressing this problem would be to extend the payment systems to include direct debits of bank accounts but just as many people do not have credit cards there are also many who do not have bank accounts or would prefer not to debit them without being sure exactly what is in them to cover expenditure. Neither are credit cards or direct debits convenient for handling micropayments. Much Web commerce will want to depend on selling very high volumes of very low priced products or services. This could include the sale of access to content on a time basis measured in seconds or minutes leading to charges accumulating a few pence or cents, depending on where the server is located.

All this suggests the need for something that sounds deceptively simple. As well as credit card or bank-based debit mechanisms, there is a clear need for some form of digital money. Money is an excellent basis for trade so long as those using it can rely on it being genuine and also rely on the underlying promise of those supporting monetary systems that the money tokens can be converted among currencies and ultimately redeemed in terms of the value they purportedly represent. There are a number of electronic money initiatives already being promoted, the best known being Cyberbucks from the Amsterdam-based Cybercash. But while simple in concept, the idea founders because of lack of concerted international support by the government and financial institutions vital to giving digital cash its trusted underpinning. So far, therefore, digital cash looks like a distant prospect so far as genuinely pervasive influence is concerned and-despite their evident limitations-credit card and bank-based systems are likely to be the most widely available systems, at least until the turn of the century.

At the time of writing, there are about 30 schemes either suggested or under development to provide secure payment systems. Among the most promising are collaborations between Visa and Mastercard and moves by banking consortia in both the United States and Europe. The importance of these lies in the trusted nature of the partners. By 1997, the first of these mechanisms will be widely available and it is likely that the market will rapidly settle down into a handful of leading products all operating within a single agreed standard and all widely supported by current browser technologies. By the late 1990s, therefore, the catalyst for Web commerce will be in place and we will see an explosion in the use of the Web for all kinds of trading activities.

THE CHANGING FACE OF THE WEB

The conversion of the Web from being an arena for a few computer enthusiasts to a vast, sprawling environment filled with the bustle of commercial activity is not merely based on underpinnings such as security and payment mechanisms. The subjective experience of individuals using the Web is crucial to the pace and character of its future development.

Most times today the Web still seems a silent, infuriatingly slow and confusing place to visit. In fact, it is often such a dispiriting experience to surf the Web, it seems incredible that there is such widespread talk of the Web's creation as being almost on an equal footing in terms of global significance with the invention of digital computing. Is it really going to have such a revolutionary impact on our lives? The answer is yes, in time. But while the mainstream revolution is still-as this book is written-a (very) few years away, the seeds of revolution are everywhere to be seen. In coming years, the Web is going to change out of all recognition so far as the experience of existing, Webwise users are concerned. And by looking at what is about to happen for some of us we can get a sense for the kind of place the Web will soon become for all of us.

An important straw in the wind is the launch early in 1995 by Seattle-based Progressive Networks of RealAudio, a software package available free from its Web site. In the first year following its launch, nearly a million copies of the client software were distributed free and over 100 Web sites were offering RealAudio content. RealAudio works by compressing segments of an audio stream and sending it packet by packet from the server to the client computer. As the packets arrive they are buffered in the client memory, decompressed and then played back as soon as the buffer is full as a stream of sound. During playback, the buffering process continues in background to give the effect of a continuous stream. So far, quality on an ordinary dial-up connection at 14.4 kbs is, in radio broadcasting terms, a little below AM and in long continuous streams it is possible to hear occasional blips in the flow as each buffered segment is accessed. But it is a dramatically different experience from the traditional lengthy process of downloading files and playing them offline.

One of the earliest applications of RealAudio has been radio 'broadcasting'. From RealAudio's site you can access 24-hour Internet radio, which is based on the hourly output of news from ABC. The transmission is updated every hour and the previous 24 hours of programming is stored at the site. This means that what you hear is never more than a maximum of one hour later than its actual broadcast time and that you have access to all the news broadcast during the day in a true on-demand fashion. Clearly, this is still far from a real-time experience but the effect is almost as satisfying-particularly for European ears tuned in to the world of transatlantic radio for the first time. Elsewhere, music retailers and bands are also showing interest in the technology. The Rolling Stones are already making extensive use of RealAudio samples at their Voodoo Lounge site with unreleased extracts from some of their tours while elsewhere vendors are offering a try-before-you-buy option for cyberspace music shoppers.

Other RealAudio sites have quickly emerged including popular Korean songs from a site in Seoul, NTT-AD radio in Tokyo, Fox FM radio from Melbourne and scores of music, radio and magazine related sites based in North America. The only European sites so far are a Swedish national radio station, the Wildpark from Berlin, a fortune-telling service from London and radio services from the Open University at Milton Keynes in the UK and from a site in Milan, Italy.

Later in 1995, RealAudio was joined by a seemingly more powerful competitor which holds the prospect of real-time multimedia on the Web. US software specialist Xing Technology Corporation has announced a new generation of server software that promises to deliver real-time audio and video to ordinary dial-up users. For a lucky few, real-time video and audio are already there. The only drawback is that you need an ultra-fast connection to the fastest backbones of the Net in order to get the bandwidth you need. Very few people, for example, have the benefit of links to the US M-bone (an experimental multicast backbone system) or access to expensive high speed links such as T-lines. Xing claims it is going to change this situation dramatically with a new compression-based technology which will operate over conventional telephone lines. Xing's new product is called Streamworks. Compatible with most existing Web browsers, it works over standard TCP/IP networks including, of course, the Internet itself. The engine driving

Streamworks is a software implementation of MPEG which makes it possible to draw both video and audio from a server in real-time, allowing true on-demand access to multimedia content. The technology has already been proved in private business applications using fast lines. NBC's Desktop Video and Reuters Financial Television, for example, both use the underlying server technology but send the data streams over private, fast TCP/IP networks to their customers.

The real breakthrough lies in the fact that the Streamworks implementation is designed for the World Wide Web and the considerably lower access speeds which commonly prevail. According to Xing, using an associated compression package in the server software, good quality audio can be delivered via an ordinary dial-up connection to the Internet via a 14.4 kbs modem. High quality audio is available through 28.8 kbs modems. With ISDN links Streamworks can, of course, do much better. Using the full 128 kbs available from two ISDN channels, Xing says that Stream-works can deliver in real-time, quarter screen video at 30 frames per second. Presumably frame speed can be traded against window size, enabling a bigger window to be used where there is little fast action in the video stream being delivered.

All that client computers need is Xing decompression software, which will soon be widely downloadable from a number of Web sites. With this in place, users will be able to use their browsers to access Streamworks sites wherever they emerge. Early interest-not surprisingly-is coming from radio stations. Radio Data Group-a subsidiary of EZ Communications, a US operator based in Washington State with 21 stations serving 8 national markets in its portfolio-has been the first to move. It has signed a deal with Xing to put live radio on the Web right away. The first stations to go live will be KMPS and KZOK serving the Seattle area. Michael Rau, president of Radio Data, reports that setting up an Internet broadcasting operation is straightforward and cheap. The operation of Xing software is very simple, much like the operation of a radio receiver,' Rau explains. 'When a hypertext link is selected, the radio station programme is instantly available and is the same programme material that is being broadcast at the time. It is not an audio file that needs downloading.... The operation is as simple as turning on a radio and selecting a station.'

Other radio companies are sure to follow but it is clear that non-traditional broadcasters may soon be setting up Xing sites too. So long as they have access to content, set-up costs are comparatively modest. At the time of writing, Xing's server software costs between $3,500 and $6,500 and is easy to configure and use. Client software can be downloaded free from Xing's own Web site. Registration-which buys full technical support and upgrade offers-currently costs a mere $29. RealAudio and Streamworks are just examples. Many other systems like them are emerging and the trend is towards better, faster, cheaper 'good enough' multimedia. These developments are facets of the revolution now set to reshape our experience of the Web. Elsewhere, three dimensional images are also fast arriving. Virtual Reality Modelling Language (VRML), for example, is cheating the bandwidth restrictions of conventional dial-up access, enabling Web sites to create interactive 3D environments which can be accessed by dial-up connections. Here bandwidth limitations are thwarted by an ingenious technique which makes the client computer do the grunt work. In other words, only low resolution instructions are sent over the network. When these are received by a VRML compliant browser, the client computer builds the virtual world and provides the interactivity which generates the 3D application. Worlds Inc., for example, the US software company acquired in 1995 by UK media group, Pearson, has used an enhanced form of VRML to create a remarkable real-time chat environment that features 3D rooms and visual representations (known as avatars) of other simultaneous users of the system.

Perhaps most intriguing of all is the emergence of a new object-oriented programming language from Sun Microsystems, called Java. Java is a terse, secure, machine independent language which will increasingly be supported by major Web browsers. Sun has its own Java browser called HotJava but Netscape has also incorporated the technology in its new version of Navigator, ensuring that Java becomes a widely accessible language for most Web users. Java's fascination lies in its ability to send entire applications over the Net in compact bundles of code called applets (a contraction of the word 'application').

This makes it possible to send not only data but also an entire added value package containing, say, data and analysis and manipulation software to a Java compliant browser. In practical terms, Java effectively reshapes the potential of Web sites making them capable of delivering any application from a 3D animation sequence to support text in a Web document to a complete wordprocessing or spreadsheet application. It is also possible to continuously update an applet as it runs on a client machine. This makes it possible to stream real-time data like a conventional wire feed of news or financial information. If it can be written in Java it can be sent as an applet.

Because Java is machine independent, target computers need only a simple Java viewer installed to gain access to whatever the applets contain. It is this reader technology which will soon be available in millions of browsers worldwide. There are three important points about all of this remarkable development activity. First, we need to keep our feet on the ground. Java has a long way to go before it becomes a language in which applications can be built quickly and cheaply. All the other multimedia and 3D bells and whistles are compelling and seductive but cost money. At a time when the Web is still generating only modest revenues for its commercial pioneers, building all-singing, all-dancing sites is a big roll of the dice. Annual budgets are today increasingly numbered in millions, even tens of millions of dollars to build and maintain leading edge sites. While the power to transform the Web experience is being delivered fast, its use has to be wedded to the economic limitations of existing Web business models.

Second, and despite this cautionary note, the Web is clearly in the process of being transformed and our experience of it today is no guide to what it will be like in only a year's time. In other words, if we are building a Web strategy now-aside from economic housekeeping issues-it must not reflect the capabilities of the Web as it is today. We have to look ahead at the interactive, multimedia future.

Third, we need to understand this transformation as something which both changes the possible uses of the Web and the audience of users. Once the Web ceases to be the slow and silent place it is today and comes to life with sound, images and real-time interactivities which can be accessed via plain old telephone lines, it will attract an ever-widening demographic of users. Tomorrow's Web is truly everyone's Web.

11

Media, Culture and Modern Times

LINEAGES OF THE PRESENT

Many of the social institutions and patterns of everyday life with which we are now so familiar, assumed their present forms in the four decades between 1880 and 1920. Their development was inextricably tied up with the growth of modern media. The arrival of wireless telegraphy in 1895, and of automatic switchboards in telephone exchanges in 1892, allowed larger volumes of information and conversation to be transmitted instantly, over increasingly greater distances.

The ability to reproduce photographs in newspapers and magazines for the first time (1880) transformed the popular press. And the launch of the gramophone, in 1887, and the arrival of cinema, in 1895, laid the basis for novel kinds of entertainment and experience. This complex of new communications media played a central role in constructing the contemporary social order in four main ways. Firstly, they allowed both the large business enterprises that were coming to dominate the economy, and the new forms of state and government which were emerging in the political arena, to manage their proliferating activities more effectively. Modern business worked with ever more complex chains of supply, production, and distribution.

Modern nation-states were assuming greater responsibility for social welfare in areas like pensions and education. With the age of total war ushered in by World War I, they faced the problem of managing military operations spread over a huge geographical area. Even in peacetime, the operations of many large corporations and western nation-states were global in scope. Empires, whether territorial or economic, posed formidable problems of command, coordination, and control. Second, modern communications were central to the ways in which governments and business corporations secured public support. Mature industrial capitalism was based on the mass production of standardised goods, typified by Henry Ford's Model T motor car. To maximise profits in this new system, mass production had to be matched by mass consumption. Consequently, the development of modern assembly line manufacture and of mass offices using the new typewriters was accompanied by the rise of department stores and mail order catalogues that were designed to engineer consumer desire and to translate wishes and wants into purchases.

At the centre of this selling system stood the new advertising agencies and public relations firms dedicated to promoting their clients' brands, massaging their company images, and combating criticisms and attacks. Modern governments too were in the business of selling. With the development of representative democracy and the extension of the vote, political parties who wished to form a government had to compete aggressively for public support and try to ensure that 'public opinion' reflected their priorities and constructions of events. The public media, particularly the popular press and later commercial broadcasting, rapidly became the main arenas where these competitions for sales and votes were played out. As we shall see below, many commentators saw the private ownership of key news media, and the ever-present possibility of self-interested interventions by owners and advertisers, as a fundamental problem for democracies based on the ideal of open debate in the pursuit of the public interest.

Third, these concerns were part of a wider debate about the state of public culture. More and more of the language and imagery through which people understood and interpreted the world was manufactured by professionals working in media industries that were dedicated mainly to making a profit. This situation generated fierce debates over whether art and thought which challenged dominant assumptions could survive in the factory-like conditions of the modern newspaper office, film studio, or popular song-writing system. Another question was whether manufactured meanings could ever be an 'authentic' expression of popular feelings and opinions.

Fourth, questions about the central tendencies of mediated public culture led easily on to concerns about their impact on 'ordinary' people. How did popular media influence beliefs and behaviour? How were they changing everyday patterns of activity and sociability? How did people manage the relations between mediated meanings and meanings grounded in everyday experience?

When these issues first emerged, they attracted the attention of a variety of analysts and commentators - from cultural critics to investigative journalists and social activists. But a number of the most important contributions came from people who thought of themselves in one way or another as social scientists. There are good reasons why we should reread their pioneering interventions. For one thing, the issues they grappled with remain central to contemporary debates, and many of their definitions of core problems remain highly pertinent to present-day debate. For another, their attempts to develop systematic techniques of investigation have essential lessons to teach us about the potentials and limits of different methods and how they might be productively combined.

To ignore this legacy is to condemn media research to perpetually rediscovering old methods, having forgotten their previous history. We develop intellectually by climbing on other people's shoulders so that we can see further and more clearly. We have no choice, but, as a field of research, we should at least acknowledge our debt to them and call them by name.

RESEARCHERS, REPORTERS, ANALYSTS AND ACTIVISTS

The social sciences were relatively late additions to the intellectual field. Their emergence as the university-based disciplines we now know coincided exactly with the development of contemporary social and media systems. Up until then, thinking about individual consciousness, social action and the good society had been overwhelmingly concentrated in departments of philosophy, with history and law making minor contributions. Consequently, as John Watson, one of the founders of modern psychology, put it, establishing the social sciences meant breaking philosophy's 'stranglehold' over social inquiry.

This assault on intellectual monopoly began in earnest in the late 1880s. In 1887, Émile Durkheim was appointed to the first named professorial chair of sociology in France, at Bordeaux. In 1890, Alfred Marshall published his Principles of Economics, deliberately rejecting the established tradition of political economy with its strong links to moral philosophy and its concern with the relations between economic activity and 'the good society.' Instead, he argued for a new discipline that would analyse 'the economy' as a bounded sphere of action. In 1892, William James invited the German scholar, Hugo Münsterberg, to Harvard to take charge of the pioneering psychology laboratory he had established there. And in 1898, two English anthropologists, Haddon and Rivers, set off for the Torres Straits, intent on replacing the impressions of missionaries and adventurers with a study of tribal life based on firsthand observation.

Underpinning many of these initiatives was the idea that the social sciences were continuous with the natural sciences and should adopt the same basic aims and techniques of inquiry. That conception privileged systematic experimentation and testing, objective observation purged of all personal values, and the translation of 'results' into statistics wherever possible. The aim was to identify the stable patterns governing social life and to formulate the connections binding them together as relations of cause and effect. The result was knowledge that could be used to manage existing institutions more effectively.

This positivist conception of 'science' was strongly opposed from the outset by those who insisted that the study of social life remained an interpretive activity dedicated to understanding what life looks and feels like to other people. One of the founding texts for this approach was Alfred Schütz's 1932 book, The Phenomenology of the Social World, in which he argued that social-scientific inquiry must always begin with 'the already constituted meanings of active participants in the social world'. This argument-that social 'reality' is being continually built and rebuilt by 'ordinary' people as they struggle to make sense of their situation and devise strategies for action - has proved massively influential. It underpins the broad tradition of work that is now often called 'constructionism' (a term deliberately chosen for its strong associations with building work)

as well as much recent work on 'active audiences.' By highlighting the range of skills required by everyday social practices and exploring the logics underpinning unfamiliar beliefs, early contributors to this tradition hoped to deconstruct prevailing stereotypes and demonstrate the creativity with which 'ordinary' people negotiated the circumstances in which they found themselves.

CONSTRUCTIONISM

The impetus to illuminate the connections between biography and history was shared by critical researchers aiming to expose the gaps between official promises and everyday realities, ideals, and performance. They rejected what they saw as the phenomenologists' 'radically individualistic and subjective' approach to the social, insisting that people's lives and worldviews were shaped in fundamental ways by structural forces which they may misunderstand, or not even be aware of. This argument laid the basis for what has come to be called the critical realist tradition of social analysis. Its supporters saw themselves less as celebrants of the complexities of lived reality and more as critics of the processes which had produced these experiences and meanings and of the prevailing patterns of power that blocked alternatives.

MEDIA AND DEMOCRACY

Liberal democratic models of mass democracy presupposed universal access to certain basic informational and cultural resources:

- Citizens required comprehensive and disinterested information on developments that affected their personal and political choices, particularly where changes were being promoted by agencies - whether governmental or business - with significant power over their lives.
- Citizens were entitled to see their own experiences, opinions, and aspirations given a fair representation in the major media of public culture.
- Citizens had a right to participation in open debates over the relative merits of competing explanations of prevailing conditions and rival proposals for change.

Surveying the state of public media at the turn of the twentieth century, particularly the popular press which was the main forum for information and debate, many commentators detected a substantial gap between democratic ideals and press performance. As America's leading political philosopher of the time, John Dewey, noted in his influential book of 1926, The Public and its Problems, the popular media had signally failed to convert a people into a public fully involved in the political process. Their failure to provide adequate communicative resources for citizenship had, he lamented, left 'the public ... formless ... seizing and holding its shadow rather than its substance, ' a phantom, glimpsed occasionally only to disappear again. Dewey's criticism focused on the eclipse of political news and debate by coverage of 'crime, accident, family rows, personal clashes and conflicts'. As we shall see below, his alarm at this 'sensationalist' turn was widely shared.

More radical critics, however, offered another explanation of the press's democratic failure, focusing on journalism's role in providing what Upton Sinclair in his savagely critical book, The Brass Check (1920), called the 'day-to-day, between-elections propaganda' which allows the 'Empire of Business' to maintain its effective 'control over political democracy' and to ensure that its agendas and priorities prevail. In Sinclair's view, this eclipse of the public interest by private interests had two origins. First, newspapers were privately owned and therefore open to abuses of power by proprietors pursuing their opinions or those of their allies and associates. Second, they were funded primarily by advertising, leaving them open to pressure from companies wanting to promote their corporate interests.

'What, ' asked another prominent critic, Will Irwin, 'does the advertiser ask as a bonus in return for his business favour ? ... suppression of ... disasters injurious to his business'. He supports his argument by pointing to the substantial publicity given to the relatively trivial sums which some train conductors had 'fiddled' from their employer, compared with the lack of coverage given to a case of wrongful arrest for shoplifting brought against a department store by a woman who had almost died of shock when apprehended. He gleefully notes that in both cases the companies involved were major advertisers. The argument that money talks and also buys silence had been made even more forcefully by Edward Ross, a sociology professor at the University of Chicago. In one of America's leading journals of opinion, The Atlantic Monthly, a year before, he wrote a piece provocatively entitled, 'The Suppression of Important News' (1910). His major concrete examples concerned the press coverage of labour relations and strikes, which could be considered the touchstone of a corporation's treatment of its employees.

Other commentators at the time analysed the news management activities of government, focusing particularly on the mismanagement of information flows in times of national crisis. This second major 'filter' of news (alongside the filters operating within the media themselves) was starkly illuminated by the prominent political scientist, Walter Lippmann, and his associate, Charles Merz, in their case study of the New York Times's coverage of the Russian

Revolution, entitled 'A Test of the News' and published in 1920. Their detailed textual analysis revealed that, at every stage of the Revolution and the ensuing Civil War (in which the U.S.A. had intervened to support the Communists' main opponents), some of America's leading journalists had been seriously misled by 'the official purveyors of information' offering opinions dictated by vested political interests rather than 'trustworthy news'. As a result, 'a great people in a supreme crisis could not secure the minimum necessary information on a supremely important event'.

Still other critics of press performance focused on ways in which the press amplified incidents of social deviance and helped provoke a public and, subsequently, an official reaction which was out of proportion to the scale of the original threat and may well have added to the problem rather than alleviating it. In 1922, for example, Roscoe Pound and his colleagues undertook a detailed quantitative study of crime reporting in Cleveland newspapers for the month of January 1919, using column inch counts. They found that whereas, in the first half of the month, the total amount of space given over to crime was 925 inches, in the second half it leapt to 6642 inches. This was in spite of the fact that the number of crimes reported to the police had only increased from 345 to 363. They concluded that although the city's much publicised 'crime wave' was largely fictitious and manufactured by the press, the coverage had very real consequences for the administration of criminal justice. Because the public believed they were in the middle of a crime epidemic, they demanded an immediate response from the police and the city authorities. These agencies, wishing to retain public support, complied, caring 'more to satisfy popular demands than to be observant of the tried processes of law'. The result was a greatly increased likelihood of miscarriages of justice and sentences more severe than the offences warranted.

MEDIA, NETWORKS AND EMPIRES

As commentators recognised at the time, the rapid growth of the telegraph in the 1830s and 1840s was a truly revolutionary development in human communications. By separating communication from transportation for the first time in history and translating messages of all kinds into patterned electrical pulses - travelling over wires, through undersea cables and, later, through the atmosphere - it dismantled the material barriers that are presented by washed-out roads and storms at sea. The effect was to create new communicative spaces released from the confines of geographical place. These spaces inhabited a no-man's land between the point of transmission and the point of arrival.

The importance of this development was forcefully put by Charles Cooley in a long essay on 'The Theory of Transportation, ' published in the official journal of the American Economic Association in 1894. He had been a senior civil servant in the transport division, and he went on to become a significant figure in early American sociology. At the time of writing, however, he was working as a political economy teacher at the University of Michigan. He argued that any 'study of communication from the point of view of place relations ... cannot penetrate more than skin-deep into the social meaning of communication' because 'in communication, place relations, as such, are of diminishing importance, and since the introduction of the telegraph it may almost be said that there are no place relations'. Or, as a poem of 1872, written in honour of Samuel Morse, whose code of dots and dashes had become the global language of telegraphy, put it: 'And science proclaimed, from shore to shore, / That Time and Space ruled man no more'.

At the time, this vivid perception that communicative spaces were displacing geographical places as the key organising nodes of social activity was not pursued particularly vigorously by social analysts. Most saw 'society' as more or less synonymous with the nation-state. The Canadian political economist, Harold Innis, was a notable exception. His early work, The Fur Trade in Canada (1930), had explained the choices facing Canada with reference to its place within the centre-periphery systems which characterised relations between empires and their colonies more generally. His later work, Empire and Communications (1950) and The Bias of Communication focused more concertedly on the relations between communications and empire, arguing that all communication systems exhibited a 'bias' that favoured either control over time or control over space.

By facilitating coordination over increasingly greater distances, the development of portable and mobile media had facilitated both the extension of modern imperial systems and the corporate concentration of control over key communications facilities.1 Innis's dense writing style and the fact that much of his empirical material was historical discouraged many social scientists from pursuing his ideas. But the perception that communications was central to contemporary forms of imperialism was gathering momentum elsewhere. By the mid-1920s, it was clear that American popular culture was rapidly becoming a global lingua franca, led by Hollywood's ascendancy in the international film market. As one observer put it, 'Language varies, manners vary, money varies, even railway gauges vary. The one universal unit in the world to-day is that slender ribbon [of film] which can carry hocus-pocus, growing pains and dreams'.

Countries at the other end of this cultural chain were rapidly coming to see America's cultural ascendancy as a new form of imperialism, based on the annexation not of territory but of imagination. Commentators in Britain were particularly alarmed, viewing the language they shared with America as a Trojan horse. In 1937, the radical art historian, F. D. Klingender, collaborated with the activist, Stuart Legg, to produce The Money Behind the Screen, detailing the parlous state of Britain's national film industry and the extent of American dominance. It was one of the first studies of its kind and set an important precedent for future work on the organisation of the media industries. However, because it focused mainly on the economic and financial aspects of filmmaking and distribution, it had little to say about the social and cultural impact of imported movies.

Merz saw the sale of movies in overseas markets as the heavy artillery in a trade war which was designed to make the American way of life the model for popular aspirations across the globe. This assault was organised around the ideology of consumerism - the promise that consumer goods can deliver both happiness and freedom - as dramatised in the lives of the stars and the lush settings of popular films. It was exactly this incorporation of film into the culture of selling that had so angered Hugo Münsterberg when he set out to defend American movies from their critics and to demonstrate their potential to become a new artform, in his influential book, The Photoplay, the original title of his 1916 work. In his view, whenever spectators were encouraged to think of themselves as consumers, any possibility of true art was annihilated. 'The interior decoration of the rooms is not exhibited as a display for a department store. A good [film] is not an advertisement for the newest fashions'. Writing less than a decade later, Merz was in no doubt that the battering ram of seductive consumer style was breaking down resistance to 'the American Way' around the world.

The tangled connection between modernisation and Americanisation was also a major theme in studies of the waves of economic and political migrants who had moved from Europe to the U.S.A. in the two decades on either side of 1900. The shifting relations between place and space were at the heart of the immigrant experience. They were simultaneously living in the United States and being members of global diasporic cultures which linked their new homes to their original homelands through multiple ties of kinship, memory, travel, and economic remittance.

As one of the major destinations for inward migration to the U.S.A., Chicago offered a rich locale for investigating these issues, and a number of sociologists took up the challenge. In these studies, the role of mediated communications in sustaining old allegiances and identities, as well as in building new ones, emerges as a major theme. The letters collected in Thomas and Znaniecki's (1927) study of the Polish migrants contain multiple references, for example, to the importance of family photographs in cementing memories and marking change. Robert Park, with his background in journalism, undertook a major study of The Immigrant Press and its Control (1922). One of the Chicago department's graduate students, Paul Cressey, went on to make young people's movement through the imaginative landscapes of American consumerism, as offered in the movies, one of the major themes in his unpublished (1936) ethnography of juvenile delinquency in the Italian quarter of New York. In a situation where migration and diaspora are increasingly characteristic of people's everyday experience around the world (the major focus, then and now, of anthropological research) and where American brands and cultural productions have achieved global currency, these pioneering attempts to explore how place and space intersect to organise memories, identities, and desires are more pertinent than ever. Similarly, as Manuel Castells has argued in his influential analysis of transnational networks (1996), the role of electronic communications in shifting the relations between space and place is central to understanding the structural organisation of social and economic life in the era of globalisation. Other commentators, like John Urry, go further, arguing that, faced with these challenges, sociology needs to focus not on 'societies, ' but on global mobilities and flows - of images, information, peoples, and goods.

This new agenda places issues of communications at the heart of social inquiry. The point can be oversold, however. People still have to live somewhere, and many aspects of their lives are still structured in fundamental ways by institutions and processes operating at local and national level. As a consequence, national and local media remain crucial resources for people's understanding of themselves and their situation.

TRAVELS CLOSER TO HOME

Although the impact of the shifting relations between physical locations and communicative spaces was felt most acutely by migrants, it was also an integral feature of the way everyday life was being restructured everywhere, even in the most conservative-looking towns. In 1921, Robert Lynd and his wife, Helen, set off for the modest-sized city of Muncie in Indiana to assess the effects of social and cultural change on everyday life. Muncie was the archetypal small town, middle-of-the-road politically and in the mid-West geographically, qualities the Lynds captured perfectly in their fictitious name, Middletown. The study was funded by a religious foundation which was particularly interested in shifts in religious behaviour, but from the outset, the Lynds decided to look at life in Muncie in the round.

The researchers were immediately struck by how comprehensively and rapidly a town sixty miles away from the nearest sizeable city and half a day's train ride from the nearest large city was being transformed by change. They were particularly impressed by the way that 'increasingly frequent and strong culture waves sweep over us from without, drenching us with the material and non-material habits of other centres'. They saw this process as centrally driven by the increasing diffusion of two technologies - cars and radios - the first offering physical release from the confines of the town, the second imaginative mobility. They pictured the radio 'rolling back the horizons of Middletown for the bank clerk or the mechanic sitting at home and listening to a Philharmonic concert ... or to President Coolidge bidding his father good night on the eve of election'. And they were adamant that it was impossible to study 'Middletown as a self-contained, self-starting community ... when one watches these space-binding leisure-time inventions imported from without ... reshaping the city'. The fact that Muncie had a population of only 35,000 made it possible for the Lynds to study it relatively intensively, using a range of methods from documentary research to personal observations and interviews. Larger towns and cities, however, posed formidable logistical problems for this intensive style of 'community study' (as it came to be called). Consequently, urban ethnographies of everyday media activity have tended to focus on particular neighbourhoods or locales within a city.

The Lynds' central focus on the role of communication technologies in restructuring everyday life gave added impetus to longstanding concerns about the range of cultural and informational resources which the popular media offered for meaning-making.

MEDIA AND PUBLIC CULTURE

Looking at the popular press - the major forum for information and debate before the launch of radio broadcasting in the 1920s - earlier commentators had seen the discussion of political affairs and public policy being steadily edged out by crime, scandal, and human interest stories. They lamented this movement towards the appeals and styles of entertainment and theatre because it seemed a move away from the rational public debate which democracy required, and to mark an eclipse of active citizenship by spectatorship.

In the ensuing debate on 'sensationalism' (as this new journalistic style came to be called), many contributors were content to rely on illustrative examples selected for their rhetorical effect. Within the emerging social sciences, however, there was a desire to calibrate this shift more precisely. Addressing the first meeting of the German Sociological Association in 1910, the country's leading sociologist, Max Weber, urged his audience to pick up 'scissors and compass to measure the quantitative changes of newspaper contents during the last generation.' Interestingly, however, he was careful to emphasise that these initial counts should be seen as the first stage of a wider research programme that 'will proceed to qualitative [analyses]'.

In the USA, however, Weber's programme was already well underway. In 1900, for example, Delos Wilcox had published an extensive study of the differences between 'serious' and 'yellow' (or 'tabloid') newspapers in one of America's most prestigious scholarly publications, the Annals of the Academy of Political and Social Science. His painstaking 'column by column' count of the space occupied by various categories of content demonstrated that critics of the popular press were right. 'Yellow' newspapers carried more news of crime and vice, whereas 'serious' (or 'conservative' papers as he calls them) carried more of the political and business news as well as letters and exchanges, as required by classical democratic models of the press as a public sphere (Habermas 1989 [1962]). This argument is also encountered today in discussions over the 'tabloidisation' of contemporary news and accusations of 'dumbing down'. Quantitative content analysis continues to play a central role in furnishing empirical evidence for these debates. By no means all commentators saw the popular press as the enemy of democratic ideals, however. In a seminal paper on the human interest story, the Chicago sociologist, Helen Hughes, argued strongly that by incorporating the stories of ordinary people into the news, the popular press was rebuilding the empathy for strangers which modern life had eroded, and which a democracy that is based on equal respect and attention to plural voices required. In her view, 'moral speculations are not evoked by news of court procedure; they take form on the reading of an intimate story that shows what the impact of law and convention means as a private experience'. Again, analysts have recently returned to these relations between personal testimony and democratic sensibilities in detailed studies of both tabloid news and a new wave of confessional television talkshows.

While some early social scientists were mapping popular representations using content analysis, others were addressing the second part of Weber's programme, namely the development of detailed case studies1 of particular texts. Critical analysts were particularly interested in how the themes and styles of popular media constructed the world in ways that supported prevailing relations of power. Siegfried Kracauer's (1927) essay, 'The Little Shopgirls Go to the Movies, ' is a particularly good example of this tradition of ideology critique in action. Movies, he argues, 'are babbling a rude secret, without really wanting to.

In the endless sequence of films, a limited number of typical themes recur again and again [revealing] the sum of the society's ideologies, whose spell is broken by ... interpretation'. This characterisation of the critic as a guerrilla fighter in the war of signs, revealing the power behind the pleasures, has been central to much subsequent work in textual analysis. However, proponents of this model of strong media have too often assumed that audiences are vulnerable or, at the very least, not properly equipped to see through the disguises of power without the help of a professional analyst. A graduate student at the University of Heidelberg, published the doctoral thesis in sociology which she had conducted under the supervision of Alfred Weber. Entitled The Sociology of Cinema, it was based on replies to over a thousand questionnaires given out to cinema-goers, supplemented by personal observations and interviews.

In contrast to Kracauer, she sees the women at the centre of her study not as dupes of prevailing ideology, but as self-reflexive actors in the new social and imaginative spaces opened up by the cinema and the modern city. Their choices are crucially determined by the dynamics and pressures of a mature capitalist economy. However, this sociological approach to audiences as actively negotiating mediated meanings and experiences, but embedded in wider social contexts that structured their responses in complex ways, had an uphill struggle. It was faced with the growing enthusiasm for the stimulus-response models being developed within individual psychology.

LIVING WITH MEDIA: ACTIVE AUDIENCES

When Paul Cressey set out to study the place of movies in the lives of young men living in the predominantly Italian area of East Harlem in New York in the early 1930s, he declared his wish to 'avoid the "social vacuum fallacy" so prevalent in much...psychological research' and to 'see the motion picture' in 'relationship to all the other forces and influences which bear in upon the delinquent boy in these areas' and in the motion picture theatre. Cressey had already undertaken an acclaimed ethnography of a dance-hall for his Master's degree in sociology at Chicago. He decided to approach this new study as an ethnography of an urban neighbourhood, drawing on systematic observation and open-ended interviews to construct a thick description1 of the cinema's role in the social and imaginative lives of the boys he was asked to study.

Cressey produced a path-breaking manuscript which suggested fertile links between the movies' equation of success and happiness with money and consumption, his subjects' sense of themselves, and the careers actually open to them. Crime, he argued, was not a simple 'effect' of crime films, but was produced in the cracks between consumer aspirations and blocked social opportunities. 'For boys who have been restricted on all sides by poverty, the appeal of [the] expensive apartments, costly automobiles, and "flashy" clothes' enjoyed by the gangsters in the films they watched is 'in itself an invitation towards that type of activity and aspiration'.

Unfortunately, the study was never published, and the unfinished draft lay unread in the archives and was rediscovered only recently. However, if we look at other enthographies of young people undertaken in the same period, such as Frederick Thrasher's The Gang (1927), we see the same drive to anchor accounts of deviance in everyday experiences and to present young people as actively creating their own meanings. Some of these meanings (as Thrasher argued) might form the basis for a distinctive subculture with its own rituals and emblems of identity.

Again, these early studies of youth subcultures, together with the preference for ethnographic modes of inquiry and the insistence on placing everyday media activity in its wider contexts, have all been enormously influential within academic studies of audiences and consumption over the past two decades or so. This has been the case particularly within cultural studies.Prompted by the early ethnographic work of the Birmingham Centre, researchers have returned to the tradition of inquiry pioneered by Cressey, Thrasher, and others. Now as then, however, there have been relatively few full ethnographies based on contact and observation sustained over several years. For practical reasons, most researchers have had to settle for qualitative studies compressed into much shorter time periods, using open-ended interviews, focus groups, or personal documents to access grounded interpretations and everyday experiences. Given Lazarsfeld's reputation as an arch number-cruncher, it is ironic that three of the most important efforts to develop qualitative methods and apply them to the study of audience activity should have come either from researchers working on projects he helped to set up, or from his close collaborators.

REACTIONS, RUPTURES AND REDISCOVERIES

The account offered here has deliberately concentrated on work conducted in the first half of the twentieth century in order to show that current research in media and communications continually draws on traditions of social science inquiry which are longer, richer, and more varied than many contemporary writers imagine. However, there is no doubt that the majority of research in the field has been conducted since 1950.

Along with other specialisms, media and communication research benefited enormously from the rapid growth in social scientific research both inside and outside the universities in the postwar years.2 But it was also profoundly shaped by the political climate created by the onset of the Cold War between the USA and the Soviet Union. This ideological conflict dominated the intellectual landscape. In the USA, the obsessive hunt for communist 'subversives' in cultural and intellectual life, spearheaded by Senator McCarthy's investigations into 'un-American' activities, had a profoundly chilling effect on scholarship, and it comprehensively discouraged the pursuit of critical inquiry.

WHAT DOES IT ALL MEAN?

This is the ultimate, impossible question but one worth asking in spite of it being unanswerable. The immediate issue, of course, is who is asking because the answer will differ with differing agendas. We will examine some answers for only two communities: the world of content owners and originators-those who will ultimately drive the future offerings of the media industry in the new age-and the world of ordinary users and experiencers of media content.

Each sit at extreme ends of a complex value chain. For commercial players, a key question will be where they sit in that value chain and how they should move to wield influence over those sectors most crucial to their own competitive advantage in whatever markets they target. The recipients of the outpourings of the media industry-digital or otherwise-have an equally pressing issue to confront. Where and how should they spend their media dollar? What product or, increasingly, which experience will most satisfy their needs? Ultimately, their decisions determine the future of the entire media industry and, within it, who will flourish and prosper and who will go to the wall. As this suggests, digital media are not at heart a technological issue. This may be a curious thought with which to conclude a study of digital media, especially one which has offered so much commentary about technology. Nonetheless, it is a point worth making. In any consideration of digital media, we must, of course, focus on technology and its varied promises. However, we must never lose sight of a vital fact. It is people who design digital media systems and it is people who use them.

This has quite simple implications. Designers, developers and publishers of digital media offerings need to make a careful and accurate analysis of the human needs that their products are meant to address. Then they must translate their analysis into effective interface and product design. Although simple in essence, this notion is difficult to implement. True mastery of design and development in digital media-particularly in multimedia-demands more than an incremental change in existing established skills. It requires a genuine transformation or, perhaps, convergence. In the creation of effective digital products and services the professions of information scientist, designer, computer programmer, systems analyst, film maker, financier, and publisher must somehow be drawn together, either in a single extraordinary person or into a well-managed and effective creative team. By doing this we may begin to see products that people will want to buy and use. We need to remember that however dazzling the technology may become, someone must be there to pay the bill. Digital media, like any technological advance, can be driven forward only by commercial success. This means addressing and meeting the needs of the people who will part with money for the products created for them. Ultimately, therefore, the real issue in digital media is not technology but the paying customer.

Content in the Digital World

We have used the rather crude and ruffianly term 'content' throughout this book, so reducing the subtleties and richness of our literary, artistic and musical heritage to something that sounds uncomfortably like a commodity. It is well to emphasise, therefore, that content is a jargon term like any other but in this case intended to carry with it all the infinite shades of possibility that lie in the media resources which fuel education, information and entertainment in our daily lives. Even in the digital age, content is not-nor ever will be-a commodity. Value, however, will be added to the experience of content in myriad ways and, if anything, our already rich media heritage should become richer still thanks to the scope and power of digital technologies.

There is a catchy, much used phrase which gives us a starting point. It tells us that 'content is king'. In other words, however many new platforms and channels of delivery emerge and whatever the technological complexities underpinning them, the information highways and byways will be silent and empty without content to suffuse them and bring them to life. More than most gross over-simplifications, this one is dangerous. And it is dangerous because it contains an important grain of truth. It is evident and demonstrable that information delivery is meaningless without information to be delivered; that vehicles for education and entertainment will go nowhere without the content that educates and entertains. It is rather like admitting that 'I think, therefore I am' is really just another way of saying 'I think, therefore something must exist which does the thinking'. So in a very rudimentary sense content is surely king, because without it the media industry, and the increasingly digital infrastructure surrounding it, would simply have no substance. But clearly, the 'content is king' sentiment goes much further than games of logic. It contains a note of smug triumphalism. It really implies that content is the linchpin of the digital media industry and that for all the manoeuvrings of computing and communications companies, the key to the digital future-and, therefore, the strategic power determining that future-lies in the hands of those who own content.

There are a number of issues bound up in this. First, we have to be clear about whether the term 'content' in the digital media world means the same as it does in the old, analogue world. If it does not, then those who currently consider themselves well positioned as owners and administrators of important sources of content may find that their hands are filled with dust. Also, if the old understandings of content are defunct, then all the legal, regulatory and commercial infrastructure may well turn out to be, at best, inappropriate and, at worst, irrelevant.

DIGITAL CONTENT

At its simplest, digital content means the forms of content that we understand in the analogue media world turned into bits and bytes so they can be manipulated, processed and transmitted by computer systems. As we saw earlier in this book, the commercial imperative of electronic publishing is to use the new digital format as a means of adding unique value to the underlying content which, in turn, can deliver new benefits to its users and commercial advantage to its publishers and distributors. This is stating the relatively obvious.

What is more interesting is to consider whether the added values themselves create a new form of content or whether the needs of producing added value make unique calls on traditional content sources. A trivial move from analogue to digital is the conversion of a text document from printed form to digital form so that it can be read from a computer screen. A few commercial products do little more than this and while commercially damned they at least fulfil the role of demonstrating how content can-if we want it to do so-pass quite undigested through the bowels of digital technology. In a case like this, the new form of content relates very closely to the old. But in more realistic cases of commercial development, the original content may be vastly more processed. The obvious example is the use of content to build an online service. It is true that in much online exploitation the original content continues to exist in a recognisable form with the added values of searchability or updatedness helping to sell the transition to the digital form. But if we examine rising trends in Web site development, it is clear that a major genre of online publishing will rely on providing not content in its old sense but a content-based experience.

Consider a typical Web site. If it is to be successful in attracting a constituency it is likely to be based on an interest area (rather than a pre-existing body of content). It is going to leverage substantial use of communications-based services such as forums, bulletin boards and real-time chat, which means that much of its content is going to be contributed by the site's users. It is going to be dynamic so that the overall content offering will change rapidly from moment to moment. It is also going to be increasingly personalised, so offering a distinctive one-to-one experience rather than a shared, generic one. Lastly, as technology makes it possible, the site will deliver multimedia, relying necessarily on a range of content types and related sources. Whatever words we use to describe what this adds up to, we cannot be satisfied with merely the old sense of the word content. If we call such a Web site content-based, it must represent a new conception of content, governed largely by acknowledging that its uniqueness and power lies in delivering a compelling but varied and variegated experience to its users. In particular, the one-to-oneness that will increasingly become a feature of digital media products is especially distinctive.

All existing content industries-broadcasting, music, film, publishing-are based on a generic model of distribution. In other words, their business is creating a single product and either replicating it in physical form and delivering it to as many individuals as they can find who will pay for it or transmitting it identically through a broadcasting infrastructure so that the same product is received by all who are tuned-or who have paid to be tuned-to the signal. In all these cases, the creators of the content products are driven by creative and commercial models which are tailored to the generic rather than the customised. In the digital domain, this generic model can persist-as we have seen in examples from the emerging world of digital broadcasting-but more importantly it can be disposed of entirely. To some extent, interactivity means every user can enjoy a slightly different content experience depending on how they choose to interact with a product but, more fundamentally, it means that information or entertainment experiences can be exactly tailored to individual needs and can be accessed when the user wants those experiences. In this situation, the substance of the content experience is determined more by the user than the supplier and a massive shift takes place in the balance of power between the two. We have also implied that part of the new content experience on the Web will be multimedia. Indeed, it is clear that multimedia of some kind is a recurrent theme in both packaged and transmitted media. From the point of view of content development, the mere diversity of multimedia is enough to mark it out as fundamentally different from all previous forms of media. For the first time, it is possible to weave interactive experiences around a synthesis of all forms of media-sound, images and text-creating something unique in terms of the values it delivers but also unique in so far as the sourcing and editorialising of content is concerned. At its simplest, few if any traditional content companies will be able to source such diverse ingredients from their existing content assets. At a deeper level, the skills required to build products that successfully interpolate the different media forms within the envelope of a compelling experience for users are new and largely unprecedented.

What does this imply for the original boast that 'content is king'? First, it indicates that much depends on what is meant by 'content' and that traditional content companies may have much less to leverage in terms of content assets and content skills than perhaps they anticipate. Second-and by implication-there may be new generations of content originators and processors who can address the new markets as powerfully as the old players, in spite of the established brandings the oldsters may be able to bring to bear. If 'content is king', therefore, 'uneasy lies the head that wears the crown'.

New Content or Old

The problems of identifying ownership in content is complex and vital so long as we intend or hope to leverage what already exists in new electronic exploitations. If we decide to start from scratch and originate new content either for a particular electronic development or-commercially more sensible-for a range of conventional and electronic exploitations, we can at least build up our control of the content assets in a consistent and considered way. There are still challenging technical issues in the drafting of related agreements and the gathering of expert legal guidance, while never cheap, is a vitally important investment to make. No corners can be cut but the potential outcome is a clear map of content ownership in a product or range of products and the ability to sleep soundly at night thereafter.

It is important, however, to consider the question of originating new content from a strategic point of view as well as a technical one. The overwhelming temptation to which the entire digital media industry has largely succumbed is to approach product development by referring to what existing assets can be leveraged. Publishers comb their lists for books with strong enough branding or content attributes to make good CD-ROM or online products. Television and film companies examine their portfolios for gems. And music companies wonder how best to generate new revenue from their backlist repertoires. There is nothing inherently wrong about this emphasis so long as it driven in the right way. What really counts is whether the impetus to examine current assets is shaped by an appreciation of the needs of the market rather than a compulsion to find ways of building new products out of old because the old products performed so well in their own analogue niches. In other words, content companies have to be market facing. This may seem too obvious to state. But the reality is that many operate on hunch and instinct. The approach works sometimes but is a recipe for disaster when applied to new high investment product adventures.

Being market facing is tough. It takes courage, particu-larly because the answers the market gives to your probing may not be the ones you wish to hear. The market may decide, for example, that none of your existing content or brand assets is suited to electronic exploitation and that if you wish to play in the new markets you will have to reinvent and diversify your business. Or the market may indicate that your brand is powerful but that the underlying content attached to the brand needs such deep adaptation that electronic publishing becomes tantamount to reoriginating all that you have hitherto created. The vital need to listen to the market is the oldest lesson that the world of commerce has to teach us but, for a variety of reasons and in a variety of ways, content companies wishing to play in the new digital media markets have partly or completely ignored its universal message.

It is not a simple matter to identify the voice of the market although classic research techniques such as surveys, focus groups and pilot products are all useful starting points. Most powerfully, however, the market can be heard in its myriad responses to existing media and to the new generation of interactive products and services. For example, it is clear that running different CD-ROMs-each of which make small but different adjustments to a PC's system software-can cause conflicts within a user's machine resulting in the longer term in knock-on problems for a whole range of other applications. Yet few titles reassure users-many do not even work properly or they contain worrisome bugs.

The message of the market which is deafeningly obvious is that it wants CD-ROM products that load and operate consistently, reliably and without disturbing the equilibrium of the machine on which they run. Not merely products that work-a blindingly obvious conclusion-but products that convey strong trust at a technical as well as creative level. Similarly, if we look at the judgement of the market in the world of online services, we see that users above all else enjoying using online services for communi-cation. The message therefore is to strand communications-based experiences within an overall online offer ing. By contrast, some companies are merely trying to shift their real world business sideways into cyberspace. Taking publishing as our example once again, book publishers are tending to see the online world as just another opportunity to sell books. It may well be-but the message of the marketplace is that online users want much more from their experiences than access to a publisher's catalogue or to the cyber equivalent of a bookstore. This puts the position bluntly and with some exaggeration to make a point. But even if we wish to refine and tune the argument, the overwhelming issue is plain. Commercialising the digital media market-place starts where all markets start: with the needs and desires of the paying customer.

Strategies for Exploiting Content

There are three options for content companies and while each can be followed independently, most electronic media strategies are an interplay among all of them:

- Licensing
- Joint ventures
- Going it alone

LLCENSING

First, content can license its assets to third parties and step back from direct exploitation altogether. There are a raft of complex issues determining how best to handle a licensing strategy but it is generally understood as a low risk route to added value revenues. It is not, however, a 'no risk' route even though a third party is assuming the investment and marketing load. A bad product created by a poorly performing licensee can do untold and irreparable harm to the future electronic prospects of a content asset. This is particularly true for high profile, crown jewel assets where failure, if it occurs, occurs in the full glare of the public eye. The message is more than merely to choose partners carefully, it is to choose then monitor carefully and-despite the distance introduced by licensing-to be continuously involved with the quality control of the product and the marketing plans surrounding it.

Defining the nature of the rights granted is also a fundamental and non-trivial task. Time plays a role here, particularly since both technology and terminology is so fast-changing. In the early 1980s, some licensors permitted contracts meant to confer video disc rights to describe them as 'optical disc' rights. If the term of the agreements had been a few years, no damage would have been done. But some such contracts endured for ten years, long enough for 'optical disc rights' to embrace (arguably) the whole raft of CD-ROM based platforms.

Even in the late 1980s, when CD-ROM was an established reality, the danger remained. Rights granted which did not clearly specify the operating system of particular platforms to be included in the grant, risked being interpreted as giving away rights to every CD technology in existence or thereafter invented! Short terms, therefore, make sense for licensors if only to allow them to escape from dreadful contractual bungles. But it makes less sense to licensees who need a reasonable contractual period to recoup their own investments and make commercial sense of the deal. The lesson is an important and general one in rights licensing. It is always possible to spell out the technical issues relevant to both parties but, to conclude a deal, there must be a meeting of minds over the commercial logic of the agreements reached. Assessing the value of any given licence is a vital but immensely difficult task. In an industry where there are few established norms it would be easy for licensors to put their tongues firmly in their cheeks and bargain for as much as they can get while prospective licensees do the same but try to pay as little as possible.

The mature reality is that the terms of the deal must ultimately be equitable. And an equitable deal has to be based on a realistic assessment of the value which each party brings. Content clearly has worth but so does the value to be added by a multimedia publisher through collateral content, interactive programming and access to the market. Ultimately all deals can be measured by this interplay of relative valuations of contributions. It is clear, of course, that strongly branded content, in particular, is in high demand and that brand in itself can confer substantial-even overwhelming-value. There is no doubt about the reason. As the platforms and channels of delivery multiply, users of media and information-the paying customers-increasingly need guidance and reassurance to aid their choices. They need trusted advisers and brands have long played that role in the real world and can do so again in the digital one. Indeed, branding can be so cherished by electronic publishers that the value or extent of the underlying content supporting that brand may become secondary.

A few years ago, for example, multimedia publisher Grolier Interactive acquired CD-ROM rights to the Guinness Book of Records. It paid a substantial upfront royalty not merely because Guinness had an interesting database to trade but because the name of the Book of Records is one of the most widely recognised in the world. In other words, Grolier paid a premium for a pre-existing franchise which it could then leverage-even at the cost of funding substantial additional content to support a multimedia production-successfully in the CD-ROM market-place. For Guinness Publishing the deal made good sense so long as it did not lock up the rights for too long a period: the term of the licence was crucial both because strategies and the value of licences change. A consumer CD-ROM licence negotiated at the end of the 1980s would hardly command huge value simply because practically no consumer market existed at that time. A few years later, however, the story looked very different. In other words, granting rights for short periods, as we noted above, is an essential element in licensing strategy in sectors where markets and technologies are changing fast. In another sense too, it was important for Guinness to be able to reclaim its rights in a relatively short period. In the early 1990s, when it licensed Grolier, its strategy was confined to licensing-it had no interest in becoming more directly involved in digital media markets. But by the time the licence expired, the company's management had changed and its strategy had become vastly more proactive. It now looks as if the Guinness Book of Records will be exploited directly by its publisher, either independently or in joint venture.

Joint Ventures

Licensing will probably form a part of every content company's strategy because the company will always possess elements of content of value to potential licensees and licensing of it need not-if handled wisely-conflict with the company's more proactive ambitions in the new markets. Apart from its technical complexity, however, licensing is not a good way, taken on its own, of gaining substantial experience of new markets. For most companies with serious interests in electronic publishing, therefore, joint ventures designed to spread risk and create an effective portfolio of business strengths often make the most obvious and immediate sense in strategic terms. This is not the place to deal in detail with structuring joint ventures but we can at least touch upon the underlying question of choosing partners. After all, if the appropriate commercial strengths are not leveraged in the first place, the issue of correct structuring is barely relevant because the joint venture will fail at the first hurdle.

Sometimes successful joint ventures are created through happenstance meetings of companies in different sectors who find almost by accident that there is convergence in their objectives and synergy in their business strengths. However, more commonly the best marriages are not made in heaven but worked at in a professional and committed fashion. The objectives governing a choice of partners are largely shaped by an assessment of the strengths that are needed to form an effective partnership. Those strengths are fairly clear: access to content, content skills and technological knowhow, and appropriate marketing muscle and secure, long-term access to market. Beyond this bedrock, the permutations are endlessly varied. Content companies may partner with other content companies to draw together the diverse range of materials (and, possibly, brandings) needed for multimedia products. Distribution companies may be wooed to create a secure pipe for marketing efforts. And technical knowhow may be brought in to ensure deep control over effective product-building processes. What ultimately decides the quality of the joint venture is whether the partnerships provide a powerful enough synergy to give the outcome of the effort a strong competitive advantage. They also need to work at a human level so chemistry and culture are also ingredients that cannot be neglected.

Sometimes obvious-seeming alliances do not work well in practice because the reality is that the benefits conferred are unequally shared. For example, in 1995 a leading European distributor of packaged media products (audio CDs, books, computer games and videos) called Total Home

Entertainment (THE) acquired a multimedia entertainment publisher called FunSoft. About a year later, leading US direct marketeer CUC International bought educational multimedia publisher Davidson & Associates and games publisher Sierra On-line. In both cases, the deals made excellent sense for the two content companies for whom access to market was vital at a time when distribution channels were dangerously congested with too much product chasing too little shelf space. For the multimedia publishers, downstreaming themselves towards distribution, retail and ultimately the end users themselves had a powerful commercial logic. For the distribution companies, however, the deals made little sense. While they gained secure access to content, this hardly offered them value at a time when they and all their colleagues in the distribution and retail sectors were being pursued by thousands of content sources, every one of them yearning for some bandwidth to gain access to market. Worse, the deals distracted the distributors from their core competencies into new and unfamiliar business territory. In other words, in the packaged media world, content downstreaming itself for distribution makes good sense; distribution upstreaming itself for content makes none.

Importantly, this kind of mismatch in partnering does not necessarily apply if you transfer the same alliance structures to the online world. Here distribution-or online access provision which is the closest analogue to the notion of distribution as it exists in the packaged media world-is rapidly being commoditised and it is going to be increasingly difficult for the main players to leverage business value simply out of providing online users with access to online environments. There have to be other strings to their strategic bow. For some, as we have seen, offering access remains a means-if properly managed-of owning customers with all that implies for long-term commercial advantage. This is the game being played by Internet access providers such as AT & T, Microsoft and MCI. Others see the future in providing access but directing it towards content in which they have a stake. Here is where distribution and content combine well online in a way they do not offline. This is why proprietary majors such as America Online and Prodigy are busy investing in joint ventures with content companies. They want a stake in the revenues derived from Web sites at which they will point their constituencies. Of course, the majors do not play a single game and the reality is that distribution and content online is forming a variety of marriages, all of which are designed, one way or another, to leverage strategic influence and competitive advantage.

Joint venturing therefore, merely at the level of building intelligent partnerships, is complex. Structuring the deal thereafter is also challenging. Key issues are frequently overlooked or mismanaged. In the multimedia field, a classic blunder is for partners to co-operate in creating a new product made by fusing their joint skills and assets without defining who owns the outcome of all their efforts! Another related howler is to forget to determine what happens to the assets (including revenue flows) created by the joint venture after it has ended. Such detailed structural issues are numerous and beyond the scope of this book. The brief points made here, however, are intended to illustrate just a few key issues so that joint venturers are better prepared for the fray when they enter it.

GOING IT ALONE

The third option for content companies is to invest directly and independently in electronic publishing. This is generally an expensive, high risk option which-in consumer markets particularly-requires confidence and consummate business skill. Above all, going it alone needs a firm commitment to a clear and ongoing understanding of markets, productbuilding processes and the ways in which the digital media world is changing and developing, almost on a moment-by-moment basis.

It is, of course, possible to tackle this strategic option like a mouse nibbling a piece of cheese-particularly in low volume, high priced market sectors-and wherever possible such caution is admirable as a means of building expertise while simultaneously minimising business risk. The danger in a modest piecemeal approach is always that too little will achieve nothing of substance in terms of gaining expertise, establishing brand profile in electronic markets or generating sufficient revenue flows and margin to feed the vision and ambition of top management.

THE VISION THING

While everyone involved in the emerging digital media industry needs to keep their feet firmly on the ground, there is also an urgent need for vision, particularly among the captains of commercial enterprise. There are plenty of foot soldiers ready to evangelise the future potential of digital media but too few top managers capable of real and sustained insight into the opportunities and threats of a fast-changing market-place. Without their commitment, corporate activity will become aimless, misdirected and ultimately self-defeating. But such commitment needs a quality of belief and foresight.

Not, of course, in a specific, well-defined future but in a landscape vision of where broad trends of development are taking us. But such vision, in spite of its broad canvas, needs to be focused accurately. And accuracy implies a base of knowledge and understanding rooted in the events of today that are driving and shaping the business environment of tomorrow. In other words, vision thrives only on comprehension, a realisation of implications and significances. This means that vision must be founded on finding out, among all the myriad events of the day, what matters and what does not. Because change is taking place at breakneck speed and the processes of change are still accelerating; because the interactions of the digital media industry now involve a convergence of many different industry sectors; because the meaning of change is often obscured by difficult, even incomprehensible technologies; and because the controlling brains of major business are (quite rightly) immensely busy tending their core assets: commitment to gaining insight and understanding which is, in turn, capable of accurately informing strategic plans, implies a substantial investment of time, money and corporate will. The real vision required, therefore, is the vision to see that the investment must be made. There is no alternative.

All of this implies that vision must be constrained by the imperatives of business. While we have persistently argued that the commercialisation of digital media is the principal engine of development, there is thankfully room for a human dimension too. All of us involved in building the new media industry, and changing the old, are attracted by the excitement not merely of a revenue opportunity but of a tool to change the way that human beings experience the world. None of us can see clearly where even the next decade will take us in terms of our access to education, information and entertainment but there are few true believers in the digital media future who do not hope that as well as generating an industry, all our efforts will succeed in bringing people across the world together in mutual understanding, appreciating differences but stressing commonalities. The most important human vision, therefore, is that our whole global community-both the possessed and the dispossessed-can share equally in a rich future of media, information and global communications that will ultimately make our lives and the lives of our children richer and more meaningful.

12

The Production of Media Fiction

Since the mid-1980s, the most intensively researched topics in media studies have been audiences, their reception and uses of mediated texts. Following the preponderance of prior research that made claims about the meanings of such texts, their ideological significance and their social effectivities, the emphasis on audiences seems both predictable and warranted. One result of this focus, however, is that during the same period far less work has focused on production processes.

This also follows, in part, from the presumption that mass-mediated fiction remains, in many cases, a 'factory product, ' standardized content emerging from routinized production processes. We suggest, however, that the situation is more complicated than this. Variations within routines, the points of tension engaged in contests between standardization and differentiation, are of equal significance and equally instructive in exploring the significance of media fictions. It is necessary, then, to provide a more thorough and detailed analysis of production practices than the usual generalizations about 'media factories' allow.

One approach is outlined in David Bordwell's concept of 'historical poetics'. Under that category, he suggests that it is necessary to explore options open to mediamakers at given points in time and in specific social contexts, attending to industrial, economic, and regulatory factors. While Bordwell tends to focus on those options generating the standardized elements found in much mass-mediated material, we believe it is possible to discover important manipulations of production processes that indicate the 'relative autonomy' of individuals, groups, even organizations within media industries. What this suggests most importantly is that any study of the production of media fiction must recognize multiple types of influence.

Factors ranging from policy formation to the application of new technologies may affect the production of any particular media fiction. While research taking account of multiple causal elements usually provides stronger explanations, it often remains the case that specific instances of production studies privilege particular aspects over others. In some cases, this results in reductive assertions about causation or influence, although in most instances it simply means that one factor is taken as dominant, overdetermining all others. These factors and the relations among them may be described as 'levels of analysis.' We emphasize that this term should not imply a universally effective hierarchy of influence or determination, but it is the case that such a categorization of influence works from more general to more specific sites and applications. The most effective production research will seek to identify the interdependence of the influences, while demonstrating their variations in different cases, settings, and systems.

LEVELS OF ANALYSIS

NATIONAL AND INTERNATIONAL POLITICAL ECONOMY AND POLICY

The production of particular media artefacts within specific industrial systems obviously takes place within more general contexts. Among the most influential works at this level are those exploring differences between commercial broadcasting or film industries and media reliant on various forms of state support. Although analyses of production practices generally acknowledge such differences, broad assumptions rather than detailed analysis commonly guide the study of the relations between policy and production. This is so, in part, because descriptive and source material related to media policy often focuses on generalizations rather than cases, while detailed case studies take the constraints of political economy for granted. Overlooked in both models is the fact that individual productions are enabled as well as constrained by general conditions. Varied responses to those conditions illuminate the complexity of the larger structures, reminding us that while media production is indeed a modern, factory product, the differences among the products are as telling as their similarities. Nevertheless, a number of policy works provide useful contextual information for production research. Among them, Alexander et al. (1998), Hoskins et al. (1997), and Moran (1996) offer extensive overviews of contemporary media industry policies that can be applied analytically.

Some studies do, in fact, bring together the macro-levels of policy and economic structure with analyses of cases. They include explorations of the ways in which media products are affected by social problems, such as 'censorship' or 'violence.' Doherty (1999) and Gardner (1987) provide examples of the first topic, showing how particular American films were produced before and during periods of heavy social control. Cowan (1979) focuses on engagements with policy by individuals (e.g., Norman Lear) and institutions (e.g., The Writers Guild of America) with regard to sex and violence on television, and shows how production strategies were affected by congressional actions mandating a 'family hour' for commercial television. As these publications suggest, a major approach to studying the relationship between policy and production has been historical.1 Boddy (1990), for example, explores relations among television executives, the U.S. Congress, and television critics in the 1950s. He carefully establishes how, in the struggle among these groups, industry executives managed to secure their economic interests through legislative and judicial decision-making.

The outcome of these battles led to major industry developments, such as the shift from 'live' television production in New York to filmed programming from Hollywood, resulting in fundamental changes in aesthetics, altered production practices, and ultimately the distinctive place of television fiction in U.S. culture.

Methodologically, all these works have depended on the analysis of archival data.2 While public policy records are usually freely available, corporate papers have sometimes been deposited in reference archives, making access for researchers relatively simple. In other cases, such materials may be proprietary and access severely restricted. These records are essential for production research, because the documents contain evidence both of conflicting points of view and of concrete decision-making related to particular media artefacts.

SPECIFIC INDUSTRIAL CONTEXTS

Historical approaches have also been prominent in research examining the institutional configuration of media industries, but here analysis is focused more precisely on specific industrial practices. Among the strongest examples is The Classical Hollywood Cinema, which examined the development of the Hollywood film industry and the resulting reliance on a particular narrative style, as indicated in the title.

The study tracks the establishment of regularized industrial strategies, consequent divisions of labour, instrumental applications of new technologies, and other features of the Hollywood film factories. It suggests that, after a period of experimentation, the U.S. film industry narrowed into certain industrial operations that were developed in the service of particular narrative conventions. The analysis also demonstrates how this general pattern of regularization was realized in particular films. The central argument points to the reduction of possible narrative strategies and, ultimately, of the styles, genres, and meanings within an industry that was increasingly successful on its own terms. The ideological result was the establishment of a particular cultural meaning of 'cinema' to the exclusion or marginalization of alternative forms.

Here again, researchers rely heavily on primary historical records - contracts, inter-office memoranda, extant interviews, handbooks, production manuals, instructional pamphlets, variously revised scripts, and story conference memoranda recording decision-making processes. These are explored in order to describe, analyse, and contextualize the actual production practices involved in film- and television-making. Because sustained archival research is needed to uncover more evidence, and because the study of media fiction, in particular, is of relatively recent development, new histories continue to refine our knowledge of much-needed background and circumstances. Hilmes (1997), for example, provided new information regarding the shifting arrangements among media industries, including the radio industry, which have altered the cultural definition of 'film' and 'television' in the U.S.A. A contemporary example illustrates how this level of analysis takes research beyond more generalized descriptions.

Montgomery (1989) focused on the different ways in which interest groups engage television networks in order to gain a more favorable representation. Using interview and ethnographic methods, as well as analysis of records and contracts, she also examined individual television texts to show how these groups variously succeeded or failed in their attempts to alter detailed television production practices. A similar case is in progress, and invites study, as we write.

In the U.S.A., the National Association for the Advancement of Colored People has recently secured contractual arrangements with major television networks that will lead to the employment of more people of colour in television's executive and creative communities. In this case, as in cases studied by Montgomery, interest groups have used strategies, such as boycotts or threats of boycotts, which recognize the role played by political economy and government policies in media production.

PARTICULAR ORGANIZATIONS: STUDIOS, PRODUCTION COMPANIES, NETWORKS

Studies of institutional relations often rely on the next more specific level of analysis, exploring the connection between an organization and the industrial configuration in which it operates. Textual analysis of individual works or collections of films and television programs is much more prominent at this level, frequently with an emphasis on genre and format as indicative of an organizational 'style.'

An outstanding example of this type of analysis is Schatz (1988), who focused on regularized and systemic aspects of the film industry, using sources and approaches similar to other histories of cinema. In using archival sources, however, his primary method was the case study, and by focusing on several studio organizations, the production of particular films, and the roles of powerful individual studio heads, he placed greater emphasis on human agency and documented important variations. The findings, again, indicate greater diversity within 'the studio system' than is sometimes assumed in studies of the general institutional arrangements.

For television, a primary example is Feuer et al. (1984), a study of the MTM production company, which argues for the existence of a 'signature style' associated with a number of its productions. The identification of that style enabled the authors to describe variations within the general structures of both genre (the situation/domestic/workplace comedy) and the U.S. television industry as such. Cunningham (1988) provided a similar example of house style from Australian television.

Such studies must rely heavily on company histories and production case studies in order to support the textual analyses that identify particular elements as a distinctive 'style.' In addition, they may make use of interviews and observations when access to individuals and ongoing productions can be arranged.

13

Budgeting and Decision Making

Managers use a variety of types of information in the process of making decisions. Media managers use accounting information for making decisions, planning the future, and controlling organizational behaviour. Most people think of accounting as indecipherable and sometimes meaningless columns of numbers representing debits and credits. Indeed, accounting information often is presented in annual reports and budgets as rows and columns of dollars and cents. Despite the financial emphasis, accounting provides meaningful, nonfinancial information describing the past, present, and future status of an organization. Without accounting information, managers would lack the necessary information for planning, decision making, and evaluating performance; organizations would have poorly defined goals, if they were to have goals at all; and managerial learning and organizational growth might never occur. Consequently, accounting provides essential information for the day-to-day activities and long-term growth and survival of organizations. A manager is faced with a wide range of accounting information. The information a manager chooses to use in making a decision depends on several factors, including the manager's level in the organization, the long or short-term nature of the decision, the organization's size and complexity, and the nature of the firm. Regardless of the variety of types and forms of accounting information available to managers, one form of information managers use extensively is the budget.

TYPES OF ACCOUNTING INFORMATION

Accounting activities are divided into financial accounting and managerial accounting. Financial accounting provides information about an organization's health to outsiders. Managerial accounting provides information about the day-to-day operation of the company for managers to use in planning and budgeting. Although both are related to managing an organization.

Financial Accounting Information

Financial accounting refers to the preparation of materials, such as annual reports, for use primarily by individuals external to the organization. Such materials are used by the general public, regulatory agencies, owners, investors, creditors, taxing authorities, and industry associations. For example, a public media company's annual report may reveal the culture and values of that organization. The annual report's cover design, letter to shareholders, and information about planned investments and acquisitions reveal what management considers important to the firm's long-term success.

A balance sheet also reveals a great deal of information about a company. Let us consider how to analyse a balance sheet using an example for a fictitious broadcast group with seven television and two radio stations called Callas Communications. The long-term objective of Callas Communications is primarily to acquire more television stations and, if possible, other media and communications-related properties in the future. Another goal is to identify and acquire stations that have the potential for substantial long-term appreciation and profitability. Callas' management looks for personnel who can aggressively manage these stations to maximize profits, allowing the company to purchase more stations. Callas' seven TV stations are network affiliates of ABC, CBS, NBC, or Fox.

This background information is important for evaluating Callas' balance sheet, which reflects the financial status of a corporation by listing its assets and liabilities. It serves as a stop-action photograph of a company on a given date. When a series of balance sheets are examined together, they reveal how the company behaved across time. The balance sheet is divided into ma or sections called assets, liabilities and shareholder's equity. Assets are resources that a company owns or that are owed to a company. Liabilities are amounts of money that are owed by the company in some form to a person or organization. Both assets and liabilities take many forms, but the total assets minus the total liabilities reveals the company's financial health. The difference between assets and liabilities is shareholder's equity, which represents the value of the company that belongs to the owners. The balance sheet gets its name from the

Assets.

Current assets include money or other resources that are converted easily to money. For example, accounts receivable include money owed the company for services or products rendered. Inventories are those objects that can be sold readily for cash. Investments and other assets are resources that come from investing other resources. Property, plant, and equipment include land, buildings, and equipment owned by the company. Because some media organizations, such as daily newspapers and television stations, require a large fixed investment, this category is often a large portion of assets for these firms. Depreciation represents the value of property, plant, and equipment that has been used up in the operation of the organization. If a newspaper or TV station buys a computer system, a certain percentage of the cost of that system becomes depreciation each year until the value reaches zero. One can look at property, plant, and equipment as investments in future production. As that investment is used for production, it declines in value, which must be represented on the balance sheet.

Goodwill, publication, and broadcast rights represent the value of any legal rights a company has to publish or broadcast and the value of how people feel about the company. Goodwill is the value of the company's reputation. A problem with these categories is that they are hard to measure. Quite often, a company will figure its liabilities and owner equity and the difference between these two and its assets will be goodwill. Just as equipment depreciates, goodwill has a limited life. People who watch television stations have viewing preferences that change, have multiple viewing options due to DSS, cable, and VCRs, and have outside TV interests. Goodwill for these people ends. This loss of goodwill is amortized across the line and is placed in the balance sheet to show this loss of this asset.

In reviewing Callas' balance sheet, a large part of the company's assets are listed as intangible assets, especially network affiliations. It appears that Callas may have simply listed the difference between assets and liabilities as intangible assets. Given the aggressive acquisition stance the company takes, one would expect to see a large amount under intangible assets and under liabilities in the next section of the balance sheet.

Anyone considering an investment in Callas would be wise to be cautious. All of Callas' stations are VHF network-affiliated stations. Network affiliations are valuable, as there are a limited number of very high frequency (VHF) channels available in each market. Television station broadcasting on the VHF band have had some competitive advantage over ultra-high frequency (UHF) stations. This advantage is diminishing, however, as viewing options increase. Plus the major networks' share of the viewing audience nationwide has been declining for several years. Such a high reliance on intangible assets may indicate a company in, or potentially in, financial trouble.

Liabilities and Shareholder's Equity.

Current liabilities are debts that are due within a relatively short period of time. Besides the typical short-term debts that many companies pay like salaries, a company like Callas has interest payments on the high level of debt the company carries, given its goals of acquiring media properties. Also note the long-term debt or noncurrent liabilities. These are liabilities that extend for I year or more. For example, if a company sells bonds, the amount owed the bond holders would be noncurrent liabilities.

The large amount listed under long-term debt also indicates the company's long-term goal of acquiring properties. For example, during the past year Callas acquired a Fox affiliate in a top 10 market for approximately

$175 million in cash and the assumption of certain liabilities. The purchase price and liabilities are reflected in the long-term debt column for 1997. Another acquisition the previous year is reflected in the 1996 long-term debt. Obviously, the owners and stockholders believe that these station purchases will pay off over the long term; otherwise they would be unwilling to acquire so much debt.

This debt is reflected in the shareholder's or stockholder's equity section, which shows a deficit. Shareholder's or stockholder's equity represents the resources of the company that belong to the owners in one way or another. For example, if the company had earned a profit, any retained earnings listed would be the amount of profit that remains in the control of the managers of the company. In the case of Callas Communications, both preferred (voting) and common (nonvoting) stocks are listed under liabilities. Should the company ever liquidate, the holders of preferred stock would be compensated first. Presently the stockholders' equity is a deficit, so anyone considering an investment in Callas must be cautious.

Although a balance sheet is used generally by outsiders to evaluate the financial position of the company, a series of balance sheets also can help managers. They are not so much generators of information for decision making as they are warning signals. By monitoring the balance sheets across time, one can get a sense of whether the company's financial position is improving or deteriorating. If the ratio of assets to liabilities is increasing, the company is doing well. If the ratio is declining, it could be doing better. In reviewing Callas' balance sheets for 1996 and 1997, it appears that the company could be doing better. Intangible assets increased slightly in 1997 when the stockholders' equity showed a deficit.

Another item to note is the "Note receivable from officer" listing under stockholders' equity. The company made a personal loan to an officer of the company with an annual interest rate of 8 per cent. Other stockholders or potential investors might legitimately question the wisdom of making personal loans to officers from company funds. Such a loan may indicate that questionable accounting practices are used by the company.

MANAGERIAL ACCOUNTING INFORMATION

Managerial accounting emphasizes the accounting information needs of the manager for decision making. Budgets and income statements are developed to aid managers in assessing whether organizational goals are being met. Budgets and income statements are the accounting information formats most frequently used by managers.

Budgets and Income Statements

A budget is a statement of the planned use and acquisition of financial resources for meeting specific goals during a particular period of time. Budgets quantify the objectives and specific goals of the manager's department or company. Budgets provide direction for decision making and are an integral part of the planning process. Consequently, budgets are used as detailed and coordinated plans for the future. Budgets also set performance standards or criteria for evaluation.

At the end of the budgeted time period, an income statement is generated. The income statement reflects the actual expenditures and revenues for each category listed in the budget for the time period. A comparison of the budget and income statement for the same time period allows the manager to evaluate the unit's performance and provides necessary information for controlling the functions of the department.

Annual budgets are prepared for the business and each of its departments, and each budget is subdivided into 12 monthly periods. The budget for the business is called the profit plan or master budget plan; departmental budgets are known as operating budgets. Long-range budgets also are developed, but typically only at the level of the business as a whole.

A master budget plan for radio station KHIT-FM, which was recently purchased by Callas Communications. KHIT is a top-40 hit music station serving a geographic area with a population of about 250,000. The area includes a major state university and several smaller colleges with a combined student population of about 60,000. KHIT's market serves as a regional medical centre and has an automotive manufacturing plant and regional recording studio. A major regional discount and grocery retailer maintains its headquarters here, as well as a national insurance and investments company. The area's median income is around $45,000.

The actual profit plan would include operating budgets from each department. The budget is comprised of expenses, which are the costs associated with running the radio station, and revenues, which are the sources of income for the station. The major source of revenue is generated from the selling of airtime for advertising. The advertising revenue is categorized by geographic source; local advertising accounts for 77.8 per cent of the station's sales revenues, and national/regional advertising accounts for 23.2 per cent of revenues. Total expected revenue is calculated by subtracting the sales representatives' commissions, which depend on the amount of sales. Miscellaneous additional revenue is added to calculate the projected total revenue for the coming year.

Projected operating expenses are itemized by department and indicate each department's forecasted financial needs. The two types of expenses itemized in the budget are operating and nonoperating expenses. Operating expenses include the day-to-day costs of running the radio station. The operating expenses of a radio station might include the cost of using an outside news service, music license fees, subscribing to an audience ratings service, and the compensation of employees.

Nonoperating expenses include other costs that are not incurred from operating the station, such as the depreciation of equipment and interest to be paid on any outstanding loans. Depreciation is a common nonoperating expense because equipment loses its value and eventually needs to be replaced. The departmental operating and nonoperating expenses are summed to calculate the projected total expenditures for the coming year. Total expenses are subtracted from total net revenues to calculate the projected business profit before paying taxes. For radio station KHIT, the expected profit for the coming year is $89,977.

A comparison of last year's actual expenses with the projected figures developed by the new owner shows some important differences. For example, more revenue is expected from local and national advertising sales and other revenue. A spending increase is planned for programme production, engineering, advertising, and promotion. These figures reflect the planning and decision-making activities of several managers at KHIT. The budget for the coming year was developed by the new sales manager, general manager, and the existing programming director over the course of 3 months of discussions, data gathering, and decision making. Callas Communications brought in two new managers from other stations with track records of increasing revenues. The company purchased the station because management felt a strong additional profit potential was likely, given the large student population and diversified economy in the market.

Presently, the economy is strong in the market, so the new managers want to take advantage of this quickly. The auto manufacturing industry often experienced downturns, so profits must be increased quickly to improve performance before another downturn begins. Also, the new managers want to educate local and national advertisers about why increasing their advertising budgets would help their businesses. The new sales manager had successfully retrained sales personnel before to increase sales and develop new accounts. The revenue projections were based on this manager's previous successes.

The general manager felt another strategy should be developed to increase other revenues over the coming year to satisfy the owners. Several general strategies might be utilized:

- The staff could work harder to maintain existing revenues;
- Costs could be cut; or
- Other types of revenue could be sought.

The sales manager was already working on the first solution. The second solution of cost cutting would improve the situation in the short run, but the long-run consequences could affect the station's ratings negatively, thereby reducing advertising revenues in the future. Budget amounts were increased slightly for engineering, programme production sales, advertising, promotion, and general administration to maintain the station's quality. These increases were judged to be the smallest possible to maintain quality and cover planned projects for the coming year. The news department budget was not increased as management felt the station's 18- to 44-year-old core audience listened because of the station's music selections, not its news coverage. The general manager also noted that she would work with all department heads to trim the budget where possible without sacrificing quality.

The programming head, who had been retained by Callas, proposed an idea to promote the station while generating additional revenue. The station could align with the city, local advertisers, and the regional recording studio to promote a concert on the riverfront every spring. The city had an annual spring festival to celebrate the end of the area's long winters and foster community spirit. The programming manager thought a free concert featuring artists who recorded at the regional studio would be a natural tie-in.

The station might conduct a T-shirt design contest to be entered by students from the local university and colleges for the concert. The winning T-shirt design could be produced and sold by sponsoring advertisers at their businesses, and at the concert itself. KHIT could promote the contest and concert on the air and locally through its cosponsors. In addition, the station could attract business for their advertisers by selling T-shirts in their stores. Any advertising for the T-shirt promotion also would be advertising for their participating clients, the station and the concert.

The extra $5,000 in the advertising and promotion budget for this year reflected the minimum cost of promoting the event. The extra $10,000 in other revenue represented a conservative estimate of the additional revenue to be gained from T-shirt sales. The increases in engineering and programme promotion represented the estimated minimum cost to broadcast the concert. Presumably the recording studio could be counted on to share production costs. The three managers agreed that the concert and T-shirt idea was worth a try. The recording studio also featured artists popular with the station's target market. If the concert was successful, as expected, it would only become more profitable in years to come. And it might lay the groundwork for establishing another concert in the late summer/early fall when college students returned to school.

The budget developed for KHIT's coming year represents the desired future status of the radio station based on the decisions of the management team that prepared the budget, keeping the corporate owner's goals in mind. The budget provides spending guidelines for the department heads and sets performance expectations for the sales staff. In particular, this budget sets a criterion for evaluating the short-range decision to promote the station through the concert and T-shirt promotion. If T-shirt sales generate additional revenues of at least $10,000, and advertising sales are increased as projected, then KHIT might choose to repeat the promotion the next year. If the outlined expectations are not met, then the radio station probably would not choose the same strategy for the coming year. The example of radio station KHIT illustrates how annual budgets are developed and used for short-range planning and routine decision making. Long-range budgets are used for plans of 5 years or more and cover more nonroutine decisions. Whether a manager makes a fairly routine, short-range decision or a nonroutine, long-range decision is often a function of the manager's level in the organization. The types of budget information a manager needs and uses for decision making are affected by the long- or short-term nature of the decision itself.

The steps in the decision-making process are reviewed in order to explain how managers use budgets. Two important aspects of the process also are discussed: how short-range versus long-range decisions affect the use of information and how the differences in organizational levels affect managerial decision making.

MANAGERIAL DECISION MAKING

Managerial decision making, like most decision making, is a process that consists of six stages, as shown by the decision-making wheel in chap. 1. Collecting and analyzing information plays the central role in the this process, but managers at different organizational levels collect and use information differently.

The case of KHIT illustrates this process. The sales manager identified the possible increases in advertising revenue through discussions with sales personnel and advertisers, and by evaluating local and national economic indicators. The sales manager viewed the opportunity from the perspective of how it would affect the department during the coming year. The general manager, on the other hand, specified the overall organizational goal of increasing profits in comparison to last year. The sales manager informed the general manager of the opportunity to improve sales performance through training and mentoring the sales staff. The general, sales, and programme managers reviewed several strategies and selected the concert and T-shirt contest because they appeared to be relatively cost-effective ways to increase profits. But all managers were involved to ensure that the organizational and departmental perspectives were considered. This example also demonstrates how the budget is used for implementing the solution. The income statement will be used to monitor the solution because it provides information about the performance of the solution. Both can be reviewed to refine the solution in future years. All three managers understand that if profits are not increased in the next year or two, all may lose their jobs.

Long-Range Versus Short-Range Decisions

Short-range decisions are often routine decisions, the type that a manager has some degree of experience in making on a regular basis. Because of the manager's experience with a routine decision, information about alternative strategies, and the results of the those strategies are accumulated. As a result, routine decisions usually involve less risk, and the decision outcomes are more predictable than in nonroutine decisions. Routine decisions are evaluated within some short period of time, perhaps a few months. So, if short-range decisions have unexpected negative consequences or do not produce the expected results, changes can be made quickly to minimize the impact of the undesired outcomes.

Nonroutine decisions are made infrequently and have long-range effects and consequences. Such consequences are difficult to anticipate. For example, the decision to invest resources in new equipment, such as a new system of computers for a newspaper, has a short-range consequence of increasing costs during the fiscal year of the purchase. However, the long-range consequences may be more difficult to determine and forecast. For example, desired long-range outcomes would be increased writer productivity and efficiency in the production of the paper itself. But an unanticipated, long-range consequence of using video display terminals was repetitive motion injury, which could have been avoided by purchasing ergonomic furniture and materials. So background research is needed to evaluate the likelihood of those outcomes, and to predict the value added to the paper in the long run.

Managers should also evaluate problems to see if an unexpected, and more cost effective, solution may be found. For example, major metropolitan papers like Newsday and The New York Times have tried to find a cheaper and faster way to make colour proofs. Some newspapers have purchased high-end colour copies to use for making page proofs and ad proofs. Such copiers cost $50,000 or more, but can print a proof in 3-4 minutes for $0.37, rather than 20-30 minutes at a cost of $7 each. Presently these copiers are more cost effective for papers generating large numbers of colour proofs (Toner, 1997a). But these copiers may come down in cost over time, making such a system cost effective for smaller papers. Newspaper managers can keep up with such innovations by reviewing the "Operations" section of Presstime each month. Managers in other media firms can check their trade publications each month for similar cost-saving ideas.

Even more difficult to predict than expected positive long-range outcomes are long-run negative, unexpected results of decisions. An example of present concern is whether the Internet will draw readers away from newspapers. Many newspapers have published online editions to retain readers and prevent erosion of classified advertising. Yet publishing online may discourage some potential subscribers from purchasing a subscription. Newapaper managers must keep abreast of Internet trends to ensure that readers and revenues are not lost to the new medium. The fact that future outcomes must be predicted makes long-range decision making more difficult than short-range decision making. Long-range decisions often involve some large investment of capital, making the decision even riskier. In a recent survey,

347 respondents reported that the average daily newspaper planned expenditures of $1.8 million in the coming year. Respondents planned $83.4 million in software purchases, up from $46.3 million the year before. Publishers are continuing to replace proprietary systems and first-generation desktop publishing systems with personal computers. The planned expenditures for such computers grew from $104 million in 1996 to $150.5 million in 1998. And newsprint expenses alone represent about 15 to 20 percent of a newspaper's advertising budget.

Obviously, companies have more to lose if the purchase does not produce the desired outcomes. The decision also is evaluated over a longer period of time. For example, it will take I year or more before newspaper management will notice all the effects of purchasing new personal computers and software. Broadcast managers must consider whether, when, and what to buy when making a decision about updating to a high-definition television system.

Long-range decisions most often occur at higher levels in organizations, and shorter range decisions occur at middle and lower levels. Higher level management makes the riskier decisions and takes responsibility for decisions that affect the entire organization. Middle and lower level management make decisions that are more routine, are less risky, and result in consequences that directly influence their departments. The level of decision making and the nature of the decision affect the type of information the manager needs for the decision-making process. Indeed, the type of budget information managers use and evaluate varies based on these same factors.

DECISION MAKING AND INFORMATION NEEDS

The nature of planning and decision making varies with the organization level at which each process occurs. At the highest levels of management, decisions are made determining the firm's policies and general guidelines for evaluating the company's performance. This is what the owners of Callas Communications do. The information top management uses is often summarized and future-oriented.

For example, information about future market share, economic indicators, and other market performance measures are forecasted and then used by upper level management to predict revenue and profit goals for the coming year. Middle level management typically deals with using resources efficiently and effectively. At this level, managers need information to develop operating budgets. Often decisions need to be made about investing in new equipment, services, or people. For example, KHIT middle managers may recommend purchase of better remote broadcasting equipment if the planned concert becomes an annual event. A newspaper's managing editor might decide to buy a new advice column about the Internet if readers indicate an interest in this service and information. Lower level management deals with more structured, routine tasks and uses information from inside the organization.

Decision rules are communicated, preferably in verbal and written form. The information used is very detailed and typically unambiguous. At this managerial level, information is not necessarily forecasted for future concerns. For example, KHIT's engineering director must decide which engineer will work overtime at the remote concert broadcast.

DEPARTMENTAL BUDGETS

Developing budgets is one part of the planning process where decisions are made about the available resources for achieving goals. Generating the master budget plan for the entire business can take some time, usually 3 to 6 months, depending on the size, nature, and complexity of the organization. Managers at all levels of the organization participate in the effective development of the master budget plan.

At the highest level, a budget committee might consist of the company president, the controller, vice president of sales, and vice president in charge of production. In a media organization, the budget committee includes the top manager, the controller, and all department heads. This committee establishes budget goals for the company that directly affect the budgeting at the departmental level. The budget committee also reviews and approves departmental budgets.

A budget director, who reports directly to the controller, coordinates budgets at the departmental level. The budget director prepares a timetable for the development and approval of the operating budgets and works with managers in the development of each departmental budget. The master budget plan is assembled and submitted to the budget committee and then the board of directors for approval. Finally, the budget director is responsible for preparing and distributing performance reports, based on the previous year's budget, to the budget committee and department managers.

Forecasting

A key element of generating budgets is forecasting. Forecasting is an effort to predict future events and trends and anticipate their implications for the company. Granger (1980) listed three types of forecasting: event outcome forecasts, event--timing forecasts, and time series forecasts. With event outcome forecasts, a manager tries to predict the consequences of an event. For example, how will the closing of the regional recording studio in town affect KHIT--FM? With event--timing forecasts, a manager attempts to predict when a specific event will take place.

For example, if a growing city has only one network-affiliated television station, that station's management would be interested in knowing when a second network affiliate might enter the market. With time series forecasting, a manager attempts to predict the effects of a series of phenomena on the business. For example, what effects will the listing of employment notices on the Internet have on a newspaper's classified ad linage?

The benefits of accurate forecasting seem obvious, given the central role of information in decision making. As with most valuable things, accurate forecasting is not easy. So many factors can change and the possibility of measurement errors is so great, that accurate long-range forecasting is as much an art as a science. Despite the limitations, however, budgeting requires some forecasting. Kreitner (1986) listed three types of forecasting: informed judgment, surveys, and trend analysis. Informed judgment involves the forecasting of events and trends by an individual or group, based on a knowledge of the topic being forecast. Informed judgment is used extensively in the creation of most short-term budgets. Surveys are efforts to anticipate the future by comments from a small percentage of that group.

Trend analysis extends historical trends found in data about the past into the future, with some alterations based on assumptions of change. Because everything changes to a degree, all trend analysis must address key factors that shape the event being forecast. For example, if KHIT's advertising staff is extending trends in advertising sales, the staff needs to specify assumptions about changes in overall business sales. The staff might assume, based on predictions by government economists, that retail sales in their market would increase 5 per cent during the next year. Using this figure, the staff could come up with an estimate of retail sales. From this figure, they could estimate their revenue during the next year by applying the percentage of local retail sales that they have received as advertising revenue during the past 5 years.

All budgeting requires some forecasting. And it is important to deal explicitly with assumptions about the changing economic environment. Otherwise, a station will underestimate revenues during a booming economy and overestimate revenues during an economic downturn. Two principles tend to hold true: the longer the range a budget covers, the more important forecasting becomes, and the longer the range a budget covers, the harder it is to forecast accurately. This in effect is the forecasting dilemma. The only solution is to invest in several methods of forecasting for the long range and to hire competent forecasters.

Index

N

O

P

R

S

T

W